C000173529

THE ROAD TO
ST JULIEN

THE ROAD TO ST JULIEN

*Letters of a Stretcher-Bearer
from the Great War*

by

WILLIAM ST CLAIR

Edited by John St Clair

LEO COOPER

First published in Great Britain in 2004 by
LEO COOPER
an imprint of Pen & Sword Books,
47 Church Street,
Barnsley
South Yorkshire,
S70 2AS

Copyright © 2004 John St Clair

ISBN 1 84415 017 8

A CIP catalogue record for this book is
available from the British Library.

Typeset in 11/13pt Sabon by
Phoenix Typesetting, Auldgirth, Dumfriesshire.

Printed in England by
CPI UK

TO DAVID, ANDREW, JOE
AND CHRISTINA

Contents

Acknowledgements

I have received a great deal of encouragement and assistance in editing the letters, diaries and plays of my uncle, William St Clair. All the encouragement and assistance has been much appreciated, and I am sorry that I cannot thank everyone with a proper mention.

My first thanks are to William St Clair's daughter-in- law, Pat St Clair, and her late husband, Norman St Clair, who saved William St Clair's papers, pictures and photographs. Without these documents and Pat's wealth of personal recollections of her father-in-law, which she has shared with me, this book could not have been attempted. I am profoundly grateful to her. To be allowed to edit such a unique archive is an exceptional privilege.

Secondly, I would like to thank my brother, William, to whom William St Clair's papers were entrusted over thirty years ago, and who very kindly suggested that I might like to edit them. I am also grateful to him for his unstinting help and advice at all stages of the preparation of this book.

I am also very grateful to John and Patience Bagenal for giving me free access to the papers of the late Hope Bagenal DCM. It has been one of the pleasures of writing this book to have got to know them and now to count them as friends.

For particular encouragement and help from further afield, I must thank St John's College, Johannesburg, for giving me access to the papers of their former headmaster, the late Reverend Captain Eustace Hill MC, and especially for allowing me to publish for the first time the photograph of Eustace Hill at Delville Wood in 1919.

As regards the pictures and photographs of the war in the book, all were drawn by William St Clair or were selected by him for inclusion in a family album as authentic to the subject matter. In helping me to choose what pictures and photographs to include in the book and for encouragement and help, I am most grateful to my friend Roger Tarr of Edinburgh University History of Art Department. Immediately he saw Willie's coloured pictures, he appreciated their importance as uniquely evocative of the events portrayed, especially in showing that our imagery of the Great War, from old newsreels, of a war fought in black and white, is misleading. I was also fortunate that Roger's colleague, Norma Henderson, so expertly photographed all the pictures, photographs and maps for inclusion in the book.

Thanks are also owed to Kenneth Shirlaw for help and encouragement and correcting any military errors, and to my cousin, William Roy St Clair, for helping me with the religious background of William St Clair's family, and to my brother, David, for encouragement and sharing recollections of our uncle which I had forgotten or misremembered.

I would also like to thank Brigadier Wilson and all the editorial staff at Pen and Sword. Their help, advice and suggestions have been greatly appreciated and have added much to the quality of the book.

Finally thanks are due to my wife, Emma, and my children, David and Andrew, for all their loving support, while I was engaged on the book.

Introduction

Like many of the men who marched away, my uncle's life was defined by the Great War. Memories of the Battle of Loos used to come round every September to haunt him — the gas, the shells, the screams, the laying out of his fellow-countrymen for burial still in their kilts. The memories never went away, but became more vivid in old age when bouts of depression returned with increasing frequency and intensity. He talked quite freely about these things to my brothers and myself when we were young.

Although it was the memories of Loos he most dreaded, Willie took part in all the main operations on the Western Front from 1915 to the Armistice, including the Somme in 1916, Arras the following year, and the desperate battle in April 1918 round Mount Kemmel in Flanders during the German onslaught that almost won the war. But the 'hell of hells' according to Willie was Passchendaele in the autumn of 1917, where he said the sights were unimaginable unless you had been there. He described bringing men in on stretchers across the swamps, the duck-boards under constant shellfire and one slip and you would drown, and spoke of the exhaustion of carrying the patient just a few hundred yards which was the distance between staging posts from the front to the dressing-station. As children we asked him if he had won any medals for his bravery. He would recount how at Passchendaele they had picked up a badly wounded soldier whom he recognized as Richmond, from his home town of Kirkintilloch. They carried him two shifts so that he would get to the dressing station sooner. He lost a leg but survived. About forty years later, having always met my uncle before with a blank stare when they crossed in the street and no word ever spoken, he came into my uncle's barber's shop. He put two gold half sovereigns into my uncle's hand, muttering about them being a token of gratitude for my uncle's action which had given him all these years of life. My uncle would take out the two half sovereigns which he carried in his wallet. He would show us the gold coins with the face of the young Queen Victoria on them and say, 'These are my medals'.

Apart from talking, Willie also wrote a great deal about the war. From the time he enlisted in August 1914 to his discharge in May 1919 he wrote of his daily life in his letters to his wife Jane*. As far as the censor would allow, he described his thoughts and feelings and the events he was living through. Call it counselling if you want, but it meant he had someone to unburden everything to and alleviate the stress. This communication he thought preserved his sanity and he felt sorry for the young men who did not have such an emotional lifeline. The price, of course, was the gnawing worry about his safety, which Jane had every minute of every day until 11 o'clock on 11 November 1918. Pack up your troubles in your old kit bag and smile, smile, smile was a mental attitude the soldiers could adopt to control their thoughts especially if they were busy, but it was more difficult for those at home. Willie's constant exhortations to Jane not to worry about him have a slightly hollow ring. He repeatedly says that he himself prefers to be busy, even in the trenches, because away from the lines at rest camps he gets broody and depressed as well as bored and much more conscious of his loneliness and isolation.

Many of Willie's letters from the front were passed by Jane to Willie's father, who read them out to the rest of the family. His uncensored letters about the Battle of Loos also appeared in *The Kirkintilloch Herald*, a local newspaper, having been sent to the editor by Willie's father. The practice of proud parents sending letters from the front to local newspapers was common at the beginning of the war and was how a lot of news about the war was disseminated. Willie's letters in the newspaper were picked up and printed by national newspapers, but subjected to a tighter censor-

---

* Although William St Clair did not go through a formal marriage ceremony until 1917, they addressed each other as husband and wife throughout the war.

ship regime. Although these early published letters had a wide circulation at the time, Willie had not written them for publication, and angrily insisted that no more appear in the newspapers. In 1930, however, Willie wrote about the war for a wider audience in his play *The Prayer*, which is based on an incident in a pillbox near St Julien during the Battle of Passchendaele, of which he had given Jane a factual account in a letter in 1917. The play, which was widely performed in Scotland, struck a new note with the Scottish audiences and with his fellow veterans by whom and to whom it was performed the following year. It coincided with the publication of other works about the war, such as *All Quiet on the Western Front* and *Journey's End,* which began to portray the war realistically, bereft of patriotic sentiment, and as a tragic sacrifice. It had taken a decade after the war before highly traumatized young men like Willie could face revisiting in the imagination their recently escaped horrors. Writing about the war was often part of an attempted therapy. In Willie's play, he cast himself to act the main part.

In 1919 Willie returned home from Germany to unemployment. He scratched a living at first painting portraits until he got back into a hairdressing business. He also had to start married life more or less at the beginning again, having in his two and a half years of marriage seen Jane only a matter of weeks. They had three children. His marriage was very happy from all accounts. However, at times he had immense difficulty in coping psychologically with the continuing stress of the war. Willie said much later that he was only saved by the sympathy and loving kindness of his wife. But again he was conscious of the price. She had nearly died during the war from stomach ulcers and was never again in good health. When she died in 1938, Willie attributed her early death to the strain of helping him back to health after the war.

Despite the feeling shared by most of the old soldiers that others had prospered while they gave so much, Willie both before and after Jane's death, lived life to the full with many friends and interests. He founded *The Kirkintilloch Players,* an amateur theatre group that is still active, and was secretary of the local archaeological society, which he also helped to found. In his sixties he married Margaret Swan, a lecturer in psychiatry at the University of Glasgow, who was in her forties. They were ideally suited. She loved and cherished him, and protected him like a piece of her prize porcelain. Whether at Glyndebourne or at an academic conference, with his thick wavy white hair and jaunty bow tie, he was always the most distinguished looking man in a room, able to hold his own in conversation with a new range of friends. At a function at Glasgow University Willie got into a violent row with the Lord Rector of the University, the first director-general of the BBC, Lord Reith. Reith had recently published a worked-up version of a diary he wrote during the war under the title *Wearing Spurs*. Willie just could not understand how Reith could say he had enjoyed the war. There was also far too much in Reith of the gung-ho and the glory hunter for Willie to stomach. Much to his disappointment having missed the main fighting at the Battle of Loos, on 8 October 1915 Reith was hit in the head by a sniper's bullet, which effectively ended the war for him. He said he thought he had been hit in the head by a cricket-ball, but then remembered the Germans didn't play cricket.[1]* The German sniper probably saved Reith's life, for he never returned to active service again and resumed his ambitious life after the war with his bellicosity intact.

Several years before his death Willie began to look back over his past life, poring over old photographs and papers. Freud had said this was a normal form of grieving, Margaret assured him. He talked more than ever about the war, but it became insistent. He had been a great hoarder of documents that had meant something to him. The most treasured papers were those relating to the Great War. They consisted of a continuous correspondence between himself and Jane. He also had pictures and drawings, which he had done in France and Belgium when he had been able to snatch a moment. They complemented his written records. In 1915 and 1916 he had kept uncensored diaries, a serious offence at the time.† In addition he had kept cards from the front, Christmas decorations, menus, and other documents not normally preserved.

The diaries had become faded, and he transcribed them into an exercise book, calling it his diary, but also taking in some passages from letters. Probably with no intention other than to draw out a

* See Notes p. 220
† Officers censored their own letters and diaries.

point here and there, he made some subtle changes of phrase or language, which reveal critical shifts in his perception of the war, as well as the slippery nature of memory. On his letters to Jane he occasionally superimposed a place name from where it had been sent, if this was not clear in the text, or a reference to a trench or dug-out subsequently having been taken by the Germans and then retaken by the British. Otherwise they are unaltered. One inscription from this time is a pencilling on an envelope, 'Oh Jane Jane Jane!', suggesting a surge of grief at the lost years.

Willie sought the advice of my brother, William St Clair, as to whether his letters could be published. He wanted to see them in book form but not until the time was right. In particular, since many were intimate letters to his first wife, he made William promise that they would not be shown to his second wife Margaret. By the time Willie died he had handed over a number of bundles of letters to William, but others he held back. Willie seemed reluctant to part with his remaining letters but said that William was to get all the material in due course and could decide what was best. There is no doubt that he wanted to see them published as his account of the Great War.

After Willie's death Margaret told William that she had burned Willie's letters from Jane while she was sorting out his things. It was also thought that she had destroyed the rest of Willie's letters, diaries and other papers connected with the Great War. Since there was not enough in the surviving letters to make publication worthwhile, that seemed to be the end of the matter. However, in 1997 Willie's daughter-in-law, Pat St Clair, told William and myself, in great excitement, that she had found another archive of Willie's letters and diaries in her loft which her late husband, Norman, had saved. This archive was found to contain probably all of Willie's remaining papers that had survived the Great War. It dove-tailed into the first archive, which William had, and so enabled the continuous narrative in letters, pictures, diaries and plays to be read for the first time. Willie had held back most of his best letters and those that meant most to him. It is this continuous narrative of Willie's experiences of the Great War throughout his life which is now published in his name as he intended. What we do not have are the letters which sustained Willie during the Great War – Jane's letters to her beloved Willie.

Willie's account of the Great War is exceptionally comprehensive. Not only did he serve right through from the outbreak to the Armistice, surviving physically almost unscathed, but he wrote home nearly every day. Apart from the normal letters which were read by officers before being sent, he, like every soldier, was allotted a ration of green envelopes, in which they could send letters which were not censored in this way, but by random checks at base, soldiers being on their honour not to reveal anything of operational importance. Willie managed to obtain far more than his share of green envelopes by buying them from other soldiers, or – a favourite story of his – getting them from some high-ranking officer in return for cutting his hair. The green envelope privilege was intended to help soldiers keep in close touch with their families by enabling them to be occasionally intimate about personal matters. Willie exploited the green envelope privilege to the full, including long passages of frank descriptions of the war which would probably not have passed the censor if sent by ordinary post. He also commissioned friends going on leave to take letters home in order to circumvent the censor.

Willie's writing range is unusually wide, comprising both immediate on the spot descriptions of experiences and events and later recollections and reflections as he tried to understand the events he had lived through. Being a private in the RAMC gave him a very good vantage point to observe the war, whether as a stretcher-bearer going over the parapet behind the infantry or listening to their accounts as he brought in the wounded and tended and nursed them in dressing stations and field hospitals. Even his hair-cutting gave him opportunities to observe and listen, cutting the soldiers' hair when they came in from Passchendaele like 'wild men', or, at the height of the Battle of the Somme, being summoned to Corps HQ in the General's car to cut the corps staff officers' hair.

Like Thucydides in an earlier war, Willie knew that he was living through decisive events in the history of the world and was determined to record them honestly. To this task he brought two special talents as well as a good education and an ability to write well. He was an artist and brought an artist's eye to describing a scene. In fact, the recognition of a good scene from the artist's point of view often comes first. Thus, before his description of the Ypres trenches in winter, Willie wrote, 'As I sit here on a dirty coke bag, the scene

6

before me looks a picture of real war and has a very sad side as well as an artistic side.' The other talent which Willie brought to bear was his ear for dialogue, which he was later to develop in his plays. Throughout the war he kept asking himself what the thoughts and attitudes were of the ordinary soldiers in the face of the hardships and risks they were being put through. Sometimes he answers these questions by describing the soldiers' behaviour as they prepare to go into battle, bury dead comrades or bear the pain of their wounds. But often he adds the soldiers' remarks, capturing their moods and thoughts in quiet and in danger, the humour and the pathos.

Willie's accounts of the Battle of Loos, written immediately afterwards, are among the fullest and frankest accounts of that battle that were written. At this time, when censorship was still light, his descriptions of the battle are so detailed that we can place him precisely on the battlefield at any time during his days and nights of desperate work attending and rescuing the wounded, uninterrupted except for a few hours when he was carried off the battlefield suffering from the effects of gas. His accounts leave us in no doubt why at the time he knew that the battle was going to leave an 'indelible impression' on him. After Loos stricter censorship meant that no subsequent battle could be recounted in such detail by anyone in the Army, and Willie himself mentioned just a few weeks after the battle that 'for writing about things that were considered other than "family affairs" in a green envelope, a corporal of the Engineers has been sentenced to 6 months' hard labour and reduced to the ranks'. Willie's accounts of Loos are not only full and frank, but they are innocently honest accounts unmediated by knowledge of the wider picture or later reflection. In their power to convey the experience of being a soldier caught in the fog and chaos of a battle, they compare with Stendhal's imagined account of the Battle of Waterloo in the *Chartreuse de Parme*.

Willie speaks not as a gentleman in the ranks nor as an officer but as a soldier. He entered the war with a clear idea where his duty lay and with deeply held convictions. As the war went on, he was conscious it was changing him. Then and later he reflected much on the nature of war, and its implications. The account he has left is his personal account of the Great War. His is a distinctive voice, very different from the romanticising enthusiasm of Rupert Brooke or from the deep disillusion of Wilfred Owen, but a much more representative voice of his generation, and one that deserves to be listened to and respected.

Note on the Text

The letters in the book represent about a quarter of what William St Clair wrote during the war. A reliable postal service enabled British soldiers, for the first time in history, to communicate rapidly with those at home, and it is Willie's sense of sharing the immediacy of his experiences with his family that gives his letters their unique value. A disproportionate number of letters were written during the first two years of the war, an effect of changing circumstances, notably the comparative lack of censorship in the early years. I have tried to offset this by giving what I believe are representative samples of Willie's writings at all stages of the war.

I also offer only a small sample of his repeated expressions of love and deep longing for his wife and of his homesickness. The samples cannot fully convey the power of these sentiments, which are woven deeply into the whole text. Nor, I fear, can the examples of the many letters written during the long periods between military offensives reveal how difficult he found the emptiness, repetitiveness and interminable boredom of life on the Western Front. I hope, in trying to avoid unnecessary repetition, that I have not been unfair to Willie, or distorted, or in any way romanticized, the impact of his writings taken as a whole.

Transcribing the letters necessarily loses some of the meanings of the crushed and water-stained originals. Some are in pencil, others in indelible ink, some as carefully written as in a school exercise book, others hurriedly scribbled crouching in a dugout as the guns roared. Paper was at a premium, with every corner written on and the writing often compressed. After the battles of Loos and Passchendaele it is many days before Willie's handwriting settles to its normal rhythm. In order to reduce some of the difficulties for readers, I have spelled out some abbreviations in full, e.g. noting that '10 A &S' was the 10th Battalion of the Argyll and Sutherland Highlanders, and ADS is Advanced Dressing Station. I have also, on occasion, made the punctuation more regular and corrected small errors. Otherwise the text is exactly what Willie wrote.

J St.C

Chapter One

Call to Arms

William St Clair was born on 22 January 1889 in Kilsyth, by then a predominantly coal-mining town of about 8,000 inhabitants on the main road from Edinburgh to Glasgow. He was the eldest of eight children of a painter and decorator, William St Clair, and his wife Mary Linn. His paternal forebears were Calvinist weavers, with every birth and marriage recorded in the local parish records back to the seventeenth century. Willie was twenty-five years old and planning to get married when at 4.00 pm on 4 August 1914 the German army marched into Belgium seven hours before a British ultimatum was due to expire. At 11.00 pm war was declared on Germany and the following day Kitchener joined the Cabinet as Secretary of State for War. On 6 August, Parliament authorized an increase in the size of the army by 500,000 men and Kitchener personally drafted a 'Call to Arms' for publication in the national newspapers, asking for 100,000 volunteers.

In response to this Call to Arms, on 21 August 1914 Willie walked with his brother-in-law, Peter Edgar, up the Garrell Burn from Kilsyth, and over the hills to enlist at Stirling Castle, becoming one of the original 'First Hundred Thousand' of Kitchener's 'New Armies', the biggest volunteer force in history.[2] In Willie's under-standing of patriotism, the claims of the nation transcended those of the individual. He wrote on 6 January 1916, 'Many more lives will be lost but a life or a hundred lives means nothing to a nation.' After his patriotic decision to enlist, what mattered was doing his duty as best he could. Everything else was in the hands of God. In a letter of 24 March 1916, he wrote, 'God has each of our ways mapped out and we have no choice of how we will die and so on. As for me at present, I live each day and try and do my duty whether it is congenial or not.' Patriotic duty and duty to God went together, a theme of the Recruiting Officer in Kirkintilloch, who was a minister of religion.

Willie joined the Royal Army Medical Corps, with units attached to each Brigade of the British Army. Before the war he had attended ambulance classes with the Territorial Army and this humanitarian work of the RAMC fitted with his family's pacifist outlook. Not being a fighting unit, the RAMC had the protection of the Red Cross, but the nature of its work at the front meant that its personnel expected to be often under fire.* The training was a mix of military and medical. After a day or two at Aldershot the new recruits were sent to Tweseldown in Hampshire and put up in tents on a racecourse. Military training consisted of learning to march in the Hampshire countryside and to get the RAMC column in and out of trains. The medical training was both practical and academic.[3] On the practical front, the recruits were taught how to put up a tent, how to carry men on stretchers, and load them on to horse- and lorry-driven ambulances. On the medical side they were taught about the nature of wounds, how to apply a 'field dressing', what cases should be given morphia, how to classify wounds as slight, serious or fatal, and the Latin names for parts of the anatomy. Dr Gompertz taught that when one organ was injured, the adjoining organs could often take over some of its functions – a sort of reassurance from Nature herself.

Aldershot

We are fairly in it now. Arrived down here yesterday and had to wait till 9.30 pm before we had any idea where we were going to sleep. We met five London chaps who were just like us so they chummed up so we kept together and managed to get into the same tent and got on all right. We had no prospect of getting blankets, so had to get our coats well about us and lie close to keep warm as it was a little chilly. I got to sleep all right (being tired out). However

---

* *Casualty figures for the war of 27 Field Ambulance are given in the footnote on page 84.*

10

they wakened us up between 12–1 and served out blankets. We were very pleased I assure you. We get up at 5.30 every morning on parade at 6.30. We were sent up to the doctor this morning where we all passed as fit for any service. Will be vaccinated tomorrow. So will have all the preliminaries over. We are being fed fairly decent but are hard up for knives and forks. My pocket knife has had to do for everything. We drink the stew out of our cups up to now, plates being at a premium. The food is well cooked. So we get outside of it as best we can. Some of us are separated into different tents today but we are going to try and keep together if possible.

This experience is right good for us. It is bringing out our strong bit. There are 1,400 in D Company RAMC here with about 4,000 RAMC all told. That represents all sorts, plenty of our own class. Our London chums are gentlemen and are very pleased they fell in with us. The tent here is terrible. We are dark brown already and look as if we had been through a campaign already. We saw some Belgian refugees in London at the hotel where we had breakfast – (which by the way cost us 3/- each). It was a reminder about what is really going on over there. They looked as if they had suffered. The kiddies were fine looking and unconcerned. Plenty wounded here from the front. One hospital full and we're getting tired looking at aeroplanes. They are flying over here every day.

Our blue suits don't suit the conditions here. So you might please dear get my Golf Jacket from the club house and patch it up any way and get my grey trousers and my heavy golf shoes and send them on. Johnnie will help you to pick them out. The shoes I have are no good for marching. They make my feet sore. Two forks and two knives. We have no prospect of getting our uniforms for some time yet. We are feeling quite fit and like the life all right. There is about 80,000 men here – so that gives you an idea – being drilled every day Sunday included. The Highlanders have very hard training to go through. Kitchener was down inspecting them all last Sunday and we expect him again shortly. They are all fine fellows. It makes one feel proud to be in it.

No date Tuesday 1. 20

We had the King here yesterday. He was to be in the Camp about ten in the forenoon, but did not come and everybody thought he wouldn't. We did our parades as usual and were dismissed at four o'clock and were all in our huts when we were told he was outside the hut. We went out and there he was riding between the huts with the Princess Mary and a few Generals. We all clustered round about him. The officers were just being dismissed by the Captain when he got to the top of the lines. He halted and shook hands with one of them and gave a fine speech about what the Medical Corps has done and how they have suffered. We heard every word, and close up against his horse all the time. There was no formality and he seemed to like it so. He saw everything at its usual. We were not even called to attention. He was just like an officer among his men, chatting to them. It was a very interesting visit which we all enjoyed. The Princess was riding about at her ease. She looks plain but nice, and one had not the impression that they were anything out of the ordinary. I was struck with the care-worn look of the King, and he did not appear to be in the very best.

4.30 I was disturbed at this stage having to rush out to parade. I was talking about the King. He did not look in the best of health and looked as if he understood the responsibility of his position during the present unprecedented crisis. His beard is turning quite grey.

Wednesday, 13 January 1915

We have all been arranged into our respective squads for good. The officer came in this morning and picked us out. We were all on parade in the hut and he said that he had chosen those who were to be in charge of the stretcher squads. My ambition was to be a No. 4 as I told you when I was at home and I was pleased when I heard that I had been chosen for the position which is a very responsible one as one has to be well up in the work in all its branches. The No. 4s (there are six in C Section) were told to pick their own men. So I chose Peter, Bob Peter, Cooper, and Shaw and another Scotch chap named Gardner and we are all very pleased as we will always be together when we go out there and we have always to drill in the positions named.

They have everything ready now to move whenever the order comes. I don't know when that will be, but very soon. Of course the longer we are kept here the weather will be improving and the spring drawing nearer and it will not be so bad when the good weather comes in again. It must really be awful at the front just now with the rain, cold and the usual conditions with troops on active service. You need not worry too much darling as our work will not always bring us into the fighting line and I will always take good care of myself as I have promised.

No date (after 14 January 1915)

We were a little anxious lest we should be taken out of the 27th. They drew lots for those who had to go. Nobody desired to change as we feel at home with the officers and men, and another thing we are the first Field Ambulance to go. We are lucky, as those who came on today are attached to the 46th and have been seven weeks in the Army. They are running about the lines looking for bread and eatables as nothing was ready for them. We know how they feel and have given them all the eatables we had left. I had a letter from home yesterday and was pleased as I had not had word for some time and there was a wee note enclosed from Peter which was very nice. I must try and answer it if possible.

Well darling, I had a new experience today. Of course I told you I was on Police duty for a week. We had a prisoner to look after today, charged with a very serious crime in the Army. We had to march him to the doctor (two of us) to see if he was fit to be Court Martialled, and at eight o'clock this morning, the doctor passed him as fit. So we marched him between us with the Police Corporal behind, down to the Guard Tent. We went for him again at ten o'clock to take him before the Major, and all the Captains. I did feel in a strange position walking at 'shun with my Regimental Police badge on my arm, and all the fellows looking on very seriously as he was to be charged with something akin to treason, cursing his Superior Officer – and what was more serious – cursing His Majesty. He was liable to be shot on the latter charge. So you will understand, we felt a little excited about it all.

13

We arrived at the orderly room all right and were marched in, the prisoner bare-headed, and sitting on one side of a square table was the Major with four Captains and a Sergeant Major. It looked very solemn, I assure you. The witnesses, four in number, were on our right. He was charged. The witnesses gave their evidence and then the prisoner gave his statement. He is a Jew by the way, and some think he is a little off. However, he spoke very well for himself and proved conclusively that he did not really mean any disloyalty and that spite caused a great deal of the trouble. Of course they willingly dropped the heavy charge, as the fellow had not meant what he said, and besides, it would have been awful. He was given fifteen days in prison but he had a narrow escape.

No date

Most folks thought the war would not in fact last more than a few weeks, and now seven months – eight I should say – gone and the position is about the same 'as you were' to use a military phrase and nobody can foresee what will be the real outcome of it all and when it will finish. God knows this country will have to pay dearly for anything she gets out of it and our own beautiful country Scotland is paying very heavily for her patriotism.

P.S. Please send on my copy of Dickens' *Tale of Two Cities*, the bound one when convenient and Victor Hugo's *Les Miserables* if you can find it.

Bordon Friday, 7 May 1915

Just had tea and what a great feast we had with that grand parcel that came today, beef and ham, hame loaf and a nice cigarette to finish up with. We have fed like fighting cocks today. We have not done much today but give in everything but what we wear and can carry, even our kit bag had to go. We are strictly forbidden to give any news as to our movements and you know why. I have some clothes I am going to send on if I get the chance. I will keep you well posted with PC. Be very brave, my beloved. I enjoyed that wee note in today's parcel. Write as usual and everything you feel write. Never forget my true and pure love for you. Remember all I have told you to be careful about.

The weather is very beautiful still. Dearest you must know my feelings which I am sure now that I will not get home before we go. I cut Pete's hair today all over the front. You would not be able to keep from laughing if you saw it just now as he sits up against the tent reading while I lie on the grass writing my letter. I also have got mine rumpled but I still have a wee bit left on the front. You see it will be rather warmer in a day or so. We did not go out yesterday. Cancelled at the last minute. I will not forget all your instructions darling. I have the Bible you gave me in my pocket and will keep it there till I come back. I will read it often over there.

Chapter Two

1915
The Glamour of this War
is All at Home

*When the New Armies started to arrive in France in May 1915,
there was already a permanence about the line of the Western
Front, which ran from the Belgian coast to the Swiss border almost
exactly where the armies of the two sides had fought each other to
a standstill in November 1914. The armies of the warring Great
Powers were now housed in opposing underground trench systems
over a 470-mile front, which had the features of a fault line between
tectonic plates. The British sector was a ninety-mile stretch which
ran roughly from Ypres in Flanders to the Ancre River, a tributary
of the Somme in Picardy. There had been static trench warfare
during the American Civil War and during the Balkan Wars but
nothing comparable in scale to the Western Front.*[4]

*The 9th Division underwent training prior to taking over full
military responsibility at the beginning of July 1915 for a sector of
the front line at Festubert. During this period Willie worked as a
medical orderly behind the lines, gradually moving up towards the
trenches. His letters record his education in the squalor, hardships
and dangers of life on the Western Front even away from the lines.
As a medical orderly dealing with the wounded and dead as they
were brought in from the battlefields, Willie was seeing aspects of
war which were hidden not only from the nation at home but in
some respects from the fighting soldiers. His letters show that he*

already appreciated the huge gap which was developing between the public perception of the war and the realities of France. At no point is there any hint of pre-war ideas about war being the supreme test of a nation's efficiency or states being in a Darwinian struggle for survival, or any indication of feelings, shown by others from more comfortable backgrounds, that war might be welcomed as a cleansing of effeteness and decadence.

France
Monday, 10 May 1915

We arrived here from Southampton this morning. We had a horrible passage. It was terribly rough and I was very sick. As a dog. Oh I am glad we are on dry land again after last night's experience. But I feel not so bad now we are waiting at the place to entrain for our destination near the firing line. They are putting off no time with us. It is so strange to hear all the many soldiers talking and they like to try and learn us their language. The weather is very fine. Well lovey I suppose you will know ere this that I am here.

I was thinking about you at the Church yesterday as I was lying at Southampton and also last night on the boat. We crossed in the boat that took you and I to Inveraray. It was packed and we lay on deck all night. Bah it was horrid. When I think about that trip I feel quite sick. You know how I am longing to hear from you but when our letters will arrive we don't know. Now deary don't worry too much about me and go and get ill. That would never do and I am quite well and strong. I will write you whenever we get to our destination and always keep you posted as to my welfare. Of course it is impossible to give you news as to my whereabouts. I have the letter I got the night before we left Bordon. I will feast on it till I get another from you. Pete is busy shaving himself just before me. We are learning to keep ourselves shaved and clean under all circumstances.

From 31800, Somewhere in . . .
Friday, 14 May 1915

We have got sort of settled down in this place now and are fairly comfortable in the school where we are billeted. There are eighty of us in the one room and we, each of us, have a bale of straw for our bed and blanket and waterproof sheet. So we are not so badly off in that direction. But we eat nothing but bully beef and biscuits and it takes some time to get to like it. Of course I cannot say anything about what is going on here. We have to give our letters to our officers and they have to see that there is no information in them before they will be posted. We would not have minded so much if it had been strangers who read them but nuf said. You understand the position. I have sent PCs every day to you. I hope you have got them all right. We have not seen any of the fighting as yet, but train loads of wounded passed us when we came up here. But we are sufficiently near to hear the guns. We will be nearer very soon. It was a beautiful train ride coming and we found the cattle trucks very comfortable. The scenery was beautiful and one would not think there was a great War on passing through such a beautiful and fertile country.

It was a very long roundabout route we came, but all for the best I suppose. It has been very wet these two days and makes our work very miserable to us. However we are healthy and strong and have nothing to complain of. Over in the trenches it must be awful. Few at home know what this war really is and the horrible sacrifice of lives that we are paying for our position.

All the French soldiers we have met are very friendly and nice, but we found it rather awkward not knowing the language. But we are learning a few words as we go along. Cigarettes, we can't get here meantime and the French cigs are rotten. Tell our John this. He will know what I want. Our address is 31800, Pte. W. St. C. 27th F.A. RAMC, 9th Division, British Expeditionary Force. That will always find me.

Tuesday, 25 May 1915

Most of our fellows have had sickness, etc with the change of climate and especially the water which is horrid owing to the fearful state of sanitation. We guessed what the consequences would be so we rather went without when we were dry than risk it and we are well paid for it now, never having had any trouble and in the very best of health. Thank goodness we were inoculated or there would I am certain have been an epidemic of typhoid. This country in the sunshine looks beautiful, cultivated to the last inch, right up to the trenches, and the little ditches by the wayside look so nice with a covering of green cress, but disturb it with a stick, and 'whew' what a stench and when it rains, what an atmosphere. All the muck and dirt of the place run into those ditches, sometimes in the street too and would give a Scotchman the 'bock'.* Our own country looks so clean and fresh to us as we remember its clear fresh cool air and its modern sanitation. I have not seen a village yet that one dare compare with auld Caurnie† and still they talk about la belle France. Scotland for me. I just wish I was there now.

Saturday, 29 May 1915

We have not had much of that sort of work as yet, just a little, any amounts here from the trenches, sick and all sorts of troubles that come through hardships. The explosion the other day there killed eight and one a staff officer. He was riding past at the time when the explosion occurred. They were all brought here and as I was on duty at the time I had to help carry them in and one of the injured who had some very bad wounds about the face. It was a bloody sight. For a start one feels a little queer, and so sorry for the unfortunate chaps, and would just like to work our hands off helping them. Pete and I carried one of them at the burial (a Scotchman in the RE). It was a very impressive ceremony, seven in one grave who the day before were strong healthy men like ourselves. They all died together and all lie together (the staff officer in a grave by himself) in the little cemetery outside the town. The service was short and simple, but every man there, officer and private alike, knew that at any time their turn might come. A common wooden box with no adornments, a little tag tacked on with name, regimental number and religion, and very far from their dear ones at home. Yes and thousands of our countrymen are 'going west' every month. Some are buried like this, others where they fall in a hastily dug grave, and still others it is impossible to bury, the shell, that sometimes kills forty at a time, doing its work too effectively, but this is the worst war in the world's history.

* Make him vomit.
† Local name for Kirkintilloch.

19

We have got our respirators and practice every day how to put them on in quick time. They are a precaution against that terrible gas. We have not been to the trenches as yet, but have plenty of work here at present.

Monday, 31 May 1915

You would laugh if you just had a glimpse of us as we prepared for 'bed'. We have a waterproof sheet and the clothes we wear. We lay the sheet on the floor, take our semmit* or cardigan and put our feet in the sleeves and then button it round our legs. We then tie up our feet in the sheet, lacing it up to our knees. Our spare shirts and socks for a pillow, our great coat on top of us, and there we are quite comfortable and sleep as soundly as ever we did at home. Of course we have to change our position from side to back during the night or our bones get a little sore, but this performance is done automatically sometimes without us wakening. We are so used to it now. Up at five every morning and lights out at 9.00 pm. Of course we never have off our trousers, I forgot to say.

The news all over seems to be more favourable and this may finish sooner than the most optimistic judge would imagine. We are all hoping so, as the country hereabouts has been literally steeped in good brave British blood, and the longer the worse. Hundreds of thousands killed and fearfully mutilated every month. Better far to be killed than to be as some are, with only life and a body that will be nothing but a burden to themselves and others after the war. It has always been the order to forget those who have given their best for their country and left with permanent injuries, and I suppose this will be no exception. It is all right as long as it is the fashion to look after the soldier, but already they are beginning to forget. One only needs to be out here to make their consideration lifelong.

2 June 1915

It is a very beautiful day and hot. I am so sunburned, yellow in fact, with a dash of crimson, is about the tint of my complexion

* A knitted woollen undershirt.

20

at present. But I am very strong and in the very best of health.

We are still in the same place and there is no prospect of our shifting as yet. Pete and I are in a tent now, were shifted there yesterday, and find it not so bad. The ground is hardly so hard as the stone floor. We had a cricket match last night with some of the Motor Transport boys. Pete and I were playing for the 27th and of course we won. It is a good recreation and all the time we were playing, there were aeroplanes up and the Germans battering away at them in the usual style. Quite a nice atmosphere for a cricket match. We are so used to them now that we take no notice whatsoever. There has been very little firing these two days past except during the night. Never a night passes but they are at it tooth and nail.

Last night an aeroplane passed overhead and we lay on the grass and watched it as usual. It had not gone very far till the usual thing happened, shells rose from all directions and, what riveted our attention at once, bursting dangerously near the aeroplane. These shells when they burst give a clear flash and they look for a second just like stars, and then the smoke hovers in the air for a long time. It was a British machine and the Germans had got the range right off, an unusual occurrence at this game. They fired fast and furiously and we lay there expecting to see her come to grief. These airmen take some fearful risks and seem to delight in playing with death. He dipped, circled and absolutely seemed to be playing with the shells as they came up. We knew it would end in grief and so it must have. He disappeared in the smoke and the guns ceased firing and it was left to our imagination what followed as he had gone into a mist and we could not see his machine, but he did not return, as we watched for a long time expecting that perhaps he would turn up, but no. The firing ceased and we knew he had met the fate of many of these brave men. Yes and there are others at the same game tonight 'doing their bit' and a very important bit too.

Pete and I had our portraits drawn by one of the chaps from the trenches, whom we have been attending. He draws for *Punch* and has made a fine job of them.* We will try and get them sent home if we can. Our routine is much the same every day just now with

* The artist was Hedley Hobbs according to Willie's diary.

21

little variety and so there is very little fresh news. In fact those at home know more from the papers as to the movements than we do.

3 June 1915

Some of our convalescent patients are playing at football in the top part of the field, hardy warriors who have been out here since the war started, and overhead (this evening is perfectly clear and there is a nice cool breeze blowing) the aeroplanes are scouting the enemy's positions, as they score off shells trying to bring them down. You can imagine the ammunition they waste at this game when I tell you that I have just counted fifty shells fired in the last five minutes at an aeroplane a little to my right. Germans short of ammunition, it is absolute nonsense, and, as to their bravery, every soldier out here recognizes the Germans as good fighters although they have many bad qualities in other respects.

10 June 1915

What a war this is. Nothing short of wholesale murder of Britain's very best manhood. Every man who has been in the trenches a month has done his bit for his country and more than his bit. But strange to say it is left to a few, comparatively speaking, to slave and suffer for months and months and still some at home enjoy themselves. They would not surely if they knew what was going on here. But then we are not allowed to say what really is going on. Perhaps it is for the best. Heroes, thousands of them, every one in fact, are being butchered to save our country in this the greatest peril of its history.

   Britain has a tremendous task before her and the sooner the folks at home get to realize it the better. Our asylums will be packed after this war. What with old feeble-minded men? No, but with Britain's youngest and best men as a result of the horrible injuries they have received out here, while a big number that could have done their bit hang back and reap the benefit of what our soldiers are sacrificing themselves daily for. Bah. It makes me sick to think of some of the supposed men at home. Some getting married and settling down to enjoy their selfish happiness. We will see, perhaps. God will repay those who have denied themselves at this time. I don't say our country will. She too often forgets those whom she should never forget. Yes, every man is needed who can get away and there are millions still and it would hasten this slow murderous war and perhaps in the long run save countless lives.

We are fighting an enemy that knows what fighting is and an enemy that stoops to all the lowest possible ways to destroy life. They are well supplied with everything, men, money, brains and what is sometimes thought not to be the case, ammunition, and this gas is beyond speaking about. It is deadlier in effect than millions of shells. How we curse that gas. One never knows the minute that the breeze blowing on our faces is going to be turned into one of the deadliest poisons. Britain is too honourable to fight such scum as the Germans but she will have to drop that honourableness if she means to win. We must play them at their own game, and that very soon. If we don't, God alone knows what will happen.

Sunday, 20 June 1915

We have not moved from here as yet, still waiting and this waiting may last a long while, we can't say. We are in no great hurry to get into it, time enough, when it comes. So we content ourselves. There is absolutely no doubt about it being hell over at the line, to lie and listen as we did last night to the awful firing, big guns firing almost as quick as a machine gun, raining shells. Right enough awful and horrible to be under such a fire. Well well but that is war.

You see this leaf has got a little torn as I had to stuff it into my pocket and go on parade. We often are interrupted thus, with our letters, but I can't waste paper by writing a new sheet as it is very difficult to get pads here and in this place impossible, and besides the French know how to charge. Oh yes, they are up to that game and there is a good lot of Tommy rot in the papers re their attitude to the British Tommy. Of course the papers put anything in. We notice that more so now since we came here. They have tried to put a glamour over this War and this life and I can tell you there is no glamour about it, nothing but stern facts and work and death and, as to soldiers anxious to get back again, I have not met one as yet. Most of the fellows who say they are anxious to get back to the front again are those who have lost a limb etc and know that it is impossible for them to get there again. It is a great nerve strain and everyone who has gone through have a great bright nervous eye and always as if they were ready to dodge a shell. It is different when they get to England. They recover all right, knowing they are in peace and safety. But one may be in a quiet place there and nice and peaceful one day, and the next be rushed up to that eternal hell and never come back, and through time this has an effect on the most of their nerves. Not that they are afraid. Oh no, that is what I have not seen out here in any man. It is just the strain of the thing. The glamour of this war is all at home.

Thursday, 24 June 1915

Ah here comes the post, but we must wait for some time till the officers get theirs. That is the prevailing custom in the army between officers and men. As long as they are right, they don't give one single scrap for the men, not in one thing, but in absolutely everything. The motto is 'I'm all right d---- you'. To give you an example, there are five tents out there for ten officers, and three and a marquee for 200 men, with the result that the most of us have to sleep out. They have their own special cooks and dinner every night. We get dry bread, and cheese and tea without milk. They have their 'valises' for sleeping on, their servants and more comforts than some of them even had at home. When we march, they ride, when we get there they have to be looked after first, and we get the crumbs and the swearings. 'I'm all right d---- you' every time. It may be different in other corps but I assure you this is the way of it in 27 FA, and of course after the officers come the sergeants, and they also have the same 'motto'. After everyone with the slightest grain of authority has been served, the private is allowed to look after himself and even then, they don't get peace to do that. Yes we will have a lot of things to tell you when we get home, when we are again in the position to think and speak for ourselves, when we will be 'men' again and not dogs.

I tell you we are getting so used to scratching that we will be doing it likely after we get home. Pete and I will be standing together speaking, but there, I will stoop to my knee and scratch and go on speaking and scratching. Pete the while with his hand inside his shirt, over his shoulder and half down his back, also speaking and scratching, both of us like contortionists, and then we will laugh at the ludicrous position of the other. 'For king and country Peter?', 'Aye for king and country, Billy' we both remark, and then a-hunting we will go, right off till it comes back again, and we are clean compared to most of the others. What a life. This is one of the 'experiences' and one of the hardships of active service. We use a lighted match for destroying purposes and it is quite a common sight to see a fellow in front of his bivouac running a match or candle up the inside seam of his trousers, and a very serious intent expression on his face. Till someone gives him a shout such as 'Business brisk?' and he looks up and laughs, 'Oh, I am doing a roaring or "cracking" trade'.

And yet I have never yet seen one on any man's head since I joined the Army. It is not our fault. Every man washes all over every day, and still they come. It is with lying out in all sorts of places. That does it, and in the trenches. They are fifty times worse, what with vermin, rats and bullets, shells. No wonder it is termed 'Hell'. That's the soldier's name for the firing line.

3 July 1915

Last night I was going out the gate of the Hospital when I saw two officers coming along on ordinary bikes. One was a big fellow and the other the Prince of Wales looking as hardy a soldier as any I have seen and sweating profusely as he pedalled that old push bike. One could hardly believe it was him, dodging along without any escort whatever, and on an old bike, but I was sure before he came up to me. I gave my very best salute and he gave me a good one back. So most of the stories one hears of him are true and not got up. He is very young-looking and very small, but looks a hardy sun-tanned soldier and was coming down from the lines.

7 July 1915

My friend left here yesterday to take his commission and promised me he would write. I gave him fifteen francs to send to you to put in the box. Get Duncan to send me a box of Munro's cigarettes if he would be so kind and give him the money for cigs and postage please and dinna flite on* me for asking cigs. There shair you'll no flite.† Well you see lovey the cigarettes they sell here are awful and would do me a lot of harm if I smoke them, and you are really doing something that will do me good sending these on. Oh Willie Willie I hear you say when will you stop smoking? Please not yet dearest. We'll see when I get haim.

We are still sleeping wrapped in our coats at nights in these old barns and a stone floor on the one we were moved into yesterday. It is for such scenes as these that I want a sketch book. It looks all so weird to see us all lying quiet wrapped in our great coats and stretched out on the brick floor at night in all directions, the most prominent absentee being comfort, men with their feet in the sleeves of their tunics, others with large stretcher gloves on their feet, others with their waterproof sheets laced round them till they look like an Egyptian Mummy, all sorts of devices to keep in the heat (or out the cold, whatever you like) and in the morning you see them all doubled up in all positions. It is very funny, I don't think. If some of those at home had a peep behind the scenes, they would hae sair‡ hearts. Our officers have beautiful billets, nice beds, and a fine mess where they have their five course dinners and so on.

9 July 1915

Oh how grand. I see the Kaiser says there will be no winter campaigns. I hope he is correct, as there is no more depressing sort of warfare than this trench fighting. No variety about it. In a real brush in the open men have a better chance to fight for their lives than lying in a shell-raked trench.

11 July 1915

I have just been disturbed. 'St Clair.' 'Yes Sir.' 'Can you come to my billet and cut my hair just now?' 'Yes sir.' 'Bring your tools and I will wait and show you.' 'Right oh sir.' (I have got into the way

* scold.
† I'm sure you won't be angry.
‡ Sore.

of saying 'right oh' to them and they don't mind me so much as they would others. I walk up with the officer and he cracks away and so do I . We meet the S. M. and a sergeant and they have some business with the officer (who is Orderly Officer for the day). They halt at the side of the road and salute. 'Half a mo, St Clair,' and he speaks to them. It is evidently a case of sickness, so they follow up behind and I continue my crack. 'Go round and wait for a few minutes till I get my hair cut.' They salute and go off. Up to his room. Of course. I walk in and have a good look around, and look at the grand bed with beautiful lace hanging all round it, and every convenience. 'What do you think of my billet St C.?' 'By gum it looks all right sir.' 'Yes we are all well billeted.' '<u>You</u> will be all right if we are here for a winter,' I say emphasizing the 'you'. 'Oh yes. Is it comfortable in the barns?' he asked. 'Oh well it is not so bad, except for the cold, the rats, the lice, etc,' I say and he laughs quite so. That's how they take it.

I proceed to cut his hair and the window is open, and the hair is blowing all over the place. 'I had better close this window,' I remark. 'Yes'. So I turn round and shut the window. He says something about 'take care' but I can't make him out. I close the window, and here there is a string with fly paper attached to it and a little fancy dresser hanging on the wall with a lot of fancy ornaments on it. Of course it comes down with a crash. 'I didna notice that string.' 'Oh don't trouble about that. There is no damage done.' If it had been his servant, that had done it, my word what a hot five minutes he would have had, but 'St Clair, the barber', well you see, there is no possibility of them getting a haircut unless they come to me for it, and knowing the Colonel and Lieutenant Colonel come to me for haircut, a mere Lieutenant, well he puts up with a little more than he would if I did not have the Colonel. You see the point dearie? This is the style all over. I make my apologies about pulling down the ornaments, say that I had got out of the way of being in a furnished room and consequently was a little clumsy, sarcasm of course.

I just relate this simply because I was disturbed in my letter writing and tell you where I have been. I have many a laugh in my sleeve at some of these chaps who I am sure have more luxuries here than some of them had at home.

I see by the *Herald*, they are having a French Flag Day. It would suit the home country if they had Flag days for their own, instead of the French etc. They like the Brit. soldier only for his money so far as I can see, and plenty in Flanders are better off than they were, at least so far as we have seen.

15 July 1915

We had a most unfortunate accident here yesterday with one of those bombs. Four of our fellows were working in a ditch cutting nettles and cleaning it out just where I used to shave the fellows and where I wrote that letter you say I was terrible homesick in. Of course this place is infested with these bombs and hand grenades that have been carelessly left about by the last company that were billeted here, which was a Grenade Company. One of the chaps lifted a grenade, just like the one I had and (I believe I had this one in my hand too as we did not know the danger of them) lifted it out to put it on the grassy bank when it exploded and blew the half of his hand off and wounded him severely and his chum was beside him. I was only fifty yards away and rushed over and what a sight of blood, and such a hand – ghastly. It gave us all a shake to see our own chaps lying there. The one with the fingers off stays at Falkirk. They are off and we won't likely see them again. Of course we all got a fright, and after us having one lying at our heads for four nights. We will all be more careful in future. It might have been any of us. Everyone has handled them since we came here. There is a small pin. If you take it out, or if it comes out any way, the grenade goes off in about five seconds. They are used extensively in the trenches.

There has been a horrible waste of ammunition in this war. Everywhere we have been, we have found 1000s of rounds of ammunition, rifles, and everything thrown away. It is always a source of danger to the company coming up behind us when cleaning up. One never knows what they are going to strike. There was straw in the barns when we got here first and of course we started right away and got it all out, as we knew the state it must have been in, and when it was burning, there was a constant crack crack of cartridges going off, and some of us had some narrow squeaks.

Friday, 16 July 1915

There must be ever so many sad sad homes and sad sad girls who have lost their best out here. What a brave hardy race we are when put to it. We often hear grousing, but never one flinches, and the specimens of manhood that are out must be our country's best. I saw the other day a battalion going up into the trenches. They had only been out a few days for a rest since September last, and they were going up again, serious-looking but still cheerful under the circumstances, and what fine fellows, but very few of the first battalion that went up at first, almost wiped out, new drafts sent to fill the vacant places and into it again, and the same story repeated, big gaps every time and then fresh men fill up the vacant places, and this has been going on since the start. The country will get a great shock when everyone is accounted for. But we are spared, lovey, and it makes one very thankful, even although we have our hard hard bits. Many both where I am and you are have it ever so much harder.

I have had all that knocked out of me long ago. I know myself better now, where I am weak and where I am strong, and know will make a better and stronger man for you now than I would have been otherwise. This life is full of lessons, and does the man who takes them, a right, a lasting good. It brings some down, but others it raises. We chafe and grumble often but we are ever learning.

Monday, 26 July 1915

I have been on Guard as I told you last night. We came on at six o'clock and I did my sentry from eight till ten, two until four this morning and am on again from 8.00 till 10.00 pm and I do my last sentry from two till four. I had to keep my eyes and ears open all the same, as being on Guard on active service is no joke, and every person who passes has to give a clear account of their self or be put under arrest. A few Frenchmen and a despatch rider or two was all that troubled my reverie. Of course this country is under Martial Law and everybody has to be in by 9.00 pm and all lights out at that time and armed Guards have the power to shoot at sight. It is just starting to rain. So I must get a more sheltered spot.

We have also a prisoner to look after. He is made to do hard work during the day and then tied to a wagon wheel two hours every night and gets four biscuits and a tin of bully beef for his day's rations, all for hesitating to obey an order by a Sergeant. Of course we don't have anything to do with him, with his work or the wheel. There are Military Police for that job, but he sleeps and feeds in the Guard Room. Ah yes one gets severely punished out here for next to nothing. Yes your Aunt Liz was quite right, but have no fears my Darling, I have sense enough to keep myself in hand. We have learnt how to bear being treated like dogs. Thank God, we will be as we were some day, free.

ROMANTICISM AND CHIVALRY

It was normal for a soldier to carry in his breast pocket a testament or other book. Books were one of the few resources available to the soldiers to relieve the boredom of military life and take them out of the trenches into the world of the imagination. Officers had better access to everything, including space to keep and carry books. The ordinary soldier had only his tunic pocket and his kit bag. Accordingly books had to be small and compact. One such book was given to Willie on 21 July 1915 by a sergeant in 27 Field Ambulance, called Hope Bagenal, with whom Willie had become friends. It was a small limp leather pocket edition of the English poet John Keats, in a type of edition that was really first popularized by the Great War. The format followed the style of the testaments of the Bible Societies, and whether a book came out in such a format during the war was as good a guide as any to its circulation on the Western Front.

Hope Bagenal chose 'The Eve of St Agnes' to introduce Willie to Keats, and recalled forty years later that Willie was so entranced by the beauty of the poem, that he requested Bagenal to read it again so that Peter Edgar could hear it. After 'The Eve of St Agnes', Bagenal read Keats' 'Ode on a Grecian Urn' and his 'Ode to a Nightingale', his masterpieces of subtle chimes and exquisite inner harmonics. Keats' poetry appealed to many soldiers not just as literature that expanded the vistas of the imagination, but as beauty born in Keats' struggle to overcome his *mortality and imminent death. Educated at Uppingham School, Hope Bagenal's style and mental habits were influenced over-whelmingly by the classical authors of antiquity touched with a neo-romanticism. For example in a 1915 draft[5] for his book about the war, Fields and Battlefields,[6] Bagenal spoke of the British soldiers before the Battle of Loos as, 'from the four quarters of the British Isles, summoned from the common ways of life for a purpose never dreamt of in past years', and as 'surely subjects of those great gods as in centuries gone by had drawn a thousand ships to Tenedos'.**

Closely linked with the neo-romance of Bagenal were the neo-chivalric ideas with which Willie entered the war, and his belief in the 'manly' virtues of courage, endurance and sacrifice. In September 1914 he wrote about being so proud to be his father's son as he read his father's straight 'manly' letter to him and then read it out to his comrades. At a field service immediately after the Battle of Loos, Willie admired the Padre's words about his dead comrades having been 'Faithful unto death' and having paid the full penalty for King and Country, and how chivalry was not a thing of the past, there having been hundreds of instances of it in the battle. What the Padre was doing was running together the notions of chivalry and Christian duty into the concept of the Christian Knight. Throughout the war Willie adhered to this concept in his attitudes to Jane and in his views about duty. He wrote that he would rather die than be branded a coward. Willie's Christian Knight had also some puritan beliefs. While reviling war, Willie believed in the idea of improvement through suffering and sacrifice. Thus he wrote to Jane just after Loos on 30 September 1915, 'These experiences of suffering will do me lasting good'.

Monday, 19 July 1915

I had a great chat with our Captain Chaplain today and he showed me a testament he got from one of the KOSB who had been shot. The bullet struck him right over the heart, went through his pocket and the books and letters he had inside and half through his

---

* Tenedos is an island in the Aegean Sea beside Troy.

testament and was deflected from his heart by the testament. He comes from Larbert and knows the Rayburns well.

There are some of us going up to the trenches next week I hear. The names are not decided on as yet. We are all anxious to know who will go. I am sure I would be quite pleased if they select me, for this sort of life here gets on one's nerves and things in the trenches are in some respects better than here. We have quite a number of young men in our Hos here who are half-mad, their nerves having given way and I can tell you its a pitiful sight to see them, and hear their ravings, and it is not surprising after dodging shells for ten months.

Thursday, 22 July 1915

This morning I saw them performing an operation on one of the patients. It is an awful game and I wish it was over. No wonder some of those chaps are down here sick. It's not only bullets and shells but dead bodies etc in the trenches and around and about that sickens them. It is nothing short of a vast cemetery and they have to stand at their posts there and legs, heads and feet sticking out of the side of the trenches of brave men who have fallen earlier in the war, and if they have to dig, what they unearth would sicken the very best.

I will sent you a PC or two of this place. The poem gives you the B.* The serg. that wrote that sonnet gave me a present of a nice little volume of Keats' poems yesterday with a nice little poem to myself on the fly leaf. I will copy it out and send it to you. He is a very fine gentleman indeed. I am going to take a drawing of him if I can, as he has a strong face. We are having fine weather out here just now, but the cold at nights is bad. I wonder what it will be like in the winter time.

Friday, 23 July 1915

In Hospital sitting beside Pete, who by the way is feeling fine and has got rid of his pain and is beginning to put some food into

---

* B refers to Béthune. See poem at Note 7.

himself. This Hospital was a mill formerly and is full of patients. Some of them are very bad indeed, two or three on my right are singing 'When the roll is called up yonder, I will be there', hardy types who have stood a bit of bashing in the trenches, and their wee blue hymn book between the three. All the floor is covered with stretchers and the orderlies moving about at their duties. It is a large place and very suitable for a Hospital, although everything is rough and ready, no polish about anything. But as Hospitals go out here, it is very good.

Monday forenoon, 25 July 1915

I have just been speaking to one of our Sergeants (who by the way is an educated gentleman). I showed him the French coin I have dated 1779 some time ago. He was extremely interested in it at the time and today he read out to me a sonnet he had composed on the same coin. I will forward on a copy to you when he gives it to me.[7] He is a very clever fellow and entirely out of place in the army, far too mild a nature to be here. He and I often have some great talks about books and history and poems.

I shall never forget the look on his face the day we left Bordon to come here. His wife had been staying at a farm close to the Camp, as she always has done since he got married at Xmas time and our train left at 7.00 am. We were all looking out of the window having a last look at the old camping ground, and when we passed it, there was Sergeant B.'s wife waiting to give her husband a farewell wave. He was in the next carriage to me, and how he looked at her such dumb misery. I knew what he was suffering at the time as I also had gone through it and understood the torture. He looks as if he was going to jump out of the carriage, and she, poor soul, was much the same. What torture this war has brought. He sleeps next to us in the dirty old barn. He dearly loves to sit and read me some of his favourite poems on a sunny day when we have not much to do and I dearly love to listen to the beautiful readings, as he is an expert elocutionist, and dream of my Darling Jane, and let my mind wander with the poet, as he reads of love, my favourite subject. Life at these moments takes on a different aspect, till the spell is broken by the gruff voice of an officer or the SM.

We had a nice Church Service yesterday in an orchard close by. Our Chaplain is with the Brigade in the trenches and so we had a new one, and he was grand, a fine address on Paul boasting about his sufferings, and took as his text, 'Ready Aye Ready', a phrase below one of the stained-glass windows of Glasgow Cathedral. I enjoyed him fine. He was so lovely and it did one's heart good to sing the old hymns, even although the booming of the guns made more noise than we did.

Chapter Three

1915
Missions of Mercy
at Festubert

'The whole system is one of evacuation. It is a very perfect
system and one of the very best in the world.'

*On 31 July 1915 Willie left Robecq and marched to a Field
Hospital just outside of Béthune. Then on 10 August 1915 he and
his stretcher squad went up to the trenches to bring down
wounded, working at night from two 27 Brigade Advanced
Dressing Stations, one at the former village of Festubert and
another at La Plantin. Despite the risks and the squalor, Willie
throughout the war seemed to prefer to work in the trenches. At
this early stage of the war he also wrote that he was keen to get to
the front. During July 1915, while his Brigade was in the trenches
he was impatient to be allowed to do some stretcher bearing, but
had to work at a Hospital at Robecq. That sort of work he detested
as repetitive and boring. In the diary that he rewrote in his seven-
ties, he harked on about the tedium of these repetitive jobs as an
orderly – to him perhaps the worst memories of the war. The
infantry at least had 'the thrill of the fight'. Willie's letter of 12
August 1915 to his father and mother, in which he describes
bringing the wounded from the trenches, was sent by Willie's father
to a local newspaper and published. The published version was
edited to give a more heroic and upbeat message.*

*After a few days' of work at the trenches, Willie left the line with
the Division for a rest camp at Gonnehem near Béthune. Then at*

the beginning of September 1915 he went to Béthune and started working again in the trenches, this time making preparations for a forthcoming military operation, details of which were not at this stage known to the men. The soldiers knew something was likely to happen, but had no idea what. In fact a letter of Willie's of 6 August 1915 (not here published) provided a clue. The fall of Warsaw told of the defeats the Russians were suffering in the east. Willie said it was disheartening 'for us out here to hear news like that' and 'It[the war] is a big big task, as we and our allies have found out'. Willie then wrote in his letter of 19 August 1915 that 27 Brigade were a fine lot indeed and had had a good taste of war and he heard that the next time they went into action they had hard work in store for them. They had a position to take before the winter and 9 Div. were chosen for the work and 'Kitchener is very fond of this Div.'.

Monday, 2 August 1915

I have been standing by as I told you yesterday for two hours. We will be relieved at 6.00 pm tonight. Our bearers of A section and half of B went into the trenches today and the first convoy of wounded will not be sent here till it is dark. We of course will wait here and relieve them in a week or ten days. We have tents here for the operations and everything ready for the grim work. I stood outside the bivouac we have here for the squads in waiting last night and watched the star shells for a long time. It is a very fascinating thing to see them for miles and miles along the line coming from the Germans and going from our lines. They light up everything around and to hear the distant boom of the German guns and the closer roar of our own all added to the effect.

To let you know how we work, we have here our Field Hospital, five operating tents, about a dozen smaller tents for placing wounded till they are treated. Further up we have our Advanced Dressing Station where we the bearers bring the wounded on stretchers from the trenches, front line of trenches as well. We send up twelve squads of four who work twenty-four hours on and same off four squads at a time, or four squads at a time and not so long a spell. They carry on for ten days or a fortnight and then the remaining bearers go and relieve them and they come down here and do the work we are doing now, unloading convoys of wounded and arranging them out according to the nature of their wounds, seriously wounded by themselves and slightly wounded by themselves, and so on, everything in order; so that whenever a case is looked to – that is properly dressed or operated on if necessary – they are taken in motor convoys, or barges on the canal, down to the Clearing Hospital where they are sent to the base and to England.

The Advanced Dressing Station is a mile behind the firing line always under shell fire, and this our Field Hospital is two and a half miles behind; so you will have a fairly good idea of the nature of our work. Bringing the wounded from the trenches is hot work. In the trenches one is fairly safe from bullet fire, or rifle fire. The ground between that and the Dressing St. is open to rifle, snipers and shell-fire and the men must be brought back and carefully at that. We will carry this part of the work of our Division for two or three months and then one of the other three Ambulances will relieve us as we did 28 FA and we will take a spell further down attending to the sick of our Div.; that is how it is done. We have had our turn with the sick, we are having our turn in the firing line, and after we will take up the Clearing Hospital duties. The whole system is of one of evacuation. A wounded man from the moment he drops is kept on the move until he gets to the base and being attended to all the way whether by train, barge or motor. It is a very perfect system and one of the very best in the world.

Sunday, 8 August 1915

I thought I would be off duty today but we got orders this morning to go on again, as 17, 18, 19 Squads went over to the trenches. Today I was writing home. Have just finished Mother's letter, and enclosed her PC like yours. We had a service, only about a dozen of us there. It is five past eleven now and you will be preparing for church. We have a bell in the Ambulance but not for church. It is the empty casing of a shell and used as a gong for sounding the gas alarm. A rapid striking of the gong, we get our respirators and smoke helmets on. We have not had an alarm yet, and don't want one.

What I am weary waiting on just now is the postman coming with the mail. We have had a few serious cases this morning dressed and sent away down. A bullet in the arm is considered a blessing, but some of the wounds we have seen are the reverse. Those trench mortars make fearful havoc amongst the men. A chap the day before yesterday was sitting writing in the trench, and had just finished his letter. 'Another one to my sweetheart' he said. As he stretched himself, the top part of his head showed over the parapet for a second and a bullet went clean through it. How very easy. He forgot for the moment he was writing in danger and how very dearly he paid for it.

12 August 1915*

I have managed to steal a few minutes to myself, not that we are fearfully busy up here, but well, we never know the minute we will be required for some job, if not up in the trenches doing something or other. But at present I am supposed to be working in our dug-out keeping it in order, and as there are many at it, the job, which by the way is finished and in good order, I thought I would slip away to this corner where I can get peace to write my letter. I know you are all very anxious to hear all my news, but it is so difficult to get green envelopes, and to put the news that would interest you into an ordinary one would in all probability prevent it passing the censor. As Jane's letters are not for our officer to read, I generally always give her a green envelope and put all the news there, knowing that she reads all the general parts to you on Thursdays. Of course the general part is small comparatively speaking, but well ye ken she and I have a lot of private business to talk about, such as but I need not mention it. Today we had one green envelope issued, the first since we left R[obecq] to come here about three weeks ago, and I managed to get another one in a little way of my own. So you both can have one. Too much of a preface this. Wull get on wie the letter, and let's hear frae ye. Well here goes.

Of course you know what sort of work we had at our Field Hospital where I was for ten days after we made our last move, night and day on for thirty-six hours at a stretch and getting used to seeing the awful consequences of war. I did not mind in the least

* This letter, most of which is reproduced, was to Willie's father and mother. A less detailed letter was sent to Jane covering the same events.

the overtime as we were doing our bit to relieve suffering, what I enlisted for. Of course we were anxious to get up to the firing line but had to wait till our turn came, to relieve the squads who went up the first day. We got orders on Monday and came up here about midday. Everything was very quiet for an hour or so and of course we could not see much signs of war, not so much as we expected till we all got our first start, an eighteen pounder let off about twelve yards behind us (these guns are so well concealed that one would have to search a long time to discover them, and anybody caught at that game, well, thumbs down).

It and some more batteries all around us – we are right in front of them – let it rip for a considerable time and the first shells passed over us (British shells of course) but what a creepy sensation they give one hearing them for the first time. The report of the shot makes everything shiver, and to hear the shell speeding overhead (Whistling Rufus, they call them) makes one wish for anything than to be in the way of it or near it when it bursts. To give you an idea, an officer came up the road last night on a motor bike. He was evidently a newcomer. He was just passing our Dressing St. when big Lizzie let go – clean into the dry ditch at the roadside he went with the fright. They are passing over my head now as I write. We are quite used to it already, as it goes on at intervals all day and night. Three squads went up into the trenches to bring back wounded the first night, and we were detailed to waiting duty, or to go up if any other squads were required. It was a quiet night and the squads sent were sufficient for the work. I watched the star shells going up and also the relieving of the Battalion who had done their time in the trenches.

It is a very well conducted performance and, my how pleased those coming out are, and how serious those who are going in look because every time they go in, there are some who never return. I stood by myself against a wall watching them go by, very quietly except for the heavy tramp of many feet on the hard road. The light of my cigarette let them know I was there. 'Goodnight lad,' some out of every platoon said. 'Goodnight boys. I hope you enjoy your rest,' I answered and on they went till I could not hear the sound of their feet. I stood for a long time watching the beautiful effects of the German star shells (which by the way are much better than ours) and thought of those boys going down and the others who

39

had just relieved them and the sorrows and hardships they all had to go through, and the sorrows of those at home, and of course my mind and thoughts were in my own home with you all in 58 and I wondered and wished I was back with you all again. One gets very homesick, standing there in the position I was in thinking of Jane, and you all in bonnie Scotland.

It was a beautiful dark night and, what with the lights and stars and the passing men, ideal for a dreamer but my reverie was broken with the batteries opening fire on the Germans, and reminded me of my work and that to be able to do it I would have to get a sleep as I had had none for two nights. I lay down just as I was and was not awakened till morning. We were in waiting for twenty-four hours and that meant that any work to be done during the day was ours. In the forenoon I was ordered out with my squad and got my medical bags shoved into my hand and told to go to one of the batteries and attend one of the gunners.

When we got there, we found the poor fellow lying with his back broken.* He had been up a tree taking observations and had fallen off. I did what was necessary for him and brought him back to our Station where he was immediately sent down to our Field Hospital in another Wagon. After dinner I thought it was not likely I would be called out again, so I got a grassy part, took off my boots and socks, stretched out my waterproof sheet and settled myself down to have a nice little nap to make up for lost time. I was only down ten minutes, 'St Clair, get your squad together and report at the First Aid Post in the trenches'. Not bad for a start, I said to myself as I called the others, meantime slipping into my boots, respirator, smoke helmet and bottle of solution to soak them (we have always to carry those in case of gas attack). I found the Regimental Stretcher-bearer there to conduct me to where the poor fellows were. I had another two squads with me besides my own and three stretchers on trolley wheels.

We set off. Five minutes up the road we crossed a field and came to the reserve trench, passed that, and up one of the most exposed roads hereabouts, till we arrived at the communication trench. Any further it was impossible to take the wheels; so we got our stretcher off and into the trench. By this time I had learned we had six

* A letter to Jane on the same events mentioned that the man had a 'DSO up'.

patients to bring down and while going up that trench I wondered how it was possible to bring a stretcher case down, but well it must be done I suppose and thought no more about it. We twisted in and out expecting every minute that one of the many shells bursting about would drop in beside us, but nothing happened and we arrived at our destination without mishap. We were 500 yards from the Germans and the new sights about the trenches, dugouts etc, men standing to, and the sensation that we were there at last, took our attention for a moment.

I went over to the dugouts where the wounded were and found the Regimental Dr., got the stretcher up and then I entered the dugout, down three steps into a dark hole and further in another hole where I could see a chap's feet covered with blood sticking out. We found four bad cases and two dead (the dead we leave to the care of their comrades who take them out and bury them). I get their particulars and kits together and bring them out of that hole as carefully as we could. The first one out has four toes blown off, the next his right arm smashed, and the next covered with wounds, and the other wee chap has a wound in his foot and one in his hip, and each as he goes out called something to his mates. A soldier or two gives us a hand. They are all in the Black Watch and Scotch. 'Noo Wull if they take you to Edinburgh mind and ca on my old wife, and tell her I getin on fine.' 'I wull that Jock.' 'Say Dave, ye're likely to go tae Dundee; they hive an Hospital there, if ye dae ca on my mither and tell her hoo am getting on, there's the add.' 'A'll dae that, Wull, so long, tak care o yersell and watch those shells.' 'A widna mind a deecent wound tae get out of this.' 'So long, a'll meet ye at Glesca cross,' and remarks like that make one feel a lump in the throat.

My word but they are brave fellows, three stretchers and four lying cases. 'We'll come back for you,' I said to the wee chap. 'No no, I am all right. You look after the aithers and I'll hobble alang.' (What a bang. I made a bad job o'my last g. with the start. There are some shells bursting on my right and some on my left I hope they don't come this way or I will have to shift.) We got them all out and proceeded to manoeuvre them down that trench, the heat was awful, my two bags of medical gear and purents water bottle feel heavy. We have to halt often, and are forced to put one of the stretchers down and get the men on the others. I shall never forget

41

that experience coming down that trench, the way we had to twist about and crawl along. Every man's heart was in his work or we could never have done it and still the little fellow hobbled along and never a murmur either from him or those on the stretcher.

These chaps are heroes, no mistake. I give some of them a drink but the water in my bottle is quite hot (the banging of those guns is terrible just now). The fellow we are carrying asks a drink but it is impossible owing to the nature of his wound. 'A right chappie, ye ken best, don't gie me it if it will dae harm.' I feel I would give my life for him, he is such a brick. Off we go again. Oh that heat. We are soaking with sweat, men pass us and crawl along underneath the parapet, taking care that not a part shows, as there are plenty snipers about. We hear the whistling of the shells overhead and also the bang of German shells bursting. We halt to take a rest and take a peep at the effect of the shells on the German parapet – bang, whiss through the air and then a cloud of dust right in the German trench. Our gunners are deadly every time and to get a peep outside the trench is an education – desolation, everything that has been a tree is stripped. Just there many famous charges have been made, charges you and I have read about in the papers and a few VCs won. I feel the effect of the thing on me and would dearly love to get on the top of that parapet and take a good view of the scene, but that soon wears off when we think of the many who have paid dearly for their curiosity.

While in the trenches a German aeroplane flies overhead and our guns are banging away at it. We proceed with our work and work down another few yards till I feel nearly exhausted, but the sight of the wee chap hopping along on one leg braces me. I never worked like this in all my life. All our thought is getting our patients down to the end of this trench as comfortably as possible. We come to a part of the trench where it divides and halt a little to allow one of the killed, being carried by his comrades to be buried, to pass on. The chap I left with the other patient up the trench comes down and says we had better get some more assistance, what I knew all along, and intended sending for when we got to the end of the trench, but that will be too late and so I hurry down and tell those on ahead to send for some more bearers when they get out.

We get them down eventually after about two hours' work. I have a look at the wee chap's wounds and find that one has not been dressed, the fault of their Reg. Doctor. I dress it up. He is done up but sticks it like a brick. We have a long road to go and the sentry tells us to take care as the road is dangerous and that the Germans are sending over shells. This road is very open and in view of the Germans. At night time they sweep it with machine guns. Our work has to be done. We try our patients on the wheels, but find they can't stand the jolting and so decide to carry them. The little fellow drops, his leg can't stand it. We take turns of carrying him on our back and helping with the stretcher. A shell bursts thirty yards on a right in an old farm yd., nothing of the farm being left but the walls. We have to halt and rest or we will not be able to finish our job. The other bearers come up. I send them on for the other chap and we get on with our work (I can hear the ping, crack of a sniper not very far away as I write). We at last get our patients down to where the wagon is waiting and get them in. The others bring down their patient. We get a drink of water and watch the German aeroplane just overhead. Our gunners fire shell after shell but not one hits the mark. The wagon goes off and we walk back to our St. after one of the hardest day's work we ever did, and quite pleased with ourselves and our experiences.

Pete Edgar worked like a Trojan. Pete, like myself is very soft-hearted and would have done it all himself if he could. The other two in our squad did everything without a grumble, better taking a pleasure in doing their best for the fellows we had to help. Their wounds were caused by a shell. A part passed through the little fellow's kilt. I saw the torn kilt while I was dressing him and asked about it. A part of a shell as large as my hand went clean through it, took a bit of his hip away and killed his comrade and still he hobbled along all that road. Does anybody wonder that we would risk ourselves to help them? I would I could do more for them. I shall never forget the fortitude of those four Black Watch. They will be sent home and I wish them the best of luck and hope they don't require to come out here again.

We go up to the trenches tonight again at 8.00 pm and stay there till tomorrow, my squad and two others. What a bombardment, it is awful just now. I expect we will be required there tonight.

14 August 1915

This is the first moment I've had to write you since my last letter. So I will start and give you our movements since I wrote you last. To start with, we are away from the trenches now at our rest camp. We left yesterday afternoon. I think, if I remember correctly, I left off where I told you that Pete and I volunteered to go up one night in place of two chaps who were a little timorous and I also wrote a page while up there and finished my letter the following forenoon. That was our last visit. I received your letter just after I had posted yours and how much I enjoyed them you know. It is impossible to say how much your letters mean to me lovey often while on the verge of despair and utterly downhearted.

19 August 1915

Our Div. are all round about this district, just now, and I am sure I have met forty from Kilsyth and Kirkie mostly in the Argyll and Sutherland H. 10th Battalion. It is fine and brings one a little nearer home. They have opened a Recreation Room in the little village close by for 27 Brigade and they had a concert amongst themselves last night but we were not there as only a few of each Company could get in. But they are a fine lot indeed and have had a good taste of war and I hear that the next time we go into action, we have hard work in store for us. They have a position to take before the winter and 9 Div. are chosen for the work. Kitchener is very fond of this Div. and inspected them today. Twice or three times now since we came out here he has done that. You see we are part of the First Army, regulars, the only Div. of Kitchener's that are attached to the First Army and I suppose will have to do the work that follows that honour. But as to our movements we know nothing for certain but we do hear some things that turn out to be correct.

It is fine being away from those guns for a little as they do work on the nerves and give one such headaches. You can't imagine the terrible shaking noise of them. I had to show our Captain my tunic yesterday where the piece of shell struck me and tell him all about it. I was only one of our Ambulance that had that experience while up there although there were plenty of small pieces flying about and

I can assure you I don't want it any nearer again. I was forced yesterday to do some patching and do you know lovey how I managed? I had no cloth and so I cut part of the leg off where my puttees cover it and cut a piece, and as I had only white thread I had just to do it with white. It is not a very neat job, stitches going in are all directions, but much better than before and so at present I am going about with a very conspicuous patch on the seat of my trousers with the stitching very prominent for today's inspection. They selected all those with whole clothes to go (dead fly and just like the Army) so that Kitchener would not see the rags.

21 August 1915

I am going to get one of our fellows who goes on leave tomorrow to post this in England, and so I will be able to speak more freely re our movements. The parcel came yesterday, and my letter enclosed. It was a topper and I enjoyed it in full. Don't worry lovey, I will not run any unnecessary risks. Of course you know that we came out here via Southampton and Havre where we stayed a day and trained to a place 1½ from St. Omer, Wesernes. We were there a week I think and marched via Ebblinghem and Hazebrouck to Steenwerck. We were there from 17 May till 5 June. We marched from there via Estaires and Merville to Guarbecque. We were there till the 25 June and marched to St. Hilaire, left there on the 29th and arrived at Quinten at 9 pm and the following day returned to Robecq where we joined our Hospital Section on the 30th. Our Div. goes into action at Festubert.

Left Robecq on 31 July and marched to a field just outside of Béthune, where we start taking in the wounded. Our stretcher-bearers go up to the trenches at Festubert the following day and you know all the rest. We also went up to Festubert and La-Plantin near Givenchy and had our baptism, and came down here for our rest, Gonnehem near Béthune.

When we go into action again, we go to Givenchy I hear, and they have the ridge to take there before winter sets in. Our Ambulance will be stationed at Béthune for the winter I hear and the Bearers of course will go to Givenchy. There are lots of rumours of leave after, and also that there is a chance of our being shifted to the Dardenelles, but I don't believe them. Kitchener inspected the 9th at Busnes two days ago. That will give you a fair idea of our movements. It has been rumoured that we have to go to Ypres where it is very hot indeed. If we do move there, you will know by a Y for Ypres or a G for Givenchy or L.B. for La Bassée as to which part of the line we go to. I suppose you will know all this already by the loops. I think I will stop the loops and try the dot over the letters I want you to word. It gets through the censor very well indeed and the loops often look so very conspicuous. You could see mine sometimes a mile away. Lovey, well, I think that will do for names of places. We are in the First Army along with the 1, 2, 7 and 9 Div. and are considered regulars – what an honour. 7 Div. who relieve the 9th at Festubert are one of the best and have had some hard cracks. We have had a fairly miserable time owing to the cads of officers we have who are as selfish as can be. As long as they are all right, they don't give a ------ for the men although since we have been up there, there has been a slight improvement. Our captain, who is Scotch, is a fine fellow, but all the English ones except our colonel have been rotten. However we are used to all that now and I believe are not so badly off as some regiments are.

Sunday forenoon, 12 September 1915

We were up the line yesterday again and made another compartment to our dugout and had a very hard day's work. We got back at 7.30 pm and had only time to get a good wash and off to bed, very tired indeed. We may be going up there any time now to stay perhaps tonight or tomorrow. What I saw up there, I can't tell you, and sign my name at the back of this envelope, but there is something in store for the Germans. There are so many guns around us up there it is beyond description, the noise of the firing. We filled 780 sandbags yesterday and between sawing wood and bricklaying etc, we had plenty to do. I by the way and a Serj. have been the builders. So you see one gets quite versatile so far as work is concerned out here. I have had to laugh at myself often, when I stop to think about it, building away as if I had always been used to it. Never mind Darling, that will all come in handy some day, perhaps, and besides, I don't object to hard work. In fact I would work the skin off my fingers any day to be away from our present S M.

Chapter Four

The Battle of Loos

'Our beautiful Division which is no more'

After various inter-Allied conferences, Lord Kitchener agreed in the summer of 1915 to a plan of Commander-in-Chief Joffre that in the autumn the French would undertake an offensive along a wide front in Champagne and the British and French combined would attack in Artois. The offensive was primarily for political or strategic reasons to show solidarity with the Russians who had suffered serious reverses against the Germans on the Eastern Front. The fear was that if nothing significant was done to encourage the Russian nation and take pressure off its armies, the Russians might be driven to make a separate peace with Germany in 1915 as they were later to do in 1917. The place chosen for the British to attack was a small coal mining town, of which about all that was left by then in the scarred landscape were some old mining structures and slag heaps. In this place called Loos six divisions of the British First Army under General Sir Douglas Haig, including two 'New Army' divisions- the 9th (Scottish) Division and the 15th (Scottish) Division – were to charge the German positions. Kitchener ordered the attack against the advice of his commanders. Although General Haig argued strongly against the attack,[8] on 29 August 1915 he was impressed by a demonstration of chlorine gas being released from cylinders – a new British weapon they called the 'chlorine wave' – and told his corps and divisional commanders that, if the wind was favourable, and gas was available on an extensive scale, it would more than compensate for the inadequate strength of heavy artillery. He emphasized to Sir William Robertson that the attack should 'under no circumstances be launched without the aid of gas', but was over-ruled by GHQ which instructed that the attack of the First Army was 'not to be dependent on the use of gas, which, in the nature of things must be uncertain'; and that the assault should take place on 25 September, irrespective of weather conditions.[9]

Haig obtained a weather forecast at 9.20 p.m. on 24 September of a favourable west wind, and gave the order for a general offensive on 25 September 1915, subject to change to a limited offensive if the weather forecast proved wrong. Zero hour was set for 5.45 am. The following day at 5.00 am, the wind was slight and, when Haig went out, there was almost a calm. At his request, his ADC, Major A.F. Fletcher, lit a cigarette. The smoke puffs drifted towards the north-east. Accordingly, on the basis of that isolated experiment, Haig gave the order at 5.15 am for the wide offensive to carry on. A few minutes later the air turned completely still, but it was too late to revoke the order.[10]

The gas was released at 5.50 am, but the wind was slight and irregular, and in some places it blew the cloud back over the British trenches. It certainly did not compensate materially for all the weaknesses on the British side. There appears to have been some element of surprise, although at least one writer suggests that the Germans knew it was going to be used by the British.[11] Haig himself always claimed that there was complete surprise, and asked just before his death,[12] when the Official History of the War was being compiled, that the draft text be amended to flag up that the soldiers had successfully kept the secret from the enemy.[13]

The use of gas in the 9th Division sector of the front had no effect on the Germans,[14] and caused serious harm to the Division. The 9th Division was in the trenches facing the Hohenzollern Redoubt on the right and Fosse 8 on the left. 26 Brigade[15] was to attack on the right and 28 Brigade on the left,[16] with 27 Brigade in reserve.[17] The attack of 26 Brigade was a surprising success, with the Hohenzollern Redoubt, Fosse 8[18] and its Dump taken. But this success was despite the gas, with the Seaforths of 26 Brigade having to charge through gas and smoke causing many casualties.[19] The Camerons of the same Brigade, on the left of the Seaforths, hung back in the hope that the gas and smoke might move from their trenches, but they also had to attack amidst gas.[20]

The 28th Brigade had an even worse experience with the gas than the 26th Brigade. This was compounded with other factors, and it led to a complete disaster for that Brigade. What happened was that the wind direction at 28 Brigade's sector was the most unfavourable on the whole front, blowing from the south-east.[21] The wind blew the cloud of gas back over the waiting battalions, and they were also faced with a German artillery barrage on their front trench. Those few of 28 Brigade that got beyond the gas and the barrage then faced uncut wire and concealed ditches filled with stakes and barbed wire, as well as enfilading fire. The casualties of the two leading battalions of 28 Brigade were:- 6/KOSB- all twenty officers who went into action and 630 men, with not more than forty-six men under a corporal able to be assembled at the end of the day; and 10/ Highland Light Infantry – fifteen officers and 631 other ranks, with the battalion diarist estimating that eighty-five per cent of the officers and 70 per cent of the men of the three leading companies were lost in the first few minutes of the attack, some from the effects of gas.

The 9th Division was withdrawn from the trenches for a rest on 28 September 1915. All three Brigades had experienced heavy and continuous fighting. In three days the Division of approximately 10,000 men had suffered 6,058 casualties, including the Divisional Commander[22] killed, the 27 Brigade Brigadier[23] captured, and most of the battalion commanders either killed or badly wounded. The British casualties at Loos were 60,000, equivalent to a quarter of Britain's Regular Army strength,[24] with nothing gained of any significance. The Commander of the BEF, Sir John French, resigned in December over the conduct of the battle and especially the handling of his Reserve divisions, the 21st and 24th, which were ordered into the battle late in the day on 25 September, so that they could reinforce initial successes, but were faced with an exhausting approach march much of it through the night. On the following day when they attacked they suffered very high casualties without even getting through the wire in front of the German positions.[25]

From Willie's account of the Battle of Loos it is possible to plot more or less where he was at any one time. One can see on the map behind the 9th Division sector trenches at Loos, a railway running west from the La Bassée–Vermelles road. The medical arrangements for bringing back wounded used this railway line to divide

49

the areas for collecting wounded into the north and south areas, which on 25 September corresponded to the areas of 28 and 26 Brigade attacks. Willie was in the north sector. Arrangements had been made to bring the wounded down in the north area by a special trench for wounded sufficiently wide for wheeled stretchers, known as 'Guy's Alley', to a Dressing Station, called 'Guy's', in dug-outs for twenty-four stretchers at the point where the La Bassée–Vermelles road crosses the railway, and thence to a dug-out in a factory further back. They were then taken by trollies, of which there were six carrying six stretchers each, to the Noyelles-Cambrin road and thence by ambulance transport to an Advanced Dressing Station in the church at Cambrin. There was a similar arrangement for the evacuation of wounded in the southern area, with a 'Bart's Alley' special trench leading to a Dressing Station, called 'Bart's', where the special trench met the La Bassée–Vermelles railway line. They were then taken down to where Bart's Alley met the La Bassée–Vermelles road, and thence to an Advanced Dressing Station in a brewery at Vermelles. The main Dressing Stations and Hospitals were further to the rear. In addition there were some aid-posts in the trenches and Divisional Collecting Stations for walking wounded beside Annequin, just west of Cambrin, for the northern area, and at Sailly Lebourse for the southern area.[26] Willie worked most of Saturday 25 September helping and carrying in wounded to the Divisional Collecting Station at Annequin. He also loaded on to wagons wounded, who had come down Guy's Alley and been put on trollies, and brought them to Cambrin Advanced Dressing Station. Late on 25 September, on the occasion he is gassed, he went up to the Cambrin Advanced Dressing Station and met Lieutenant Hancock. They then went up Guy's Alley Trench to an Advance Post, meeting some of 28 Field Ambulance. The section of the front he then describes, where they went over the parapet to bring in a wounded soldier, was the section of front from which 28 Brigade had launched their ill-fated attack.

Willie's letter of 30 September 1915 raises the controversial issue of both sides' treatment of prisoners. It is interesting, because we can see elements of exaggeration, myth and propaganda at work in the accounts of the soldiers, as they came in from the battle. They were claiming that the Germans were shooting British wounded. This charge must be treated with care. The British Official History of the War stated that after a dreadful slaughter of British soldiers on 26 September 1915, the Germans behaved impeccably:

> *'The Germans did not follow in pursuit, but from Hulloch about 2.00 p.m. they sent out medical personnel and stretcher bearers who, regardless of shelling, worked at binding up the British wounded, sending all who could walk or crawl back to the British lines.'[27]*

The soldiers also told Willie that the German machine gunners were chained to their guns. This is often thought to be a myth but in the Kirkintilloch Herald *of 3 November 1915 a survivor of the battle, who was himself a machine gunner, said he personally saw a German chained to his machine gun and asked a captured German about the practice. Accounts in that newspaper also suggest that the British soldiers in the battle 'saw red' and killed Germans as they attempted to surrender and after they had surrendered.*

Saturday, 19 September 1915 8 pm

We were put up the line to the Advanced Dressing Station today, about a mile further on to where we have been working all week. We are just outside L[a] B[assée] in a village that is all ruins. I can assure you it is a very hot corner. I and my companions who came up today are getting our 'beds' ready in a dugout. Everybody here sleeps in a dug-out because we have shelling every day – five burst thirty yards from us tonight. It is much hotter than the last place we were in at F[estubert]. The communication trenches start about four yards from where I am writing. The rifles and machine guns are rattling away just now like mad. My word but it sounds near. Our Dressing Station is in or just outside C[ambrin] Church and one of the Engineers was killed by a bullet in the Church just round it yesterday. So you have a fair idea as to where we are.

The squads go up for two days at a time and stay in the trenches, two squads at a time, and the others go and improve the dugouts there and have had to widen the trench right up to the firing trench, work that the RAMC have never done before. The RAMC are not looked down on here – you bet, not in this Division, and as to what you say some folks in the home country say about us, well it is not

51

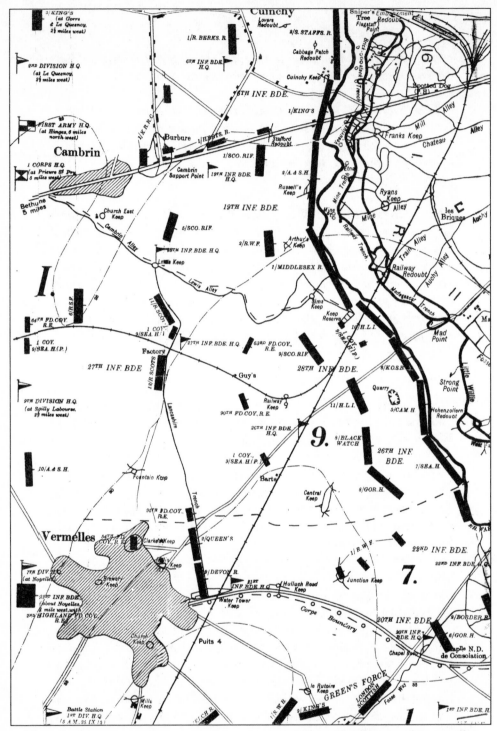

Map showing routes of evacuation of wounded to Cambrin and Vermelles from 9th Division sector of the front at the Battle of Loos.

worth taking notice of, as we belong to the Corps that possesses the most VCs in the British Army for body-snatching and robbing death off many victims who would never have had a ghost of a chance if it was not for the devotion to duty of this same Corps – but enough of that. Darling you know, and that's all I care for.

Sunday night again inside our dug-out in my old corner, writing.

We went up into the trenches this morning early with water and rations (¼ loaf, one tin of bully beef) for the day to do a day's digging. What we had to do was to make small dug-outs or rather crevices in the side of the trench to put stretcher cases in when we get the big rush of wounded we expect soon, and we have them right up to the firing trench. It is not the work of the RAMC to do this, but the Pioneers. But our officers, or rather Commanding Officer volunteered for us to do it ourselves, as every man has to do his share to get everything perfect. We had only got the length of the fourth line when they started shelling our part with shrapnel and 'whis bangs', and we had to duck and get on with our work between times. It was a hot and exciting job, I can tell you, with the shrapnel, bullets smashing against the inside of our trench. These shells burst in the air and everything comes down.

We had a party of the Scottish Rifles working with us, and what with shells coming over our heads from our own guns – and one often feels as if they were going to drop short (as they sometimes do) and come in amongst us – and those coming from the Germans (who are only 250 yards from where we were working all day), we have rather a hot day of it. But our Artillery gave them a hot time of it today sending shells into their parapet all day long. I and another chap were told to clear out an old French trench, a part where it joins ours; so that we will be able to put some stretchers in there. It has not been moved for months and was almost level with the parapet, the sides having come away and for about an hour we had to work exposed from the shoulders. Our officer told us to work and keep ourselves well down but that was impossible. However, we got our job done, but while at it we had a great view of the shells bursting in the German lines which are right in front of a rather large village a mile from where I am now in C[ambrin].

53

There were plenty of bullets whistling about, but we were as careful as we could possibly be under the circumstances. There is a row of houses just beside a coal mine where the Germans are, and we could see our shells doing havoc there, one single shell brought down to the very ground the fourth house in the row, as neat as if it had been cut out. It was a great shot and I pity any Germans if they were in it at the time. Our Gunners are absolutely great and can lick them every time.

One of our chaps, who was widening a part of the trench, came on a dead Frenchman buried in the parapet and had to throw a part of his leg over to do his work properly. And it looks rather ghastly to see the boot on the other foot, flush with the side of the trench parapet at that part, and all the 'tackits' showing quite plainly. There is a tiny cross on the top of the parapet with his name etc on it. This is a mild thing so far as these trenches are concerned and will give you a faint idea of what it is to use a spade and shovel in them. One never knows what they will turn up next. Two dead Germans were unearthed yesterday but I will not tell you any more as it is not a nice subject. We stayed up there and worked like Trojans, as the job was to be finished tonight, and I am very tired now I can tell you.

It was rather cold sleeping in this dug-out last night and I woke early this morning with the cold and lay for an hour and counted forty shells the Germans sent into and round about this village this morning; and our guns were sending them back, two for their one, rather a novel Sabbath morning.

Monday evening, 20 September 1915

This morning we got orders to come up to the trenches and finish the job we were at yesterday. It was a beautiful morning and we felt it warm winding up the communication trenches till we arrived at our especial part, and before many minutes were much warmer shovelling dirt over the high parapet. We had no trouble for about half an hour and then they sent over a shower of bullets which kept us lively. They evidently had seen us yesterday and had decided not to let us work in peace this morning, for as we continued to shovel up earth, over like lightening came three whis bangs and burst twenty yards down the trench from us.

These things are awful things indeed and make one feel rather nervous, as you just hear the report of the gun, and two seconds it bursts on its mark. I shall never forget them. We had absolutely no cover at all in our trench which runs perpendicular with the Germans except the little crevices at the side which we made yesterday. They were getting very close, and altogether we felt very uncomfortable and I thought it better to duck in the crevice. We did and had no sooner got in, when seven came over in rapid succession and one landed right on the top of our crevice, and I thought it was all over. The explosion was beyond description to my companion and I who were right in it. The whole side of the trench came on top of us. Oh it was awful. I thought my companion was sure to be killed. I could see nothing for smoke and dirt. I felt we had been hit. I shook the debris off myself and my companion was all right at my side. We did a bolt up the trench and I saw that my companion had been hit. The blood was pouring out of a nasty wound right over his eye. I got him into the firing trench, which by the way is much safer as it runs parallel with the Germans. He looked as white as death and my own hand was shaking. I knew we both had escaped death as if by a miracle. We had no tunic on and so I tore one out of the KOSB's tunic nearest – to his surprise – and bandaged up the wound. I felt the blood running down my own face, but I knew it was nothing but a scratch I had, as I felt no pain, but my companion had a nasty wound and looked awful with his good looking face all covered with blood and as white as a sheet. He is English and comes from Middlebar, Ernie Britton is his name.* Perhaps you will see it in the list of wounded later in the paper. The whis bangs were still coming over and we remained where we were till the others came up. When they found our caps and the side of the trench blown in and blood all around, they thought our cap was all that was left and came rushing up along with our officer in a terrible state. We both looked bloody and covered with dirt but well enough to enjoy the cigarettes we were smoking. It was impossible to continue our work during the day and so our officer told us we would have to get back. But word came up the trench that the communication trench we were to go down was being shelled and so we had to try another.

* His death is mentioned in diary entry of 19 July 1916.

The others were sent on first and the two officers and our wounded man and I waited till he got a proper rest. We started going down what is known as Railway Alley that leads to Guy's Alley, the one we wanted to get to. We got there all right when a bullet passed between Britton's head and mine and lodged in the side of the trench which is very low at this part. We were lucky again although it made us start. When we got to a straight part, over came more whis bangs and we all flopped down on our stomachs. I thought we were never going to get back to safety but they landed outside the trench. We got to our dug-out Dressing Station in the reserve trenches, and right glad was I to get in I assure you. Even there they were bursting and we had to wait for half an hour before it was safe enough to get down. We arrived here at the DS just before dinner and right glad I was to slip out of that Communication Trench outside there after a very very hot time of it and as narrow an escape from death as I wish for. It is either one thing or the other as a rule when a whis bang comes near you – death or next to nothing. It landed and burst only a yard from our heads, and how we both escaped, God knows. It must have been His good mercy and I sent up a silent prayer of thanks. My companion has gone down the line but I don't think his wound is serious enough for him to get home.

I shall never forget the sensation of that awful explosion that left me almost deaf for a half hour and the feeling of being buried in the debris, and the sensation when I found I was alive and nothing the matter. My cheek is a little cut, a small scratch on the nose and also above the eye, but just the tiniest scratches lovey that you can hardly see although my cheek did bleed a lot. But when I had a wash, I was all right with no trace of my awful experience. But it has taught me more about what war is than anything. Our officers told us both we were lucky and must have been born under a lucky star to escape so easily. That's my little story of this morning's experience.

Wednesday, 22 September 1915 11.00 am

Have just come back from an hour round the trenches and out down the road a bit. We had to go up there with boards and nailed them on the different corners, so that 'Walking Wounded' cases

56

(that is chaps who are slighted wounded and can walk) can find the road to our Dressing St* further down where we made the dug-outs last week. You see we have four Dressing Stations up here, two in the trenches or just outside, that's this one and another a mile down the road and then our three Hospital in B[éthune]. So you see we have quite a lot of work for one Field Ambulance. We all take our turns in the trenches (those of the bearers who are up here) two days and two nights. My turn comes tomorrow night I think. There are plenty of cases and oh some awful sights. I would not tell you the condition of some. It would sicken you, but what a terrible effect a shell has sometimes, and other times like my own, no damage whatsoever, but very few get off so easy as I did with a thirteen pounder shell and I am very thankful.

Thursday, 23 September 1915

It is just before teatime and we are in our dug-out. There is a terrible bombardment going on now and it has been going on incessantly for three days. What a row – we can't even hear each other speaking. The Germans are paying the penalty now. Oh war is horrid and I, like everyone else here, wish it was all over. We thought we were to be shifted today to our old dug-outs but we are here still and are likely to be for some time, I believe. As I think about you going to Kilsyth just now and the peace of it all, and all this death and destruction, God but it is awful to see it in its raw state. The little cemetery just outside here in range of German bullets is full and more go in every day just as they are. A shell landed on one of the graves last night and opened it up. By gum but the soldiers on this part of the line are doing their bit and no mistake.

I don't know the date somewhere about the 28 Sept.

Tuesday morning. I think, 2.00 am

My Ain Precious Darling I am in the trenches in our dug-out and on duty although I am nearly exhausted – I can't sleep. This is the first minute I have had since I wrote you last, and God knows we

* At Annequin.

57

have been through hell a few times since that. I can't tell you everything that has occurred since I last wrote. It has been too awful and besides my brain is rather numbed. I don't know where to start, and I may be disturbed at any moment with cases to attend – shattered men of our beautiful Division which is no more.

But I have been to the doors of death scores of times since my last letter, but God has protected me and brought me safely through, and at the present moment I am sound and well except for the utter exhaustion of days and nights of awful work and also a slight touch of gas I got while bringing in the wounded. All your prayers are being heard about my safety, Darling and those at home, or I would not be here.

This Div. charged the Germans here on Saturday morning early, and since that it has been a hell on earth, but we have accomplished our task, and beat them back paying the penalty to the full. Very few of our Grand Reg. of Highlanders and all Regs. of the Div. are left – how many God alone knows just now – but we have brought in thousands and still they come, and still many are lying out. And what was left of them today charged (some out of every Reg. who were not completely knocked out) and made the Germans pay for the lives of our comrades with cold steel. They are still at it and what will be the finish I cannot tell. I have been dressing the wounds today (oh the sights and the wounds awful awful) of scores of men who had been wounded on Saturday morning and just got in today.

Wednesday afternoon, 29 September 1915

At last I have got time to write you a letter. I have tried often since my last to get a line through to you but it has been an utter impossibility. We were relieved last night and came down here B[éthune] to our old quarters. Left the trenches yesterday afternoon but I will try and relate what has transpired since my last letter and some of the experiences I have gone through. I am feeling very tired and my nerves are not as they were at present, but I am scratchless, for which I am thankful to God for. I can't just remember the day I wrote you last, but I will start on the Friday.

We had been busy all week in the trenches before that preparing for the big battle we knew was coming off at the weekend, making places to put wounded men in the trenches till such times as we

58

could get them carried back. First of all we had three days'
bombardment – hundreds of our guns that were around us at our
Dressing St. at C[ambrin] firing continuously on the German
trenches for three days and nights. It was awful, the air full of
whistling shells and the noise indescribable. We had to shout to
each other to make ourselves heard and on the other side the
Germans also shelled and we could not tell which way the shells
were coming. It was all very trying to the nerves and has had a
considerable effect on our hearing – only temporary I think – and
then the bullets that were flying about were rather annoying.
However, we knew that to be only the prelude to a very big affair
that our Division had been honoured to try and accomplish.
Everybody was talking about it except the Regiments that were to
be the first in the charge who were quiet and thoughtful and looked
anticipatingly at us and our preparations for the wounded. On
Friday last we got orders to move back to the dug-outs we had
made the week before and prepare a Dressing Station there for
cases that could walk and ten of us were detailed off as scouts to
scour the country round about the trenches, and bring in the men
in parties. I was not sorry to take up this job, as it was easier work
than carrying, and by this time my strength was not as it had been
owing to a fortnight's hard hard work, digging dug-outs both in
the trenches and out of them, and often under heavy fire – and
after the miraculous escape I had had with that shell, I was not in
the form I would have liked to be in, although the job as a scout
was one full of danger from shells – however that is just by the way.

We went back to A[nnequin] a mile from C[ambrin] D[ressing]
S[tation] and got our place in order. I had not been there long when
another party came up from B[éthune] Hospital to work there and
Pete amongst them. I had not seen him for some time and was
delighted he had been attached to this party at the last moment.
Every man was needed and they left very few at B[éthune] to work
the Hospital. He brought up the parcel and I had my letters. We
had a good tuck in in the dug-out and a good talk about everything.
We slept in all our things to be ready to go out at the shortest notice.

Saturday morning 25 September I shall never forget it. We got
up at dawn and as the morning cleared, the action started, our guns
billowed out and all along the line was a cloud of smoke. We knew
what it was and you will know when I get home if it has not been

in the papers.* The Germans were shelling our position like ------ and it was evident that our men were charging by the rattle of rifles and machine guns and the shrapnel shells bursting in the air all along the line. I was sent up to C[ambrin] D[ressing] S[tation] with a message to our Capt., and when I got there, the first batch of cases were just coming in, most of them gassed. It was the start. I delivered my message and we got a party of about thirty walking wounded cases to take back to be looked after. Before I got back, they were coming down from the trenches all roads, and some very bad cases to be walking, but that can't be helped in a big engagement as all available cars are required for men who are seriously wounded. One of them had a bullet wound right through his chest and he was walking back. I got back and found everybody busy (Pete was busy giving some tea etc and lots of jobs taking them down in the wagons to B[éthune]). That was the start, and we ten scouts walked between that dug-out and the trenches all day long bringing 100s – some we had to carry on our backs and others were able to stagger along and all covered with blood and the grime of the battlefield. It was terrible to see it – men wounded in two or three places staggering along exhausted and all of our fine Div.

We took our turn loading the wagons at the railway line where they were run down on bogies from the firing line all the time under fire. And the state of the cases going into the motors was fearful and beyond description. We were positive of the fact that we had lost very heavily. We had often to duck in a ditch or run into one of the communication trenches to escape the shells. This corner where we were was in full view of the German lines, but the men had to be got away. Often we ran short of cars and to crown it the rain came down in torrents in the afternoon and sometimes we had a score of serious cases lying on stretchers, some dying and others lying in pools of their own blood. And the moaning and calling to us to hurry it was awful. We could do not one whit more than we were doing. This went on unceasingly all day, and still the roads were busy with wounded men. I had nothing to eat, and was dead beat a few times and still I was kept up seeing such suffering all around. News of how the engagement was going on was sometimes

* There is an insertion in the original text of the word 'Gas' written at a later date after the word 'smoke'.

good and sometimes we were told that all was well. I was soaked to the skin and like to drop, and when I got back to the dug-out to get something to drink and a waterproof sheet, I was told to pre-pare my kit and go with four others – each of us with a stretcher – up to the line. I did not know how I was going to manage. I was so beat up and the rain was coming down so heavily. I knew what we were in for and being told to take our iron rations and other things with us, we knew that it was a dangerous game we had been chosen for. I made up my mind to stick it till I dropped. I could do no more, but there were others who had had an easier day than I had, who were more fit than I was. However I had been told and set off to one of the worst experiences that has befell any in this Ambulance – I must stop and continue later.

Evening sitting in our old attic with Pete at my side.

I managed to get a Field Post Card off tonight; so that will keep you from worrying. We have to be ready to leave this place tomorrow morning to go to the place we arrived at when we left H[avre] the second day we were in France. It is over twenty miles from here. I don't know whether we have to march or not. It is well up the line. There is another Ambulance in our Hospital here.

Well lovey to continue my narrative or experiences, I and my four companions set off on our mission with full kit and a stretcher each and two medical bags in a drenching rain and absolutely exhausted and hungry but with our teeth set to go through with it. We got to C[ambrin] Dressing St. expecting that we would at least get a little rest there, but no, an officer was waiting for us and told us to follow him. He entered the communication trench and our real troubles started. The rain had made the clayey trench a perfect muck hole. We were often up to the knees and often tumbled on our faces into holes and our stretchers were getting so heavy I could fair have lain down in the muck. But the thought of the lives we might be the means of saving spurred us on. Shells came over and bullets seemed to come from all directions. The rain went off and the moon came out and we had to keep our stretchers from showing over the parapet. At last we got to our Advanced Post and we met there a party of 28 FA. I threw in some of my kit. I knew it would kill me if I had to carry it any further. We had come away without

61

water and managed to get a little – as much as wet our lips as it was very valuable up there. 'Follow on' our officer said and 'keep about four yards apart in case of shells'. We knew where we were going – right up to the firing line – to bring down the wounded who were lying over the parapet. Ah dearest it seemed a forlorn hope, and I sent up a silent prayer to God and thought of you and all our love. We stumbled on and oh my God what sights dead everywhere. Some places we in the trench, we had to walk over them lying ten deep. At many parts of the trench it had been shattered and was exposed. The Germans were continually sniping at these parts. Our officer halted us when we got to the most exposed part and gave us our instructions to double past after him. He went first and rip rip went the bullets. The next fellow crawled on his stomach and we shoved over his stretcher. I passed my stretcher on and doubled over safely and ping ping went the bullets. We all got safely past.

It is near lights out. I have just heard no letters have to be taken for a week and that we are going to Y[pres] tomorrow to be in reserve there. It is too bad as the Div is beat up and it will take about 10,000 men to make up our losses. God knows we thought we were going for a rest and we need it, but it seems not. Goodnight my beloved Darling Wifie. Oh I wish I could get word through to you. x x Oh I love you dearly dearly my ain Wifie. I will get this letter finished off as soon as I am allowed.

Thursday 30 September 1915

We are waiting with our kits ready to put on to move at a moment's notice. We don't yet know when we will go. So I will make good the time and continue my letter.

We all got past the various parts of the trench where it had been blown in, and how some of us were not hit is a marvel. We were then in the second line of trenches and what sights of horror – men dead everywhere, some on the parapet and others lying in the mud in a state too horrible for me to tell you, and in all the little crevices we had made the week before in the side of the trench lay wounded men, some of whom had been there since morning, and as we passed they implored us to take them for God's sake down out of it. That was impossible as we were after those who were in a far worse plight than them, those who were lying over the parapet exposed to the enemy, who if we didn't get them in before daylight, would have to lie there all the following day exposed to the elements and what was worse the shells and bullets of the Germans that constantly raked the ground.

We got up to the first line at last and oh what a sight – over the parapet men were lying like flies on fly paper and it was almost certain death to go out and bring them in. We got one and started to carry him down the trench to our first aid post. I can't describe this experience properly lovey. It was all too awful for words and besides all those dead and dying were my own countrymen. If I had come across a wounded German at that time he would never have lived. I was so mad. That scene has left on me an indelible impression I shall never get rid of.

We had to carry our man down a narrow trench up to the knees in mud over dead men, and past groaning wounded. We ourselves were completely beat up and could only carry the stretcher, two at a time, a distance of ten yards when we sank down on our knees exhausted. The next pair would lift us up and place us against the side of the parapet and go on till they would go down on their knees and so on staggering on but careful that no injury came to our patient. How we got past the open parts of the trench and how we escaped being killed with the bullets that seem to just miss us and lodge in the parapet I can't tell you. It is all like a nightmare to me.

We got down to one of the communication trenches, and then we were shelled – about fifty shells and whis bangs came behind us and in front of us. Every minute we expected one to land amongst us, and it would all be over. We were so beat up, I don't think we cared two straws. Once I sank up to the waist in mud while carrying the stretcher and my companions had to draw me out. We were starving and thirsty. I had given all my water away to wounded men in the crevices and the bottle was lost and my rations and many other parts of our kit. Something made us halt with our stretcher, some reinforcements coming up the trench as there was only a very few men in our front trench and none in the support, and if the Germans had made a rush, there was not many to keep them back, and the way they were shelling, we thought they certainly were preparing for a counter charge – which they did in the morning but were beaten back. We had to wait till some of those troops passed.

It was getting very hot indeed and we were nearing our first dug-out after being hours on the way down the trench with this patient. We heard a roar at our back and down the trench as hard as the mud would allow him came a soldier with his smoke helmet on roaring to us that the Germans were sending over gas shells. Two of our chaps disappeared, I and the other got our helmets out and rushed them on, but I could not get mine properly fixed. We got the stretcher up and had to wait till another one in front got away. It was a terrible time. I thought of our patient. He had no respirator. I dashed down the trench to get one at the Aid Post. A shell burst in front of me. I collapsed, my helmet worked loose and I felt like bursting. I was in torture to breathe and felt my lungs bursting and like a drunk man I managed on to my feet and staggered on. Someone caught me by the hand and led me to the Aid Post. 'Send a smoke helmet up the trench to our patient,' I said and collapsed. I could not stand on my feet. Oh what a horrid condition covered up to the neck with mud. They took some time to recognize me. And they then hustled me out on to one of the trucks to be taken to Hospital. I had been gassed.

They were still shelling all the way down on the truck and how we all escaped, God knows. If anybody was struck, it was always some other body than one of 27 F A. Not one got hit, although they have been amongst it all the time – one wounded, the chap who was with me when we were buried last week with a shell and myself gassed, but only slightly. They put me in the motor Ambulance wagon and took me to C[ambrin] Dressing St., left me in the fresh air for an hour and gave me an inhaler. I thought I was finished, I felt so bad, but the fresh air revived me and when I went in to the officer I felt better. I spoke to him and the Colonel for ten minutes before they recognized me. I was such a sight of mud and dirt and had lost my cap and kit. They could not keep from smiling. 'That's three times they have nearly done for you, St Clair. You're a lucky chap to escape.' 'Yes Sir.' But I thought of the true prayers that go up to heaven every day on my behalf and knew it was an answer to them. The Captain wanted to send me down the line to Hospital. 'How do you feel?' 'I will be all right in an hour or two,' I said. 'No, Captain,' said the Colonel. 'We can't spare one single RAMC man at this awful time. Put him in the dug-out and keep him warm till daylight and see how he feels.' I felt not so bad in the morning and was sent down to where Pete was with my four companions with a note saying I had been gassed and had to get a rest.*

How we five looked. Everyone looked as if he had had a horrible nightmare and looked as dead- beat as any men ever were. All I had of my kit was my smoke helmet in my hand (the smell of the gas is on it yet). Pete could not recognize me, and had heard that I was away down the line gassed during the night and was surprised to see me 'What hae they been daeing tae ye noo Willie?' 'Gassing me, Pete.' 'The blank blank. I wish I had some of them here the noo. Get awa and get a sleep.' I slept till the afternoon and went back to the trenches about four o'clock on Sunday afternoon and was up most of the night dressing wounded men and all the following day and night. Dressing men, all Scotchmen, handsome fellows but shattered, they had been lying out since Saturday morning till Monday most of them, and oh my God their wounds were awful and their pluck beyond praise. They had a charge on Sunday night again and we could not tell how it was going. I treated scores of cases along with the officer who let me do most of them myself, an unusual thing for an orderly. He said he would never forget the work in that dug-out on Monday afternoon, the cases being the worst he had ever seen. Men were walking in with a bullet wound in the head and when we looked at it it seemed as if his brain would come out. One chap was shot in both hands and through the shoulder, his leg broken, and he said I have a wee scratch near my knee. My God when I looked at it, there was a hole in his thigh just above the knee the size of my fist, a scratch. I talked to him and kept his mind and eyes off it and gave him a cigarette and not a murmur – just a little drawing up of his face as we put splints on his leg. He was a hero of heroes and had lain out between the lines from Saturday morning, when they charged, till Monday, Cameron Highlander. We had scores of them, all brave fellows and all were the same.

I received your letters while up there and the one with the photos

* The *War Diary* of 27 FA for that day (W.O.95/1758), records thirty-five cases of gassing among the casualties. There seems to have been a suspicion that gassing was something that soldiers might be shamming as it was difficult to disprove. The note reads:- '*35 cases of 'Gassing' were among the casualties. The first lot appearing genuine enough but later appeared trivial in character – at least their symptoms were anything but urgent.*'

which are beautiful and the parcel and a letter from Mrs Hudson, a lovely letter it was indeed and to read it under these circumstances put more life in me. The first minute I got during the night, I gazed at your photo and oh dearie how I loved you. I immediately started to write a letter but had only got two pages written when I had to attend more cases, and this is my first opportunity since. We, this Ambulance, treated 2100 cases on Saturday and since then I don't know the figures but our Div. has lost fearfully. They were burying them in long trenches at our D.S. in the churchyard, a big trench for every battalion, KOSB, A and SH, Cameron H, Black Watch – 200 dead Argylls I saw in one trench just as they had fallen. What a sacrifice. But they have done what has been tried since Mons, and has never been accomplished – that is broken the German line. We saw many prisoners, and many German wounded. One of their Red Cross saved his life through attending to our wounded. It was difficult to keep even the wounded Highlander from snatching a rifle and shooting him, and no wonder they hate the Germans – I will always hate them like poison after what they have done to our grand Div. Most of them are cowards and put up their hands, but that made no difference, our men were seeing red, and that's why there are so few prisoners. The curs were even shooting our wounded, but they have paid for every life, their losses must have been awful. Their machine gunners were chained to their guns, or they too would have run.

How all the Kirkie chaps in the Argylls got on, we cannot say yet. We had two over here to see us last night. They had just come back and wanted to see if we were all right. Reed and Bell, and they could not just say who had been killed. Some are wounded but on the whole Kirkie has escaped well. It has been one of the fiercest engagements of the war, and there has been lots of tragedies, but it has been a victory. I can't remember the half of the things that happened dearie. I will be able to tell you all about it when I get home, DV.* We were relieved on Tuesday and came down to our dug-outs at A[nnequin] and were just preparing to get away when we had fourteen shells high explosive round our dug-out killing some of the horses but injuring no man. Yesterday we loaded an Ambulance train at B[éthune] Station and I saw some of the chaps

* *Deo Volente*: God Willing.

I had dressed in the trenches on the first stage of their journey to England. I am strong and well again but don't want to see any more of this horrible business of war but will just have to take what comes, and trust God to always protect me as he has done all through this awful time. Pete would likely tell you about wee D Clark of the KOSB. He is a little hero and Pete wheeled him down the railway on a truck to the Ambulance wagon. He had lain out for two days and nights with his leg broken. He managed to crawl into our lines and when the Doctor was dressing him never let out a murmur, although the pain must have been awful. I could have cried when I saw him. He will likely be home now in some hospital.

All through this lovey I thought of you and wondered if I would come back safely. I prayed often especially on that awful Saturday night when I was up at the firing line and as I leant exhausted against the side of the trench coming down with the wounded. How it was they only sent five men of our Ambulance up there, I can't say. There was work for hundreds, and many were more fit than we were. We five were all that were up so far in our Ambulance and I was the only Scotchman of the five. All the rest of the work was done further back. I am glad, now that it is all over, that I was one of them. The experiences of suffering will do me lasting good. Please dearest lovey go to Kilsyth when you get this letter and read it to them and tell them it is and has been impossible for me to write any more, or even send more F P Cs. I will keep you posted at every opportunity. I know you must have been worrying as to my welfare. I could do nothing. Others here had more opportunities than I had.

We may get leave after this and we may not. Many vacancies in the Div. will have to be made up before we can go into action again and that will take time. I can't write any more at present. Give my regards to all there including Miss Paterson if there still. I am so pleased you get on so well I thought you would, and as to her attitude to the Ps, I am not surprised as they are not in the same class. Fraser and Fergus were here in B[éthune] all the time and have never been under fire yet although they were busy in the Hospital all the time seven or eight miles behind us. Pete is sitting beside me reading. 'Tell them I wrote yesterday and my love to all' and give mine also to your Folks Darling and also thank Mrs Hudson for her beautiful letter to me. I will answer it when I get time and don't let this letter get into the Herald. All my pure love to you my beloved Wifie. That is such a nice photo of you and I can see you are thinking of me. You will look happier when I get home Darling. Aye and so will I.

Ever True and Devoted Husband and Sweetheart

　　Willie.

Saturday, 2 October 1915

My Dear Father and Mother and All,
　　I suppose you will all be very anxious to hear from me again seeing it has been impossible for me to write to you for some time. I only managed to get a letter off to Jane this morning and a F P C to you the first opportunity I have had for a long time. The letter to Jane gives full details on the cause of my silence. We have had to take our part in a very big battle on this front in which our Div. played the most important part, and with great success. We lost heavily, as was expected, and some Kilsyth chaps were killed. I was so very sorry to hear when we came back that Henry Morton, whom I have met often out here, and just before the engagement, was killed, Briton of the Craigends mortally wounded, and I believe there are others but I have not got all their names yet. Kirkintilloch was very lucky. There is a big number of chaps in 10/Argylls who were in the thick of the fighting from Kirkintilloch. Some of them were wounded but, so far as I know, up to date none were killed. I can tell you I was very pleased to see them when we came back to B[éthune]. Of course we all sought each other out to see if all was well. W. Cowan is either wounded or missing. I could not get proper news of him. I also tried to get news of Miller of the Howe Rd., 2/Argylls but could not. Don't know how he got on. Motherwell of the Seaforths was wounded slightly, I think, and I could get no news of Archie Barton. I sincerely hope they are all right.
　　It was a most awful time and I trust we have never to go through the same experience. Our Ambulance treated 2100 cases on Saturday alone and over 3000 altogether, a record for a Field Ambulance; which will give you a small notion how much work we had to do. It all appears a horrible nightmare to me now. It was

a terrible hell. I was in a position to see the effects better than most, as only five of us were sent up along with some of the other two F Amb* and I was one of the five.

I shall never forget last Saturday night and early morning of Sunday. Jane will tell you what I say about it and that description does not half explain the terrible horrors. How many times I escaped death I can't say, but they say of me in this Ambulance that I am a most fortunate man to be alive. I know that, and also what protected me. I was also gassed by a German gas shell, but it did not keep me out of action more than twelve hours, although I still feel the effects of it a little yet. What a horrible sensation of bursting, choking and pain. It turned the buttons on my tunic greenish black. The rain came on just after the charge and made the ground awful and the trenches were feet deep with clay and water and gave us twenty times the trouble to bring down our wounded. On the Sunday afternoon I was put in the dugout with an officer and had all the wounded to dress with him.[28] It was great experience medically, but the nature of the wounds we had to treat were such that the officer said he never wished to have such a day again as we had on Monday – men shattered, some perforated with bullet holes and shrapnel wounds and the flesh torn off them in lumps. What an awful state and all Scotchmen and everyone a hero, and most of them had lain between the enemy's line and ours since Saturday morning. Some had crawled in and others carried. What dreadful suffering they must have endured. One brave fellow with a bullet through each of his hands, one in the shoulder and in his leg, a compound fracture caused by another bullet, let me dress him without a murmur although he must have been suffering great pain. He told me he had another scratch in the other leg, and when I looked at it about a lb of his muscle had been torn away by a piece of shell – a scratch he called it. We used to boast about our Div. but now others boast about the 9th because they have done what none have done this war – broken the German line and held them. All our work was done under heavy fire and except for a few scratches our Ambulance escaped. It is wonderful. It was a sight never to be forgotten to see those gallant Highlanders, every one a volunteer, come back after they had been relieved, and to notice

* The other two Field Ambulances , i.e. 26 and 28 F.A.

how few out of each battalion was there to answer their name. Two hundred and fifty returned out of 1100 of the Argylls. What a horrible thing is war when you see it as we have seen it last weekend. We all lived years, and when I came back on Sunday morning, they said I and my four companions who had been with me all night up at the firing line looked like old men, and no wonder. However, I am back to my old self again.

We were relieved on Tuesday and were immediately placed under orders to remove to another part of the line. We thought it was to go for a rest what we need, but they brought us up here to Y[pres] in trains yesterday and our A Section went right up into the trenches where we will relieve them in turns. This is the first time we had been in Belgium and it is a hot part of the line as you know. There is a cemetery here where some of the Kilsyth and Kirkie Terriers are buried I suppose. We have not had an opportunity of visiting it yet. They, as you will remember, were in the fighting here in May. There is a decided difference in the Belgians and the French, and I must say the Belgians are not out to rob the British Tommy every time like the French we have met. We are likely to be here for a month or two so far as I know. We had built our minds up on getting some leave after our work at L[a] B[assée] but evidently we as a Div. are much too valuable now as a fighting force to be spared. I suppose we must just stick it although I have seen all the fighting I wish for. It is getting horrible cold out here now especially at nights and as yet we have not been supplied with a blanket. It is time we were.

I was delighted to get Mima's letter and the boy's enclosed and also a very fine parcel from Polly while up the line. We had a great feed in the dug-out that night with the square loaf she sent and the other specialities. I will write her first chance. Tell all friends I am asking for them and my thanks to Mima for her letter. I was with Henry Morton the Sunday before he was killed. No it must have been the Sunday before that, as I was in the trenches that day. Lately I have rather lost count of the days.

Evening

There were plenty of helmets. Pete during the battle and lots of our fellows got one (or rather bought one). I would get one for you but

70

it is such a trouble to carry those things about. Yesterday while at the St. the RS Fusiliers came up and one of them got his eye on a helmet one of our boys had. 'Say mate,' roars the Scottie, 'I will get you the head for that helmet.' But I suppose you will know all about our big affair in the papers more than we know probably. The papers have a decided knack of missing the truth re the war I notice. I wish I would be allowed to tell you what I know and have experienced but then we daren't, and besides we are all anxious that this should finish and we know the trouble spies cause us. They are thick as bees where we were last, and many a long roundabout march they cause us, to put them off the scent. The boys are all singing Bonnie Mary of Argyle, an old favourite of yours Father, eh? I will close for tonight. You are all in my thoughts. Goodnight.

Sunday Forenoon

This is rather a nice morning although it was very cold when we got up. We slept well last night, and had a blanket issued to us and we required it. We tuck ourselves in close for warmth and do not so badly. I was pleased to hear Miss Paterson had been to 58. She enjoyed herself alright Jane says. What do you think about her? She has been very very good to us, and is constantly sending things. I was sorry to hear about her cousin being killed. I don't think it was in our battle as their Div. was not there to my knowledge. Somewhere about here I think they are. All the officers in some of the Reg. that charged last week went down and one of the charges was led by the medical officer, he being the only one left. My but the days of real chivalry are not over. A cigarette was about the first thing a wounded man asked after a drink, and to hear the matter of fact 'thank you' made one proud of our countrymen. They thought next to nothing of their wounds. Most of them had something to avenge, a brother's life perhaps, and they did it. One fellow who was very seriously wounded said to me, 'I can die now quite happy mate, I have got some of my own back this morning for what they did to my brother.' 'Come here you, I want to speak to you,' another said. I went over. 'You're St Clair,' and there was a little fellow who was one of my customers. I saw him off safely and told him to tell everybody at home I was asking for them. But I will be better able to tell you stories by the legion of bravery and fortitude

71

when I come home. 'Take this fellow first. He is worse than I,' was a regular thing. I must close now.

Sunday, 3 October 1915
Afternoon.

Well Darling we had the first church service we have had for some time – in my case about a month. They were impossible while we were up there and that the service this morning was fine and he had a great subject re our battle, 'Faithful unto death' for a text, and he spoke about our comrades who had paid the full penalty for King and Country and how brave they all were and the fortitude of the wounded, and also about ourselves in the medical units and the splendid work. Although none of us were killed, many had been 'faithful unto death' risking our lives all the time to help the wounded, just our wonderful luck. Yes he said many of you and all soldiers would rather go out on that bullet- and shellswept battle-field than kneel and pray to God before your comrades in your bivouacs; which is very true. He talked about chivalry and some people thinking it was a thing of the past, but we who had been in the battle knew of hundreds of instances that equalled the best of it. It was a very good sermon or talk and very refreshing indeed after all the horrors and bloodshed. I thought of many things but principally of my love for you and how happy a moment it would be when I came home for good. God grant that it may be soon and finish all the sufferings.

This big battle has left on me an indelible impression that will never leave me. I think I will never forget some of the sights – to see 200 Scotchmen, A and SH all placed in one big grave just as they had fallen and ten yards off the same of another corps and still another, no covering but just the earth. My but one does get wild at those Germans when they have seen this, and strange thoughts of vengeance surge on the brain, but the day after we carried a lot of wounded Germans to the Ambulance train and were careful with them also, because after all, ours is only a mission of mercy and we have been of use to many: we certainly were needed after all and more of us if it had been possible. We used to think we would not be required but that is away, every man is certainly needed.

We had one of 9/A and SH down to see us. Pete and I were just outside the Camp to see if we could see any of our Argylls. A soldier came along on horseback, and when close to us said, 'I will have a haircut and shave'. I could not make him out. 'Hullo Bill'. We shook his hand, Aldridge from the Hillhead, of our own territorials. We were pleased to meet him, and so was he. He had heard we were here and came down to find us. We had not got many yards more when we met young Adie of Townhead. His brother is a butcher. He is in the engineers. We were the first Kirkie chaps he has seen. The Terriers are not far from here and we hope to see some more of them soon. I have got back and into the bivouac. Just outside five or six of the boys are around an old biscuit tin they have made into a fireplace. One is playing a mandolin, some silently smoking, others humming the tune being played 'Annie Laurie'. It looks such a fine picture, and if the home folks could just see them as they are around that camp fire – it is a perfect picture and I wish I could just put it on canvas, all sorts of expressions as they all watch the burning wood. One can almost tell from their faces what they are thinking about.

Tuesday, 19 October 1915

I was not pleased at all to hear about my letter getting into the papers. I simply hate publicity now and I would so much rather they kept them out. Which letter was it that was put in? I hope it does not get into the *Kirkintilloch Herald* by any means. Not that I mind in the least who reads it, but well, I would hate it if people had the idea I wanted to swank about my little experiences. It is much too serious an affair this and it gets more serious every day. I thank God that there are no more of ours here than Pete and I as the chances of those who are in fighting Regiments out here at present of getting home after the war, or coming through it with their life, are very small indeed. If you had listened as we did after we got to bed the night before last to the sound and terrible blood-curdling rattle of an engagement up here, it would have given you a faint idea what this war is. It is a Hell every time; all night long it went on – machine guns by the hundreds – oh they are very deadly indeed and it is just impossible to describe them and their effect. It makes us who know them shudder knowing their deadly effect.

It was very distressing to hear about Mrs Morton, poor soul. All that I know dearie is that he was shot through the kidneys while going over the parapet and he was just on the top when the bullet hit him. 'I am struck,' he said and 'it is through my kidneys.' I don't think he said any more. As to getting any of his belongings, unless some of his comrades managed that, I think it will be impossible; there were so many dead that day. On the Tuesday I looked to see if I could pick out any whom I knew amongst 200 A and SH who were being buried in the little cemetery at Cambrin Church. I did not see Henry but he is sure to have had a decent soldier's burial. Most likely he would be buried there while I was up in the trenches as it was on my road down that I went into the cemetery which is just outside the church we used as our Dressing Station and a tiny rough cross is generally put over everyone with name, etc, which will all be done now. We left of course and came here immediately after the battle as you know. It is possible I may see that place again. I will certainly visit it if I do.

Just a hurried note before the post goes. A paper came to Fraser today with that supposed letter of mine, the one I suppose which was in the *Chronicle*. Now these letters when they are trimmed and cut by reporters have an entirely different meaning to what one means to convey, and it would appear from that one that I was the only one doing anything. Now nothing makes one out here more of a laughing stock than letters in the papers. I don't care who see my letters as all I say is the truth but I don't want them published and if that one or any other appears in the *Kirkintilloch Herald* or any other paper, I will write no more letters home. I am angry, wild – the annoyance of the thing is rotten. I enclose a note of the same description for 58 to prevent any more of that rot. My letters are written to give you just an idea of what we are doing and are private. But when they are published in such a way sometimes that I myself don't know them, and come out here as they always do – Oh I see St Clair swanking it in the papers and I can tell you they have a way of making one uncomfortable. It is not you to blame this time dearie. But I know you like to see them in print. Well it must stop. I said before that I did not want it and the last one appeared in the KH. When I say no, I mean no. I simply hate publicity of any description. Send the enclosed letter to 58 at once please. I will answer your letters re today later. Oh dearie I am so very angry today at the foolish swank of it all.

Chapter Five

Reflections

The remnant of the 9th Division was taken out of the Battle of Loos on 28 September 1915 and ordered on 29 September 1915 to proceed immediately by train and route march to duties in the trenches in the Ypres Salient, or 'The Salient', as it was always called. On the morning of 5 October, they took over a stretch of the line south of Zillebeke, which extended from north of Hill 60 to a point south of the Ypres-Comines Canal near Oosthoek. There they stayed in the line south and then east of Zillebeke for three months. It was a period, according to the Divisional History, of 'unmitigated gloom' because, even when 'quiet' these trenches were a particularly dangerous and detested sector of the front.[29] The Salient meant enfilading fire, and the state of the ground meant that men had to sleep in dug-outs above the ground affording protection at best only from bullets. For three months it rained almost every day. The results were what might be expected in country that, without proper maintenance of drainage, reverts to swamp. Everywhere was a sea of mud, and the filth and squalor meant rats in untold numbers. Willie has diary entries for this period, with just the word 'rats' or 'mud' as the entry for the day. They took up a good part of the day's devotions. The entry for 27 October 1915 is slightly extended to:- 'Was inspected by the King. Mud.'

Before going up to the trenches at the end of November, Willie worked at a Dressing Station at Vlamertinghe, away from the front line, although, like everywhere in the Salient, under shell-fire. It was a time for reflection in the aftermath of the Battle of Loos. Willie also had time to visit the ruins of Ypres in the centre of the

75

Salient. The city was in the course of being razed to the ground by German shelling. It was Ypres' position in the middle of the horse-shoe in the line of the opposing trenches which made it so exposed to bombardment. Nevertheless its destruction shocked public opinion. Winston Churchill argued in January 1919 that the whole ruins should be acquired as a permanent reminder of the war and that a 'more sacred place for the British race did not exist in the world'.[30]

10 October 1915

Yesterday we had another march. One of the officers wanted to see a certain place and of course he marches us twelve miles out and in to suit his whim. I rather enjoyed it in a way as it was always new country. We marched to Dickebusch just below St Eloi and halted at an old mill where the Germans had been. While there they bought the windmill off the Belgian who owned it and when forced to retire, left him in charge as a spy. He used to signal to them by means of the wings of the mill any important movements of our troops till eventually he was discovered. He was hung on one of the beams of his mill*. It is to be blown up because it is rather a good landmark standing on the crest of a hill and the Germans judge the range of various places roundabout from it. It is wonderful how many spies are knocking about and the risks many will run for the sake of the money they get. Of course when they are caught it is 'na poo'.[†]

During the heavy days many turned sick and others fainted, but it would never do if all were so weak. One has to take a very firm hold on oneself and not give way. I have seen strong men look at a case we bring down a trench – they were going up and had to pass us. One I paid attention to seemed fascinated and could not look away; he hugged the side of the trench and I saw the involuntary shudder pass through his whole frame and he put his hand up to his face. Poor fellow, he was going up and perhaps before many hours would be as our patient was, and we had days and nights of this – forget them I never shall. It is an entirely different thing seeing

* At Wytschaete.
† Soldier slang of the Great War for something that is of no use or does not exist. It is a contraction of *il n'y en a plus*.

them after they have been attended to after and fed and cleaned, then to England. To see it all in its awful raw state gives one a very clear idea of what war means, and quite different to a Hospital at home. Folks at home can't realize it properly. We see that by the papers, and perhaps it is a good thing; in fact I believe it is better so. But if I continue to write like this, you will think my letters depressing and I don't want that. I just talk as I feel when writing. There is great activity here and I believe it to be the beginning of the end, although it will certainly take a long time yet and the sacrifices must be enormous. It has got to be done and the men know that.

Wednesday, 13 October 1915

On Guard at night time in this country is a time when one thinks more of the war than any other. Last night, for instance, there was something doing on the right, the Canadians have been busy there for some days. They must have either had a charge or a counter charge, as the machine guns and rifles burst into the silence of the night and the sky was lit up with hundreds of star shells. It is really blood-curdling to hear the spit of those machine guns. This is not war it is murder and butchery – for a man to face the enemy, to go over the parapet nowadays is almost sure death. He may escape the first time through sheer luck, but that can't always last. Ten or a doz. machine guns in a trench would mow down a army if properly worked and our fellows are doing it every day and every day there is the usual heavy death roll on both sides, cold-blooded murder. If it was the fighting of the old days – man to man with artillery, his rifle and bayonet – it would be different, men would have a chance. But this war, they have only – not even – a dog's chance. I hope from the bottom of my heart that militarism is crushed for ever this time.

Monday, 25 October 1915

I was rather hurried with my letter yesterday owing to being on duty till late and had not even time to explain about two or three things I enclosed as souvenirs.

The leaf I picked off a vine that was just outside what once was a beautiful villa in Y[pres] The green ribbon I found lying amongst a lot of debris in a cellar of the Cloth Hall* and the part of a painting, I cut off a portrait of a lady which was perforated and torn with shrapnel. The brooch was the only part all right; so I cut it out. The photos were lying scattered about a ruined house near the Cathedral. Talking about the Cathedral by the way, it is in an awful state. It is pitiful to see such a fine building and such gigantic pillars battered to ruins. There were lots of very valuable souvenirs but it was impossible to bring them.

You have a good idea what like the place looks from the post-cards I have sent but it is even worse now than when they were taken as they still continue to shell as we experienced on Saturday when there. You could quite easily put Monaville inside some of the J J† shell holes. The cemetery at the Cathedral is awuf‡ as it has not escaped either and the contents of the graves of long since dead are exposed all over the place and makes one understand what German 'Kultur' means. It is diabolical.

Thursday, 28 October 1915

Yesterday I was one of a party out of our Ambulance who were inspected by the King here along with our Div. We were all lined two deep on one side of the road and he and the Prince of Wales and ever so many big officers walked right down the road and carefully inspected every man. It was all very good in a way. After he had got to the end of the line, our front rank went over to the other side of the road and he came down between us. He looks very old and worried and one can see that he is bearing his share poor chap.

I have just been interrupted, I had to go and cut the ADMS hair. He is the man who could give us leave if he took it in his head. I

---

* The Cloth Hall, founded in 1200 by the Count of Flanders, was completed in 1320, and during the Middle Ages it was the headquarters of the cloth makers, weavers, and fullers. It was the pride of Ypres, as well as perhaps the greatest medieval secular building in Europe.
† Jack Johnson; a shell named after the American heavyweight boxer because it delivered a knockout blow.
‡ Awash.

was near asking him. Our Captain Nicol was in the office at the time. They were talking about shells that were bursting some distance away and he told the Colonel that I had had a few narrow squeaks. He asked me if I had had enough of it. But I couldn't say any other thing than that I enjoyed it.

16 November 1915

This day puts me in mind of one of the days of the bombardment before our big attack. I did not see much about our Div. in the papers, just the usual though. The man that pioneers seldom gets his due share of the honour. It is generally the man who comes on behind him and lays hold on what he has had to leave behind, pushing meanwhile on and it was like this during the battle and there was things happened that never got into the papers. Conflicting reports, the dispatch run, but we who were there know what happened and how our Div. suffered in consequence. Ours and the Guard's Div. were the best there, as everybody out here knows. But we dare not say much in a letter.

Chapter Six

Winter in the Trenches

On 26 November 1915 27 Field Ambulance went up into the trenches and took over duties at two Advanced Dressing Stations, 'Maple Copse' and 'Railway Dug-outs', where Willie remained for two weeks, before going to a rest camp for three weeks. These Dressing Stations were in makeshift dug-outs in a very exposed part of the line. Maple Copse was only 300 hundred yards from the German trenches, as well as being at the point of the horseshoe of the Ypres Salient. The front-line trenches were safer at this part of the line than the support trenches, because the enemy trenches were only between 400 and 20 yards away. This discouraged enemy shelling of the front lines, in case the German trenches were hit. But the nearness of the trenches encouraged subterranean mine laying, which was very trying on the nerves of those in the trenches. Was that noise below a rat scurrying or a German laying a mine? As if mines and shells were not enough, on 19 December 1915, the day before the 9th Division was due to leave the trenches, the Germans accompanied a massive artillery bombardment of the Ypres trenches with the release of their newest and deadliest weapon – phosgene gas – ten times more deadly than chlorine.[31]

Every day in the trenches meant a steady attrition of the lives of the soldiers. Dangers and extreme discomfort came in almost unlimited forms – sniping, bombing, lice, filth, disease, and the pervasive wet and cold that caused 'trench foot' and denied all attempts at proper sleep. Some men were driven to despair. Willie's time in the Ypres trenches coincided with German air superiority and with the British disadvantage to the Germans in the production of shells – which in the course of the war would inflict seventy per cent of all casualties as well as the worst wounds.[32] Because no battle was being fought at this time, the military described the front as 'quiet'.

Saturday night, 27 November 1915

I am now in the trenches arriving here last night after dark. It was a very rough journey up to the corner below where our cars come for the wounded. What with the anxiety of shells and the miserable shell holes that we were constantly getting into, I was very pleased when we got to our destination. I had to go right away with some patients whenever I arrived. We take them on trolleys down a little wooden railway made for the purpose and all the way we are in range of German rifle fire. It was a trifle exciting to hear the old familiar ring of the bullets about one again. We are right in the line this time in an old wood that has barely a tree that has not been smashed. The anxiety of the place is the worst feature. There are so many shells and always whiz-bangs every day and hour of the day.

All our clearing of cases is done after dark as the road by which we take them is in view of the Germans and our dug-out is only a shelter from bullets and whenever a shell comes over we have to go into communication trenches in case they continue to shell. The reason our dug-outs here are not underground is because the ground is so damp they fill with water. They landed a shell last night on the officers' dug-out (when they were in ours – lucky for them) and one went right below ours and did not burst. Today a big Jack Johnson came over and dropped twenty yards from us and it also did not burst and everybody cleared out into the communication trenches except us because we had cases to look after, but fortunately no more came over.

We are again seeing war as it is – horrible. Seven have died of wounds since last night and in all today we have treated forty cases and this is when everything is quiet. As I write just now our snipers are pinging away and I can hear from here the whistle of the Germans replying. It is a most peculiar part of the line this and quite

81

uncomfortable to notice at nights the starshells flashing up all around us. We seem to be right in the centre of a horseshoe-shaped part of the line and the German lights almost meet behind us. It is an enfilading fire we get and that is why it is so dangerous. One chap who died here today had a letter addressed to his mother amongst his effects and I had to write a few words to inform. He had one of these souvenir cards and a short note telling his Mother and wishing her luck, and that he was just going into the trenches. A sniper shot him through the stomach today. It is very sad but only too common an occurrence here.

Sunday forenoon

It is our A. Section who are again in the trenches and it is always my luck to be attached to them when there is work. I don't mind in the least so long as it has to be done. It is seldom the RAMC ever have a DS so near the firing line – some 300 yards from the Germans – not so dusty eh? This is certainly no-man's-land and coming up the desolation everywhere was terrible. You see the Germans can get at anywhere about here at our backs and all round except one part. It is a perfect horseshoe-shaped line and that's the reason it is rather warm.

I can't say how long we will be up here. Our Ambulance carry on here till 24 December 1915, so far as I know. But we will likely be relieved now and then with the other party who are at the other dug-outs. I suppose that will be to keep our nerves from going, although I don't feel mine any the worse up till now. We are wearing gumboots that come up to our thighs and could not possibly do without them, as for instance while out this morning early, I went over the knee in water taking those patients down. The trenches are in a fearful state of mud and trench feet are very common, and no wonder when fellows have to stand in mud for four days without getting their boots off and it has been very keen frost these last three nights and we had a lot of frost-bitten feet this forenoon and very sore some of them look.

3 December 1915 Night

I have at last got another spare moment to write. Yesterday it was quite impossible and today I have been kept busy all day long and now when most of the boys are asleep I can manage. I was relieved yesterday at the M[aple] C[opse] St. and sent on to this place or R[ailway] Dug-Outs as they are termed. I was not sorry to be sent away from the other place, as one never knew the moment that one of the many bullets that are flying about is going to get you. This is at a different part of the same line, and fairly hot. Indeed I was never under such shell fire as we have had here all day and even as I write I have to stop every minute, wondering where they are going to land. Just as this moment they are sending over shrapnel and high explosive in the dozens not fifty yards away, in fact just at the very spot where we load our wounded on the cars. We have not bullets here, but oh dear we do get shelled. One landed in the place where we get our water from this afternoon and just outside they landed one and it is a dud lying there for anybody to see.

We had about thirty shells over just now and it is not a nice sensation to be so near them and they have been at it all day. There is an old ruined farm just where we carry the patients to, only at night of course, and during today's shelling they gave it what for. There was a lot of Scotties about at the time and of course they were caught napping. We were watching from the mouth of our dug-out and of course they made a rush for the dug-outs, and how they escaped was marvellous. Shell after shell made them get behind a tree or whatever was nearby.

Saturday forenoon

We are having very miserable weather and our dug-out is almost flooded. The place we are in is alive with rats, and they had some cheek moving all over us at night. Oh, they are horrid and run about everywhere in hundreds. I received your very welcome letter of Sunday (yesterday) and right glad I was to get it. I tried to write your letter last night but round about here got such a shelling that I had to stop and they are at it this morning again. Our dug-outs are on an old railway embankment. Their positions are all right, but if anything did land on them, it would be na poo, as they are only one sandbag strong on top. Our good luck still continues and we have had no casualties yet. Everybody seems to get it except 27 FA. How we will finish up is another matter as we have to carry on till the 24th of this month.*

My turn at the Advanced Post is past and I expect a week here and I will be relieved. I will not be sorry. There will be very few of the old Div. when we do come out. There are only about 250 of one battalion left and 300 of another, both a thousand strong to start with; so you can form an idea from that.

We have eight patients in this dug-out just now, and at present it is my duty to see that they are fed till time for the cars. We have been almost flooded out of our dug-out today – the rain coming in at all parts and settling in pools on the floor and jolly uncomfortable it is. I am still in the best of health despite it all. We are lying just beside Hill . . . and the desolation is awful. Just outside our dug-out door, there are about 150 graves, mostly all Scots, and every day it gets bigger.

Monday 6th December 1915

We are having our usual 'straffing' today and every day they nab someone. Just as I closed my last letter to you, a shell burst just outside our dug-out and burst just where one of the Seaforths was crossing. We had to lift him out of the shell hole. He was in an awful state, both his legs having been blown off and his arms stripped of all the flesh. Poor chap he died two hours after and was buried just outside here. Another of the same regiment got it today, but only wounded.

I have not experienced such shell fire before. One daren't go outside the dug-out, they shell so often. I was just stepping out today and jokingly remarked that things were quiet. I had only got two yards when I heard the whistle of another and was not long – one jump I think took me into the centre of the dug-out. There is

* During the Great War, 27 Field Ambulance suffered 140 casualties, consisting of 40 killed in action and 100 wounded, gassed or taken prisoner. It won eighty-two awards or distinctions, consisting of: 1 D.S.O; 1 M.C.(2 Bars); 8 M.C.s: 1 Croix de Guerre; 5 D.C.M.s; 1 M.M.(1 Bar); 1 M.S.M.; 43 M.M.s; 8 Parchments; and 10 Mentioned in Despatches. A Field Ambulance comprised approximately 200 men.

so often a very comical element about it all – to see us all scattering in all directions and disappearing like rabbits that have been scared. A hundred shells have burst in a circle of 200 yards where we are today, not a bad straffing and only two men have been wounded, and none seriously. On Saturday we had to stay up till 3.00 in the morning as the cars could not get here owing to the roads being blocked with dead mules and wrecked transport. What a picture our dug-out presented. I wrote a little note in my pocket Testament and will copy it here.

Saturday night in our Railway Dug-Out, 12 midnight. We have fourteen cases mostly Gordons and nine or ten RAMC inside. A dug-out is about ten feet long and eight broad and a very shaky looking structure. A part of the side which is the railway embankment has fallen in and all that side is perforated with rat-holes and every now and then a rat comes out to see what is doing. In the centre is a brazier glowing red with coke. As I sit here on a dirty coke bag, the scene before me looks a picture of real war and has a very sad as well as artistic side. The rain has been coming down heavily all day with the result that the dug-out is flooded. But that makes no difference. Just at my side is a chap on a stretcher. He has two bullet wounds and is lying gazing into the embers of the fire, and quite well I can see he is wondering on his chances of getting out of this horrible place to England as a result of his wounds, and the prospect I can see absolutely eclipses his present suffering.

On the other side of the stretcher in the corner two more Gordons with bandages up to the knees are asleep. One has his head between his knees and the other his head behind his companion, hard up against the sandbags. On the other side of the brazier another lies asleep in a cramped position. They have all been in since dinner time and are so fed up waiting till they can get away. But tonight the cars are very late. On either side of the dug-out is an improvised seat where the others sit, head nodding and kilties in every position. One dour-looking chap who has hardly been awake a minute, is snoring, his head is swathed in bandages and on one side the usual big blotch of red where the wound is. I had to pick him out below the brazier not many moments ago, to keep him from burning and he did not half swear at being disturbed. A few candles or two is all the light we have and we can hear the rain and wind howling outside and in some parts it is

85

dropping in a perfect stream, but we cannot help that and have to make the best of it, and we are all wet. The only dry corner is where I sleep at nights fortunately.

One or two of our men are leaning against the supports of the dug-out and only wake out of their reverie when a shell bursts rather close to the dug-out and then gaze into the fire and dream again. One or two take a look round and a shake of the head leads me to believe they are thinking as I am and if all at home could just get a glimpse inside our dug-out just now they would get their eyes opened as to what war is, fourteen suffering men who have just come down from hell where they have had experiences but nobody but those who have been there will ever realize, and endured sufferings, and what is more, hunger while protecting their particular part of the line. They have been already twelve hours in here as it is impossible to get them away till night. They would be sure to get battered about with German shells as the roads are in full view. But tonight they are very late with the cars. Something up I fear. But they can't be long now and then we will each of us get a man on our backs and trudge through that mud that comes well up to the knees, and the same game continues after they are gone. Perhaps word will be waiting that more cases have to come from the firing line and our waiting squad will have to go up and bring them down. It is certainly a real picture and no mistake, and I wish I could sketch it, but there is no room. Every part of the dug-out is occupied and we are packed like herring in a box lying each on the other.

Today as usual we are having rain, and if it was not for our trench boots it would be terrible. Sometimes we go over them and they fill. Yesterday going down that road where every few yards there is large shell holes some of them deep enough to drown a good few men, we had a lot of trouble. I had a soldier's full equipment on and a rifle over my shoulder. We looked a sight all in a line, men with shattered arms, some had it in the head, others in the hand and some sick and all the time ready to drop into the first convenient hole if a shell came, whether it was full of water or not. It is a very difficult place this to get wounded men to safety, as the roads are all so open and in full view of the Germans, and their shells come from every side.

There come some more shells. What a horrid place and what a poor dug-out this is, but our luck is still in and I hope it continues

1. Portraits of William St Clair drawn in May 1915 in France by Hedley Hobbs, artist for *Punch*.

2. Picture by William St Clair of a barn at Robecq in July 1915. Peter Edgar is on the left and Hope Bagenal on the right.

3. Picture by William St Clair of an estaminet in France in December 1915. William St Clair is standing at the bar. To the right in RAMC uniform are Gilmour and Teddy Tighe.

4. Picture by William St Clair of Rocourt, St Pol, France, 26 June 1916.

5. Picture by William St Clair from Rocourt Rest Camp, 27 May 1916.

6. Picture by William St Clair from Roubrauch Rest Camp on the Belgian Coast immediately after Passchendaele, October 1917.

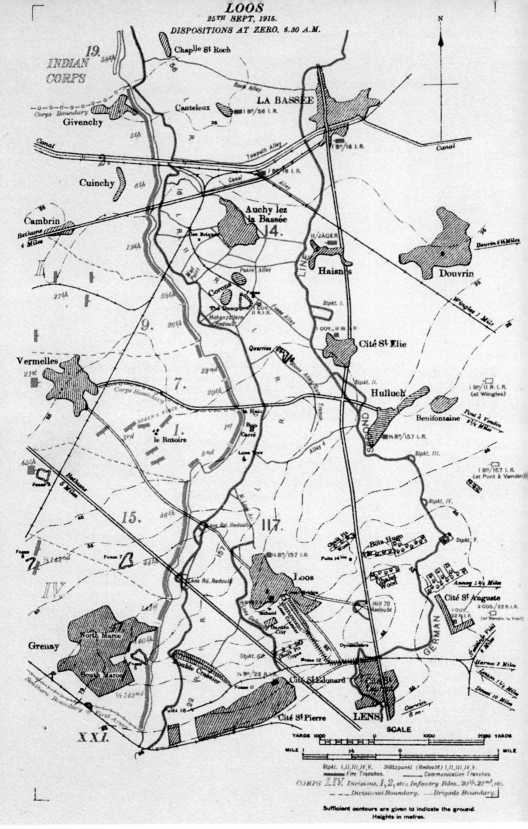

7. Map showing disposition of 9th (Scottish) Division at Loos on morning of 25 September 1915.

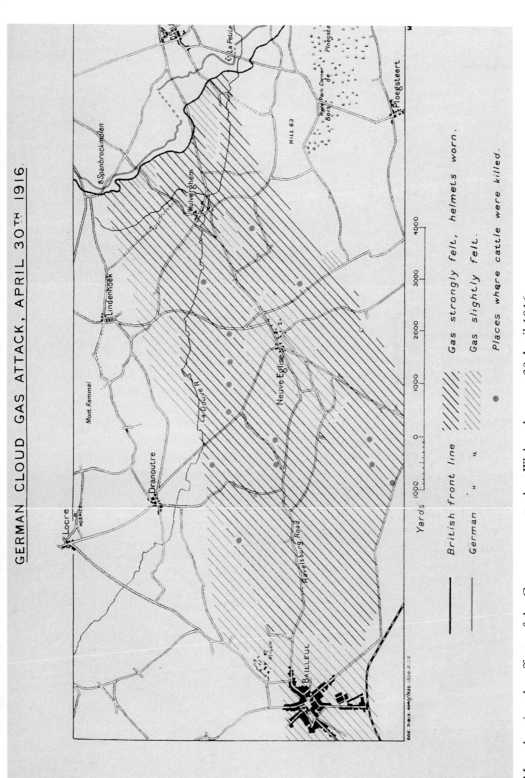

GERMAN CLOUD GAS ATTACK, APRIL 30ᵀᴴ 1916.

British front line ▨ Gas strongly felt, helmets worn.

German " " ▨ Gas slightly felt.

● Places where cattle were killed.

Yards

8. Map showing the effects of the German gas attack at Wulverghem on 30 April 1916.

9. Picture by William St Clair of a field ambulance taken from an old trench at Bazentin-le-Grand during Battle of the Somme on 10 October 1916.

10. Picture by William St Clair of the inside of an Advanced Dressing Station at Bazentin-le-Petit in October 1916 during Battle of the Somme, showing Scottish soldiers in kilts and aprons and two German prisoners in grey uniforms.

11. Christmas decoration painted by William St Clair for the celebration of Christmas in December 1917 after the battle of Passchendaele.

12. Picture by William St Clair of the RAMC bathing place at Affringues on 21 May 1918.

13. Picture by William St Clair of the RAMC tents in an apple orchard at Affringues on 15 May 1915.

– trash crash shell after shell going over us and landing in Y[pres]. They try for the transport every night and often nab it, but they pay for any damage they do as our artillery (and about here, we are their superior there) gives them what for.

Wednesday, 8 December 1915

My word warfare during the winter is quite a different thing to the summer. All the hardships are multiplied ten times and the discomforts, and also the dangers as it is difficult to keep a shelter in condition. Trenches fall in and are flooded and dug-outs collapse. My word but we will be pleased when this war is over.

I used to try and imagine when in England last winter but my imagination at the worst was not as bad as what the real thing is, especially in this part of the line where they can get at you from all corners. There are very few of the old hands and the different battalions of our Div. left now, mostly all are drafts, and every day they go down killed and wounded and the little cemeteries all near here are getting fuller every day. With Scots too.

Later. Dearest we have just had an order sent up from Headquarters to the effect that we who have been up here from the first have to be relieved tonight. So there, good news eh? We go down with the wounded tonight via Y. I trust that when we are going there, they have stopped shelling. That is the only trouble of the journey. If all goes well, I will be back with Pete about midnight tonight and that will be my turn in the trenches finished for some time. I am thankful to have been again spared while so many round about have been struck down. Our little dug-out is packed full of wounded men just now waiting on the cars and I am sitting in a corner with all my kit ready to slip on whenever they come up.

I wish the days would hurry so that I could get home to you. I have envied many of our cases their wounds and prospects since I came up here.

Tuesday Night, 28 December 1915

I wish I could come rushing home to you now and make you so very happy but your Willie is so helpless and bound with the chains of discipline, and that word means more out here than at home.

For instance, for writing about things that were considered other than 'family affairs' in a green envelope a corporal of the Engineers has been sentenced to six months' hard labour and reduced to the ranks. Oh yes they can make you do just what they want when in this country on active service. We feel the chains more and more every day. It is nearing another year and I trust that, ere it finishes, this war will be finished and us all back again. I think so, as the expense is horrendous for the nations to keep it up.

Thursday Night, 30 December 1915

They are keeping us so infernally busy that it is seldom we are free at all. Today, for instance, we paraded at 7.00 am, dismissed at 7.30 till 9.00 am, when we were marched off for Physical Drill and ordinary Drill which kept us till 12. We were forced to play football whether we cared to or not to keep us fit and before they were done with us we were soaking with sweat. A thorough good swill and dinner, letter delivered (a great treat for me) and that brought 2.00 pm when we had to parade for respirator and smoke helmet practice. An hour at that so that we can put on our smoke helmets on the shortest notice. Those of us who did not get a bath the other day while we were at B[éthune] were marched off there shortly after 3.00 pm – a distance of four miles, had a good bath and marched back. Just had tea and it is now after 7.00 pm. The result is that I am very tired doubling and exercising all forenoon and an eight-mile march in the afternoon.

This is how we are spending our rest. It is all very good and keeps us very fit, but we get so tired of it as it is a daily performance and last night just after I had got my tea I was sent for. The Colonel of 10 A. and SH had sent to Headquarters to see if they would send me down and cut his hair. It was a damp sort of night and they are two miles from us. Of course I had just to go and find my way as best I could. I got there, cut his hair and enjoyed the lonely walk back fine. I just made myself believe you were at my side and that I was at home, and I spoke to you with my love and just cracked away in our own way lovey, and the road instead of being long, was very short because I had not said the half of what I was going to say before I was in this village. Ah love, I love you so much and want to tell you and be able to kiss you too.

88

Morning, 31 December 1915

I am just closing my letter to give it to the post. But I must wish you my love good morning. I found the enclosed piece of poetry in a mag.[33] It is my feeling always. I am on Guard tonight, so will bring in the New Year that way.

Chapter Seven

The Scales of Sacrifice

The Divisional History of the 9th Division says that, 'after each devastating battle, the Division rose Phoenix-like from its ashes'.[34] *This meant, in non- military language, that new recruits had to be found to replace the men who had been killed or were too seriously wounded to fight again. The 9th Division, for example, had suffered nearly 6,000 casualties at Loos. Conscription seemed the only solution, but it was anathema to much of the Liberal Party. Lloyd George argued strongly in favour of conscription, to give the military the best means to victory. And eventually his argument won the day, and, after a short debate in the House of Commons on 12 January 1916, the Military Service Act 1916 was passed. It conscripted into the Army all single men in Britain*[35] *aged between eighteen and forty-one years. In May a second Military Service Act was passed conscripting married men into the Army. Even these measures proved inadequate and in early 1918, the age limit for conscription was set at fifty-one. All the time fitness and height criteria were being relaxed.*[36] *The era of the Kitchener volunteers, who could march twenty miles a day over an indefinite period, had long passed.*[37]

The Army did not just need men as a result of the carnage on the Western front, it needed officers, because by the end of the main fighting of the Battle of Loos, 42.3 per cent of serving officers were casualties[38] *of whom junior officers in infantry regiments were by far the most heavily represented. Before the Great War, the universities and public schools had been relied on to supply the great bulk of the officer class and had been encouraged to set up Officers' Training*

Corps. Some of the public schools, like Edinburgh Academy in Scotland, rejected the idea of a Cadet Corps on the grounds that military training was not consistent with a liberal education,[39] but by the outbreak of war all the public schools considered military training an essential part of a young man's education.[40] When the war came, the public school and university cadres were immediately mobilized. 25,000 Oxford and Cambridge men served as officers, of whom 5,000 were killed.[41] The public schools paid an even heavier toll, with whole year groups leaving to go to the front as officers. The casualties of the Edinburgh Academy were typical. Its whole unbeaten cricket XI of 1914 went straight into commissions in infantry regiments, and by the end of the war all were casualties– seven killed and four wounded.[42] About sixty infantry officers from the school were casualties at the Battle of Loos.

The remorseless arithmetic of the casualty figures and the huge expansion of the Army – 275,121 men served as officers during the war[43] – opened up the British officer class, with Willie and Peter Edgar applying for commissions, backed by their commanding officer. But why would men like Willie and Peter Edgar want to be officers – most likely in an infantry regiment – when they knew well that a commission drastically reduced the odds on your survival? First, any pacifism Willie had had when he joined had been stripped away by the Battle of Loos. Then there was patriotic duty, with Willie's commanding officer saying that he had been expecting Willie and Peter Edgar to apply for commissions. There may even have been an idea of going up in the world. 'We are out for big things,' he wrote to Jane. But in his letter of 24 March 1916 he said that he was keen on getting a commission because of the monotony and thanklessness of his job as an orderly and that the trenches were a 'boon to this sort of work'. To Jane he also hinted at something darker in the letter – 'no variation except bullying'. The bully was 'Sammy', as Willie called him in his diaries, his vainglorious Sergeant Major. Sammy was doubtless behind Willie and Peter Edgar not getting commissions and Willie and Peter instead being separated. At the time Willie wrote to Jane that if he did not get a commission, it would be for the best because he was certain there was a 'power looking after us'.* He never applied for a

* See letter written on 16 March 1916.

commission later in the war, although he would almost certainly have got one. By the end of 1916 he had seen the toll of officers killed in the Somme battles and was also planning to get married. His duty of loyal sacrifice to his country had now to be balanced by his duty to Jane, and he was perhaps thinking that the state was demanding too much from its citizens.

In his letter of 5 March 1916 Willie talked of 'sacrifice after sacrifice'. He had heard that he was going to lose his business, and indeed his livelihood when he came back in 1919, a point that caused him deep bitterness, which he often talked about in old age. The loss of Willie's business was a side-effect of conscription. The Military Service Acts provided for exemptions on the grounds of extreme hardship because of domestic or financial position, as well as on the grounds of conscience, infirmity or engagement in key war work at home. By the end of the war Willie's brothers, John and David, had been conscripted into the Army. But it was the conscription of his brother John that caused him the most problems. Willie speaks in his letters of the struggle to keep his business going with John running it in his absence at the Front. John's conscription into the Army by the first Military Service Act in 1916 meant Willie's business was lost. John did first, however, try to get exemption on hardship grounds and on the grounds that he was training to be a preacher of the Gospel.[44] His case was one of the first before the Kirkintilloch Military Tribunal, which met for the first time on 22 February 1916 and shows the working methods of the Tribunal, as well as their poor grasp of the economic realities of running a small family business. A transcript of the exchange appeared in a local newspaper.[45]

Chairman:	'Can they not fall back on the old bowl and scissors style?'
Baillie Gibson:	'It would be rather hard lines on the brother if he came back and found his business gone.'
The Provost:	'Thousands will have to do that. If nobody goes to the front, it won't be long till there are no businesses at all.'
Applicant:	'But my brother has gone to the front and is depending on me keeping his business for him till he comes back.'

Major Hope:	'I think this is a case we might postpone for a little.'

The Military Tribunal granted two months' postponement.

The Provost:	'May I add that if we were to allow our own personal feeling to come into play, we would exempt everyone. Anyway a man can start a barber's shop in an hour's notice.'

At the expiry of the two months' postponement, John applied for exemption on the 'conscience' ground. This was not accepted, but he was put into a non-combatant unit, later serving as a stretcher-bearer on the Western Front.[46]

Thursday, 6 January 1916

They are issuing us all with furskin coats and all the infantry are going through a course of b[omb throwin]g. Every man has to be able to do it, whereas up till now only a few were b[omb thrower]s. What is in store for us, we have not the slightest. And what may interest you to know, Winston Churchill is Colonel of 6/ R.S.F* of our Brigade. I don't think this news will be a fault with the censor or I would not tell it.

We are not so badly off here. It is a very decent billet. Although we had some extra blankets each and were very comfortable till yesterday, our SM came up, took every one which was extra away. Here they were being looked after and what seems to trouble him making us comfortable – a thing he positively hates to see, and this is the truth – he took them from us and now they are lying in a damp store where they will most likely rot. Yes there are plenty blankets to keep us all as comfortable as one could desire. But he would rather keep them in the store. Folks at home don't know the half of what goes on. There is something worse than that, if it was known at home, would – well I better stop. But a soldier has always a way of getting the better of a SM of that description.

* 6th Battalion of the Royal Scots Fusiliers.

Sunday afternoon, 9 January 1916
Outtersteene, France

We are still in the rest area yet and so far as appearances go are likely to be till about the 21st of the month. But as you know as well as I know, we are never certain when we are to be on the move again. We have not heard yet where we are going after that. It is rumoured that our Field Ambulance will go to Armentières and do the Trench Work, one to Nieppe or Ploegsteert (Plug Street) and one to Bailleul. We may go to any of the three places. Our Div has been putting in a lot of training since they came to the rest area and even here we are not allowed to forget the familiar sound of machine guns and bombs. The field just outside our billet is a bomb range and every day there are large parties of men and officers practising bomb-throwing and machine-gun practice.

Every man has to be able to bomb and so they are very busy learning. They evidently mean to bring the Div up to its fine state of efficiency again. Whether it will ever be as it was before the battle remains to be seen. Our Corps Commander is now Field Marshal – as you would notice – Sir Douglas Haig and perhaps that accounts for it. Of course it means that where the fighting is thickest we will be, an honour so far as a Div is concerned.

Our Sergeant Major has turned out a proper rotter and nothing is too low for him to do and nothing pleases him better than to see us squirm under his treatment. He had said that he will break some of our hearts. Yet only the other day he said that to another Sergeant. Of course he will never do that. He is paying back all those who told him off before he was a SM. He never had brains and had to depend on privates to see him through and now he hates the look of a man who he thinks knows him as he is and does not suck up to him as he wishes. Every man hates him like poison. That is our big trial, but of course nobody, unless those who know military life and especially active service, understands this. He is of a boorish lot and should never have been over the sort of men found in a Field Ambulance. I am not one of his favourites thank God and I believe that was the reason I was not allowed special leave. I had an excellent chance with the officers, but he sways a lot. However I was fairly lucky in the ballot and it is drawing near. Four more go tonight and tomorrow and that leaves me no. nineteen now I think. I am just as glad now that I did not get special leave. It would have been over long ago.

This is a beautiful day and for all the world like a spring day. I do hope it continues, for when the cold weather does come it cannot last too long. For a month or two will start the good weather. Oh I do hope there will be an early prospect of some settlement, either that or the complete downfall of Germany. This eternal bondage gets so unbearable. We who are volunteers cannot cotton so well to discipline and such discipline as we have in this Ambulance. A very strange thing is that all our grumbling is done when we are away from the trenches. So long as we have plenty of the work we are here for, we don't incline to grumble. I suppose we are very strange mortals in a way to those at home. There is a certain fact and it is that no regulars ever did better (or perhaps quite so much) as the volunteers of all Regs. did at Loos. However, we will talk about these things in the future. It will not be so long till this is all a dream. Many more lives will be lost but a life or 100 lives means nothing to a nation. A reward will most surely be reaped and our country will benefit. But I am drifting onto political things again lovey.

End of January 1916

I don't like coming home without Peter, but I will worry so much about the shop that I will simply be in misery. I must see how things are, and if possible prevent John from enlisting. One out of a home is plenty. My God it is some of the supposed men who loaf about Regent Street who should be away and allow those who have duties at home to remain. But if they will not go, the others must ruin themselves financially for the sake of their country and to prevent what few as yet seem to realize would be the consequences. It is no joke about the country needing men. She must get them, or God alone knows what the result will be. This war is only in the first stages. That soldier last night told us some things about the war that are true, which is a very rare thing to get. We are inferior to the Germans in a lot of things. Artillery is one. We have not a ghost of a chance in that direction, and it is very important in this war. We are drilling about 800,000 men just now. Germany is drilling about 3,000,000 recruits between the ages of eighteen to thirty.

That's the reliable news we have here. It makes me wild to think of some in Kirkie who swank about and never make a move. Compel them. They should be dragged by the legs and forced. Excuse this outburst dearest, but I can't help it. I don't write this to worry you, but all the suffering should not be placed on a few, and ours is bad, but there are worst cases.

Sunday Night, 5 March 1916

This is the first moment I've had to spare today to write and I have been a little miserable over a matter of discipline. To let you know, I have been in the habit of going along with two corporals at dinner time to a little place to get a cup of coffee and sometimes we get our dinner instead of in the Camp. It is a Frenchman and his wife who make it for us. He has lost one of his eyes in the war and they make us our dinner very cheap and are so homely. It was such a boon to us to get a decent meal so cheaply. While out today – it is just at the back of our Camp but evidently out of bounds as we are not supposed to leave the precinct of the Camp till after six at night without a pass. But almost everybody goes down for a coffee and nothing has been said till two days ago three chaps got ten days' First Field Punishment for going out before time at night. We did not think we were doing any wrong and so continued to go at dinner time.

All would have been well, only an officer came today for to get his hair cut while I was out and our SM asked me where I had been when I came in, and I told him the truth – I was down for a coffee. We had arranged, Pete and I, to go before the Colonel tomorrow for our Com. (for his permission to go for it) and this I knew would make that impossible if I was crimed for the fault. I told the SM but he paid no heed and told me I would have to parade as a defaulter. I went in the afternoon to cut the officer's hair and told him how I had been done for being out. He said he would do what he could. It meant if I had gone before the Colonel, I would most likely have got days of FP and that would have put a crime on my sheet, which up till now is perfectly clean, and then there would have been no chance of a Com, which would certainly have been a source of pleasure to one individual. I was sent for by the officer who went on leave with us and he asked me about it and I told him exactly the truth, and he squared it up for me, saying he would be very sorry to see my character sheet crimed for nothing – which it was and so it is all over now and there is nothing to be said.

I was terribly annoyed at the prospect of the degradation of FP for I am proud, as you know, and the idea of being tied to a wheel would have maddened me and there might have been more trouble for me in consequence.* But everything is all right now and we are going to ask our Colonel to go on with the Com tomorrow. This has made me keener than ever to get me away from this Corps. I trust you understand this properly as I cannot be more explicit in a letter. I went a few yards out of the bounds of the Camp and you see what the consequences might have been. Of course I must tell you all my troubles darling, and I feel easier. I am very thankful there is no trouble and I will know what to do again.

Yes it seems so hard about the business, sacrifice after sacrifice. We will most likely have to start from the beginning when we come home. That does not frighten me so long as we are spared with health and strength. G.F. will be very uncomfortable, poor Geordie, I would not like to be made like him. It is better to die than to be branded a coward.

March 1916

Despite all that disgusts them about the life, the petty and at times hard ways of discipline, whenever they are asked to face death with almost impossible chance of escape, and throw themselves against those murderous weapons of modern warfare for bringing men down like sheaves of corn, they only take it as part of their daily business, so far as concern goes, but with all the enthusiasm of a glorious history. To credit it, one has to be amongst it. At home we lost our memory of all this. It seems so unreal when there. And there is not the slightest doubt that the country does not realize what this war is and what is really being done out here. Whether it is better to be so, I cannot say. Time will tell. The time will come most likely, after it is over and we have won, when the country will forget about it, and most likely as of old, about those who return. Everything will go on as before, only there will be fewer men about. We will be a great nation, but the men who have been through it and know

* Willie is describing here Field Punishment Number One.

97

will never forget the hundreds of thousands of dead heroes who are left here. There is just the possibility that those who do return will alter the mouldy politics of our country. One thing is certain, it is by no means a nation who is beaten that we are fighting against at present. They have to be yet.

No further developments re commissions yet. Anxious to have your reply letter to hear your opinion. Colonel Jeffrey, our Chaplain, told me today we would stand a good chance. We take no steps till we hear from you all. But I must close darling as I am on my last ½ inch of candle and will be in darkness in a few minutes.

Monday, 6 March 1916

Well lovey Pete and I went before the Colonel this morning to request his permission and assistance to get a Com. and he has given us it and was nicer than ever we expected. He spoke about Major A. writing him and had been wondering why we had not yet applied. That recommendation from A. did us a lot of good and made it much easier for us every way. He asked us why we wanted a Com. and did we realize the great honour if we got one, to which we replied satisfactorily. Asked us where we had been educated and so on. Then he told us he had a good opinion of us himself. We were good boys and he would do all he could to get us our Com. but that he would be very sorry to have to part with us himself, spoke of our good characters and of our work up the trenches and made us blush with his good opinion. What do you think of that lovey? I was surprised and pleased as our SM was standing behind us and he had to acquiesce. He gave us our papers, which we will fill in and send home to be filled in there by people who can vouch for our character before the war and our qualifications. So far as education goes, we will tell you what has to be done. Of course there are lots of obstacles to get over yet, before we are finished with it. We will have to have an interview with our General. We told him we wanted into some of the Scotch Regs.; so may have to don a kilt yet. I hope the weather is warmer than it is now, and then we will have to wash our knees oftener.

As regards my business, it is a pity my Father wasn't able to work it. If John has to go there is no use of us getting miserable over it. This is a time when there has to be no end to our sacrifices and God alone knows how we finish up. If this affair comes off, we may be sent to Scotland to do our training, who knows? Our luck so far has always been good. So we will have faith in it for the future.

There was a young chap in the Hospital I got very friendly with this week and he is a DCM* to boot. He is away down to the base now with a knee trouble. It was with some difficulty I got the story of his DCM out of him. At the battle of Y[pres] he and five others were placed in the centre of a road with a machine gun. Along this road the Germans were advancing and the gunners had no cover whatever. Four were killed outright and the other two worked the gun till they were forced to retire a little. But they determined to take their gun with them. The gun in itself is a very heavy thing and so is the tripod it rests on. However he managed to get the gun on his shoulder and his companion was lifting the tripod when he was shot. The other stooped down, seized the tripod, doubled back a little and decided to fix the gun up again. While fixing the tripod, a shell shattered two of the legs. He looked about for something to give his gun an elevation, got his eye on a dead German, turned him over, rested his gun on him and kept the Germans at bay till our troops recovered their position. A Brigadier General noticed the machine gunner firing, with it resting on the dead German. He was recommended and got his DCM. That was early in the war when it was very difficult to get an honour. Now an action like that would most likely get a VC if it was noticed. Some men have got DCM who have not earned them, but this chap did. He is a nice chap. He wants to write to me and is going to send on a souvenir photo. He got a present of £8 along with his medal. Not bad eh?

Wednesday, 15 March 1916

We have been very busy and are still. Yesterday all our available men out of our already short-handed Hospital were sent up to the trenches to lay barbed wire – quite a new departure for the RAMC eh?† And so those of us who are left here have as much work as we can get through with. After working all day till near six last night,

* Distinguished Conduct Medal. It is won by those below the rank of officer and is a very high award. For officers, the nearest equivalent is the DSO.
† This would be in clear breach of the Hague Conventions on Land Warfare.

I was told 'off for Guard', and of course have been up all night and had just to start my usual work this morning immediately I came off at 6.00 am.

Wednesday night 8.30, 15 March 1916

We had quite a new departure this afternoon. Our Divisional Band was here and played some very fine selections for the benefit of the patients. It was quite a treat for them and us. It was a beautiful afternoon and but for the discord of the heavy guns firing, one had difficulty as to a war being on and a matter of five miles away. There was the usual game of give and take in slaughter. But I expect on the other side the Germans play the same game and perhaps the same tunes. Doesn't it seem ridiculous the whole thing? One would think the nations concerned cannot help themselves and are compelled by some influence over which none of them have control, to wage this disgraceful game, and that if they could, they would stop it. But there you are, to explain it is impossible, but there is the faith that good will come out of it all. God grant that it will. For it at present is evil.

Thursday forenoon

As to the Com, we may not get it lovey and will not be disappointed, for if we don't I suppose it will be for the best for I am certain there is a power looking after us. How I wish we could be sure that it would finish in June. Who knows the news this morning looks more hopeful, and already there is a talk of peace from the Germans, but the conditions are of such a nature at present that it will not be considered but it is always in the right direction and breaks the ice. God grant that something will come of it.*

* Towards the end of the year, Germany sent out its first proper peace feelers through various embassies, but it would have meant Germany hanging on to her gains. Lord Lansdowne, Minister without Portfolio, circulated a memorandum to his cabinet colleagues to the effect that Britain's position was becoming catastrophic and that negotiations should be entered into. His colleagues rejected this. Sir 'Wully' Robertson, Chief of the Imperial General Staff, talked about 'cranks, cowards and philosophers who think we stand to gain more by losing the war than by winning it'.

Friday, 24 March 1916

I see you want me to detail to you my Sunday work. Well dearie Sunday we do just exactly as other days and so far as I am concerned generally more. I have not been able since we returned from leave to be at a church service even – no time. We rise at 5.50 am and parade at 6.20 am. I wash and shave, get some breakfast and cut some patients' hair before 8, when I go into every one of the wards and examine every man's feet and nails etc. – chiropodist you know – and cut any who have not had their hair cut. Well this job takes me a long time as there are seven wards and four marquees. After I am finished I do some shaving, have to do it whether I get paid or not. Seldom I do get paid, and have generally a quiet time just before dinner when I write or at least start, but have often to go and do some job or other.

After dinner we get ready for the convoy which often consists of fifty patients. I of course have to cut their hair before they go into the wards and when I finish these cases, I have to go and do all the stretcher cases in Hospital and seldom ever finish before 6.30 pm, and often later. I go out if I feel inclined, which I always do, as to get outside this gate is like going outside a prison. I go down to the YMCA Hut or to the Canadian Institute an hour and back at 8.00 pm and put bed down, and there you have what it is like every day there is – no variation except a bullying order now and then. I hate it all and for that reason, I was keen on the Com. because the monotony and the thanklessness of this job gets on my nerves. But well we did not even get a chance, and so must be content. But so far as I am concerned, the trenches are a boon to this sort of work. There one is to an extent free. The work is of such a nature that one can put heart into it, and the danger is just the thing to keep it from being monotonous.

26 March 1916
Bailleul

In the job I am in at present, I get many a laugh as well as my temper tried. You see every man that comes into this Hospital of ours has to have his hair cut and the order has it that it has all to come off right over the front, like a jailbird. The result is that almost every man objects right off. 'Come in and get your hair cut Jock.' 'Hoo a ye gaun tae cut it – right aff?' 'Aye, every bit of it.' 'Am damned shair ye din'a – is this a jile* ar whit is it? Ye cae it a hospiteel – its mair like Barlinnie.' 'But it is an order,' I say and 'ye'll have to go through the mill.' 'Whoe's order?' 'A never heard o it in oor battalion. Its a d------ fine order gaun seek. A wish a had akent aboot this hair cut. A wid rather hae drapped than gaun seek. A didna want tae come doon here. It wis the Dr and they cut yer hair like that. Its awfu'. 'But it's an order Jock and I have to do it,' I say. 'I ken fine its no your blame, but dinna ye think its a da – d shame tae treat us like that after lying till oor body canna staun it in mud and water for them eh?' 'I quite agree with ye Jock. It is worse than a d------ shame but you know what an order is. See the SM about it.' 'A wull that afor a'll hae my hair cut like that. Man alive am gaun on leave in a day or twa and the wife all kull me if I gan hame wae a heid like that'. I get the SM as I am responsible to see it done and beside the Colonel is keen on it and has given me an order to do it. The SM orders them in his own way, threatening all sorts of crimes if they don't and the result is they last submit to the ordeal.

But this happens every day and often every other man that comes in – but they all get their hair cut at the wind up, but it is often very funny to hear them and breaks the monotony of the job. Before they leave they enjoy the joke of the newcomers going through the ordeal. It would surprise – the pride, unless you knew the position, dirty and ill and they will wrangle for a quarter of an hour to try and save three inches of hair in the front of their head. Others will say 'Oh take it aff – whit dis it matter? A'll na hae a heid long if we are in they trenches ony longer'. Others say, 'I suppose they copied this aff the Germans like maist things. A weel if I pop my head aboon the parapet, they'll think am wan o'their ain', and so on, many a laugh I get indeed.

Monday forenoon, 27 March 1916

Ah there go the anti-aircraft guns, firing at German aeroplanes overhead. They are on their daily prowl. Do you know what is our latest order: 'not to shave the upper lip'? The penalty being etc etc

* jail.

etc and so we are all training moustaches. As for mine, you would smile I know if you just had a glimpse of it – eleven a side and no mistake, the only time I can see it at all is when I let the sun shine on it and look in the mirror then. But I believe in a year or so it will be visible.

WAR WITHOUT A MASK ON : THE WULVERGHEM GAS ATTACK

The governments of the belligerent countries at the beginning of the war had no plans to use chemical weapons. There was mention in the Hague Conventions of not using 'projectiles the sole object of which is the diffusion of asphyxiating or deleterious gases' or 'poison or poisoned weapons' as well as a general prohibition on using weapons that cause unnecessary suffering. But it was not even known whether gas weapons were feasible or how effective they might prove. It was the stalemate on the Western Front that prompted the German military to take gas seriously. The Chief of the General Staff, Erich von Falkenhayn, became convinced that unless he could come up with some big idea to break through on the Western Front, the Germans would lose the war. Accordingly a brilliant team of German scientists at the Kaiser Wilhelm Institute in Berlin, some of whom later won Nobel prizes, began looking into the potential use of gas as a weapon.

The first successful use of gas by the Germans was when gas in chlorine cloud form was discharged against the French, British and Canadians at Langemarck on the Ypres front on 22 April 1915. By being in cloud form and not in a projectile it could be argued that the Hague Convention was not being breached. The German project leader, Fritz Haber, had also become convinced that gas used in this way was humane because it would only incapacitate. The gas attack came as a complete surprise and caused panic, but the Germans had not made sufficient plans to exploit the break- through and no crucial gains were made. But the gas attack added to the already extreme public outrage at the Germans and their behaviour and the British decided to retaliate, although there was no provision in the Hague Conventions allowing retaliation. Following the German attack at Langemarck, all the main allies, including later the Americans, used gas. Sometimes it was released from cylinders as at Loos, sometimes fired in shells or mortars. Deadlier types were invented – phosgene, mustard, etc.

By April 1916, when the gas attack described in the following letter took place, the British troops were all equipped with efficient respirators and much attention had been devoted to general defensive organization and training against gas. There was to be no repeat of the attacks in April and May 1915, when gas cloud attacks had been made against unprotected troops. Training was aimed at the men having their respirators on within fifteen seconds of the alarm being sounded. A 'P' helmet, soaked in sodium phenate solution, which had the power of absorbing both chlorine and phosgene, had been issued by the time of a gas cloud attack on 19 December 1915. Shortly after an improved 'PH' helmet, which had an increased power of absorbing phosgene, owing to the presence of hexamine as well as sodium phenate, was generally issued. Key troops, such as machine-gun personnel, signallers, and selected artillery personnel, being prime targets, were issued with a large 'box respirator', which gave even greater protection. Another protection the British had was that the wind on the Western Front usually blew in an easterly direction.

On 30 April the British sector at Wulverghem was on high alert for a gas attack for a number of reasons. First, since 22 April the wind had remained in a dangerous quarter, and from that date a 'gas alert' was in force. Secondly British artillery fire had more than once broken up gas cylinders in the German trenches producing telltale clouds of gas. Thirdly on 25 April two German deserters had stated that gas had been installed and was to be used as soon as the wind was favourable. Lastly, at 9.25 pm on 29 April 1916 two more deserters had entered the trenches held by the 3rd Division and stated that the Germans intended to make a gas attack the same night or early on the following morning. Warning was immediately circulated to all troops in the threatened sector.

The deserters were reliable in almost every detail. The gas was released at 12.35 am on 30 April, when darkness made its liberation difficult to detect. The release was also under the cover of rifle and machine-gun fire to muffle the hissing and prevent the alarm gongs and horns being generally heard. It was released right along 3,500 yards of the front from Spanbroekmolen to La Petite

104

Douce Ferme except at two small sectors, where the Germans attacked. There was simultaneously an artillery barrage on points behind the British trenches and trench mortar fire. Despite the British precautions, the wind speed of nine to twelve miles an hour and the short distance between the opposing trenches – they were only forty yards apart where the casualties were worst – meant that the gas reached the British trenches before it was noticed.* The gas cloud sent over by the Germans was of chlorine with phosgene in a concentrated form. A short exposure was enough to cause death, sometimes within an hour but usually more protracted. About 14,000 troops scrambled to put on their respirators, but, for those nearest to the German trenches, the slightest hesitation in putting on the respirator, or fumbling in adjusting it, proved fatal.

The gas cloud travelled a considerable distance with great rapidity, being quite unpleasantly strong at Bailleul – a distance of six miles from the discharge – causing coughing and in some cases vomiting. At Bailleul it was first noticed at 1.12 am, which is equivalent to a speed of 300 yards per minute. The course which the gas had taken was clearly marked by the burning or discoloration of the grass and the destroyed vegetation. Even at Bailleul, where Willie was working in a Field Hospital in the Divisional Rest Station, the young shoots and leaves of plants were withered and cattle were killed in fields just two miles short of the town. Nearer the discharge a horse was killed as well as calves and poultry, and in the vicinity of the trenches rats died in vast numbers. Among the soldiers, according to the official figures, there were 562 gas casualties caused by the attack, of whom eighty-nine died. Many more soldiers and civilians were treated, but not classed as casualties.

Under cover of the gas and artillery and trench mortar fire, the Germans raided in two places, one sector held by the 3rd Division and another held by the 24th. The attack on the 3rd Division was repelled by Lewis-gun fire from a flank and by hand grenades thrown by the garrison of the trench attacked. Two 9.2-inch and two 8-inch howitzers were turned on the German trench mortars and destroyed them. In the raid on the 24th Division the Germans

* With a wind speed of twelve miles per hour, the gas travelled fifty yards in ten seconds.

were armed with bombs, daggers and pistols and they succeeded in entering a short three-bay length of front trench, but they were beaten back by a counter-attack. The Official History of the War then states that, 'By 4.30 am, after a lovely sunrise, the front had entirely quieted down without either the supports or the reserves having been called on, and a peaceful Sunday followed.'

The idyllic weather at the time of the attack was remarked on by Willie in his letter to Jane, but with no more elaboration than giving her a backdrop of his patients recuperating out in the sun. Hope Bagenal, by contrast, devoted a chapter of Fields and Battlefields *to the gas attack, which he allegorizes as 'In an Elysian Field'. Bagenal quotes from 'Ashes of Soldiers', Walt Whitman's elegy for the dead of the American Civil War, in which Whitman had served as a battlefield wound-dresser, 'Perfume therefore my chant, O love, immortal love, Give me to bathe the memories of all dead soldiers . . .'. Bagenal's most telling point, however, was that he overheard an officer saying that 'The men had disobeyed orders in being caught without their gas-helmets. It was impossible to guard them against themselves. There had been no deaths among the officers'. But, barring wearing a helmet all the time, there was no guard against the gas, and two British officers did* die in the gas attack.

Monday, 1 May 1916

I have just received your very welcome and loving letter of Friday. It is a real lover's letter. I see you are getting the same good weather we are having here. It is very hot today and has been like this for some time now. I have been doing all my work outside today and am sitting on the long grass where the patients' tents are. But they live outside in weather like this and all around me they are lying sleeping, some on beds and others in the Hospital blue clothes lying stretched out on the grass. It is an ideal place for patients when the weather is good, and the air is of the purest, although it was not very pure yesterday morning when the Germans sent over gas at 1.00 am. We were all awakened by the gas alarm and could sniff the gas very strong. Of course we all had to wear our helmets (gas) for over thirty minutes till it was over. The breeze that was blowing was very favourable for the Germans. Some of our fellows

106

were very sick, but as we are behind the line a few miles, it was not strong enough to kill by the time it got our length. Where Pete is, it did not strike luckily as he lies more to our left where our Div are. And of course few of our Div got any of it.

Of course the Germans made an attack after and the guns were awful. The whole sky was lit up by the flashes of hundreds of guns. We stood around here with our gas helmets on our heads watching and wondering what tale this morning would tell for we knew for certain that unless everybody were very quick in getting on their helmets 100s must have died. For any man getting two breaths of this new gas the Germans are using, which is the most deadly gas known, two breaths are sufficient to kill a man in an hour. How cruel it all is. The Germans advanced and were driven back. But yesterday morning the wounded and gassed began to come down and before night 1100 gassed cases alone passed through the Hos of this town en route to the base.

The scenes of suffering are beyond description and a big percentage died and a bigger percentage will die in the course of a few days. They often linger for four days. They writhe in agony. One fellow was so bad that he pulled his razor out of his tunic pocket and almost severed his head from his body. All day every available man out of our Ambulance were unloading wagons. And today they are busy burying the dead. My God but it is a frightful stuff and no man has a ghost of a chance if he does not get into his helmet in fifteen seconds. We are expecting the dose to be repeated again before long and we are never without our helmets handy. That is here, and what must it be to be in the trenches just there and never know but that the next breath you take will be the means of killing you. Shells, bullets etc are nothing to this dreadful stuff and none of them have the same awful consequences. Last night we had another fire but I cannot say what caused it. But dearie mine, I must close. I have fifty men to do.

Wednesday night, 21 June 1916

I received your very welcome letter last night, written on Friday. I have tried to answer it before this but could not, simply because we are working so short-handed just now. Today for instance I have been on five or ten different jobs. There is plenty of work for every man now. I was sent for last night by a General of X, another Div. to report at his HQ this morning to cut his hair. I also had to do his Aide-de-Camps. It is quite a professional honour. I had a letter from Pete today telling me he had got his two stripes, and that he is expecting to be home on leave next week – lucky fellow.

We are all hoping that this next battle will finish the war. I trust to God it does and think it will. It was very nice of that man to offer me a job after the war. We will see then. I am not the least afraid of making good when I get home because I know that in civil life I will. This army life is not my style. I cannot bring myself down far enough to get on in it. It is all a very degrading system and only we who have been out here so long know just how degrading it is. But most folks at home don't know anything about it and as a rule we soldiers don't care to explain.

Chapter Eight

1916
The Battle of the Somme

Any hopes still harboured by the governments of the belligerent nations, that there might be an easy route to victory in the European War, died in 1915. Despite defeat after defeat, Russia was still in the war, and that meant for Germany the strain of a war on two fronts – the old nightmare of Bismarck. But at least, from the German point of view, it was the German Army that was in the forward positions, holding most of Belgium and parts of France. The British and the French had no such comfort. If their failure in Artois and Champagne was not to be repeated, the scale of the military commitment on the Western Front would have to be enormous. With all the luck in the world, dislodging millions of dug-in Germans could not be done except at terrible cost in men's lives. Escalation to all-out land warfare on the Continent of Europe appeared the only option. The alternative of using naval power in support of military operations in the east, as advocated by Churchill and Lloyd George, had been tried in 1915. It had ended in the ignominious disaster of the landings at Gallipoli. This failure of Churchill's Dardanelles Campaign spelt victory for the so-called 'Westerners' in the British military establishment, those who thought that Britain's military resources should be concentrated on the Western Front. And their victory was reflected almost immediately in changes in personnel in the Expeditionary Force. Churchill, having resigned in disgrace in November 1915 over Gallipoli, continued his descent by exiling himself to the Western Front to *command a battalion of Scottish infantry, the 6th Royal Scots Fusiliers, of Willie's 27 Brigade. General Haig, in contrast, became Commander-in-Chief of the Expeditionary Force in succession to Sir John French.**

The main lesson Haig drew from Loos was that, for an offensive to succeed on the Western Front, the attackers must be adequately trained and equipped, and they must attack in overwhelming superiority of numbers. Now he was in charge, Haig was going to ensure that everything was properly in place next time for his big offensive. Churchill learnt of Haig's thinking on 17 January 1916 when he was summoned to the town of Hazebrouck to hear a lecture by his friend, Colonel Tom Holland, on the battle of Loos. He described the scene to his wife in a letter full of foreboding: 'The theatre was crowded with generals and officers . . . I could not even get a seat, but stood on the wings of the stage. Tom spoke very well but his tale was one of hopeless failure, of sublime heroism utterly wasted and of splendid Scottish soldiers shorn away in vain . . . with never the ghost of a chance of success. 6,000 killed and wounded out of 10,000 in this Scottish division alone. Alas, alas. Afterwards they asked what was the lesson of the lecture. I restrained an impulse to reply, "Don't do it again". But they will – I have no doubt'.[47] And Churchill's foreboding was justified. The British Empire threw everything it could into the great offensive on the Somme, including tanks and there appears to have been extraordinary optimism among the British soldiers. But the military gains were meagre and by the time the offensive was called off on 19 November 1916 there had been over 400,000 British casualties.

The story of 1 July 1916 is well known; how the massive artillery bombardment, that for days had preceded the attack, failed to cut the German wire; how the German defences were more solid and deeper than British Intelligence had predicted; how the heavily laden British soldiers walked across no-man's-land, giving the German machine-gunners time to bring their guns up the ladders from their deep dug-outs; how 20,000 British soldiers died that day and how hope was dashed in the greatest loss of life in British military history.[48] Although Willie could see that for many of the

---

* These changes are mentioned by Willie in his letters of 6 and 9 January 1916 respectively.

*soldiers marching to battle it would mean death, he nevertheless
wanted to be in the thick of it. He was refused permission to be a
stretcher bearer and go over the parapet and follow the infantry.
His correspondence with Jane is silent in the lead up to 1 July 1916,
but we know these facts from some short diary entries he made of
this period, which are given below. They also capture some of the
feeling of action and excitement as the men marched to battle.
When the letters begin, the note of excitement is never heard again.*

21 June 1916

Met J Munro and other Caurnie* lads of 10/ A and SH on their
way to the big do. I am thoroughly sick of being here and asked to
get up the line but was told to be content.

24 June 1916

Bombardment started at an early hour this morning. W Best and
P Bell down seeing us today. Corbie full of troops and Brigade after
Brigade going up the line. I have a great longing to be in the thick
of it. Trying to get up.

25 June 1916.

10/ Arg and S H away today and Camerons and Seaforths arrive
in Corbie also the Grenadier Guards. Camerons back. Play the
Retreat in the Square. Bombardment still furious. Black Watch
arrive Corbie.

26 June 1916

Royal Scots and Manchesters and Royal Welch Fusiliers go up to
the trenches in fighting order no pack and all with distinguishing
ribbon on their shoulders. Great weather so far but this bombardment will likely break it up.†

---

* A local name for Kirkintilloch.
† The soldiers during the Great War believed shelling caused rain.

27 and 28 June 1916

At CE of 13 Corps this morning on duty. Bombardment still raging. Camerons and Seaforths and Black Watch still in Corbie. Rain most of the day. Order of attack 30–18- 9 Div. Lots of armoured cars ready to go after them. The 5/ Camerons and Black Watch leave Corbie with drums and pipes playing, one of the most stirring sights one could witness, everyone laughing and joking and many of them going to sure death. Every soldier and civilian was stirred to the core. Good old Scotland. 1/ Life Guards and 2/ Life Guards and also Scots Greys here now and many cavalry Regiments 3 DG and NH.

29 June 1916

The 30 Div, 18 Div and 17 Div have to take Montabaun Mametz and Fricourt.

30 June 1916

The weather has cleared great and it looks as if the charge tomorrow is going to be under favourable conditions. Everyone making preparations for an unprecedented number of wounded.

1 and 2 July 1916

The bombardment before the charge was awful. Great success of the preliminary stages. 7.30 they went over. So far our Div 9 has not had to go as the task was easier than anticipated. At night the wounded get to Corbie. Plenty of them but there is a majority of slight wounds. Quite different from Loos.

4 July 1916

The charge going well. The wounded coming down seem slight in the majority.

8 July 1916

Left Corbie for Dressing Station* and started right away in B. Block as noculator. God not to be rushed and such sights to stir the experienced of us today. No rest all day till 10.00 pm.

9 July 1916

On duty at 6.00 am. It is beyond me to describe what we are seeing just now. I don't think I shall ever forget anything of this experience.

18 July 1916

A disaster at the ADS.† A shell dropped right into the DS. Killed five and wounded nine of our Ambulance. Some awful cases down today.

19 July 1916

Went to Corps HQ in the General's car to cut the corps staff officers' hair. At E Britton's funeral.**

LONGUEVAL AND DELVILLE WOOD

The task of XIII Corps in the Somme Offensive was to gain control of the ridge running from Waterlot Farm to Bazentin-le-Grand, probably the toughest task on the whole front.[49] The key to the ridge was Longueval and Delville Wood, and it was given to the 9th Division to take these positions. The position of XIII Corps

---

* From 8 to 23 July during the offensive, Willie served at Dive Copse Corps Main Dressing Station, one mile North East of Sailly-le-Sec church. Dive Copse was a small wood nearby under the Bray-Corbie Road.

† Hope Bagenal was wounded in this incident at the Advanced Dressing Station.

** E. Britton was Willie's companion in the trenches before the Battle of Loos, when a shell buried them both.

was already a salient and success would intensify it, meaning enfilading fire and risk of being cut off. The ground was vital to the German defences and was held by seasoned troops.* But possession of the high ground near Longueval was the pivot of Haig's immediate plans as it would facilitate an attack on High Wood in the north, and it was essential to an advance on Ginchy and Guillemont. The 9th Division first assisted the 30th Division on 8 July in trying to clear an intermediate position at Trones Wood. The main attack took place on 14 July against well-prepared German positions with no element of surprise. The normally restrained Divisional History[50] summed up what happened to 27 Brigade attacking in the northern part of Longueval, 'The melancholy roll of the killed and wounded was the monument of the devotion with which the men had attempted to do more than men could do. Out of a total of barely 3000, the Brigade lost eighty-one officers and 2003 men, and the great majority of the killed and missing, 569 in all, left their bones in the blood-soaked undergrowth of the orchards of Longueval'.

Monday afternoon, 17 July 1916 (I think)

I wish I had found time to write you before this, for it positively breaks my heart to think you will have to wait some time on my letters especially this last week past as I have not been able to snatch time, being so full of work, and after receiving those beautiful letters of yours today. While on duty I determined at all costs to write this afternoon, but I was so dead tired when relieved that I immediately fell asleep and have just woken up. But I think I had better be more lucid and tell you the reason we are so busy. Some days ago (I cannot on the instant tell you how many) we at HQ were relieved of our Hospital and ordered up here to take our duties at the Main Dressing Station, where all the serious wounded cases are sent to be dressed and then evacuated to the place we left.† I was not an hour here till I was put in the Dressing Room for duty and have been working at high pressure there ever since, except

---

* 16th Bavarian Regiment and 6th Bavarian Reserve Regiment of the Tenth Bavarian Division.
† Hospital at Corbie.

114

about eight hours sleep every other night, taking a bite just when we could get time, and if too busy, doing without. We are sleeping in tents and our D. Stations are also in large marquees. In fact it is a camp and on the main road to the advanced positions, and all cases (stretcher) are brought here from the advanced Dressing Stations. We are in safety besides, although we can see the bursting shells well in front.

But oh my God what terribly shattered men we have had to attend and still they come in what seems a never-ending line of cars, which unburden their load of groaning blood-bespattered, mud-covered heroes every minute of the day and night. It is awful and at times, despite my former gruesome experiences, I feel a little queer. But oh how brave they all are. But even the bravest of them remark on the wonderful bravery and fortitude of the Scotties of our own Div. I have not seen one on the dressing table yet, unless those unconscious, of those who belonged to our Div. let him be ever so badly wounded, who could not smile at it all. One yesterday with some pounds of his flesh off at various places, actually while lying with his face on the stretcher, the Doctor and us busy dressing a big wound on his back, started the whistling.

Last night we had to perform an operation on a Sergeant of the South African Scottish. A hand grenade had caught him full on the arm and oh ------ but I will not tell you how it looked. His arm had to be amputated. It was a great experience for us, and the chap was so brave when told he had to lose his arm and was such a splendid fellow. We were all keen on the operation being successful (which it was) although it was very dangerous considering his condition. But his life was saved. He would have died probably if he had not had it taken off here. I was not keen on being present but the Doctor would have me there to assist him. Professionally I was pleased I did. One of us had to hold the arm, while he took it off. I had to hold the patient and the other gave him his instruments while another officer gave the anaesthetic. By the way our officer in our lines is a trump, an Australian just lately come to the Ambulance, and we all get on so well with him. There are several of us who work with him in the Dressing Room. One gives the patients tea etc when they come off the cars, two carry the stretchers, two clean up and cut dressings, one dresses and I inoculate every wounded man that comes in and also dress, and the Dr.

We came off duty today at 2.00 pm, go on tonight at 10.00 till 6.00 tomorrow morning, on again at 2.00 pm till 10.00 pm and off till 6.00 am, and if there is a big rush of wounded, we have to carry on. We are relieved at the various hours by another officer of our Ambulance and the same number of staff. Work and a little sleep is our whole life at present. We are in a Field, miles from anywhere and your parcel today my darling is more than welcome. I will not tell you about the horrors of this job, working always and living amongst wounded, groaning and dying men, Germans as well as our own (they are brought in on stretchers and treated with the same skill as our own) or of the different cases and how manfully they suffer. I could not if I would. It would take volumes and not be finished. But my God the country is paying dearly for all the great things you read about in the papers, about the advance that is steadily and surely forcing the Germans out into the open, yes paying for it all with the lives of our very best manhood. This has been a hell of hell for twenty days now and God alone knows how many will be left to see the finish. Our poor Div. has again suffered heavily, simply because they must fight in the very van of the battle. They were given, as before, almost impossible tasks which they have accomplished and held, and fight like lions. 'The Jocks will give them hell,' is what the other Div. said before. 'The Jocks have given them hell' is what they tell us now, and when they have been fighting, the German dead are heaped up around the bodies of the lads with the various tartans.

We have had quite a number of casualties since I last wrote you, one officer, a few Sergs., also wounded. Jock Fraser was slightly wounded the other day, but is still doing his work. He got a little scratch on the nose and neck, but not enough to keep him off duty, shrapnel. If his folks know nothing about it, please don't say anything as he perhaps has not told them, and it is so little, they need not worry. Jock and Peters are with the bearers now. I hope everything comes all right and Kirkie lads get through this again.

Thursday, 27 July 1916

We have had a very strenuous time and lost a lot of our Ambulance last place – forty-one casualties in the 27th, twelve killed and the others wounded and one officer wounded. I have not been able to ascertain just how the Kirkie lads in our Div. got on. J. Munro was wounded is what we heard, although I did not see him.

I have not had a green envelope issued for some weeks and those I have sent are what I had in my pocket. I don't know why they had stopped our issue and FPCs are terribly scarce. You would hardly know us. We are all scraggy and everything we have on is worn out. Some of our lads are terribly dirty-looking after the hard work they have had. It is a wonder any of them came through it. I wonder how things will go in this new part of the line. I hardly think it will be just so bad as at the last place. No I have not heard from Pete for some time. Oh yes I had a F Card the day before yesterday saying he was quite well. Things are quiet where Pete is, I hear. So he should be tres-bien. I must write to 58 today as well if I possibly can. I am well except for a cold which is a trifle considering the places we have had to sleep recently. I will let you know when we arrive in the trenches.

Sunday night, 30 July 1916

In my last letter lovey mine, which I wrote just before we came to this place, I said we fully expected to be in the trenches in a day or two but it has turned out different. At present we are working a Brigade Hospital and have no idea how long we will be here, not long as our Div. these last few months has been on the move constantly. This is a mining town near where we were about a year ago and we have not a great deal of work. Our officers seem to recognize the fact at last that we occasionally need a little rest. The weather is very hot and sultry and this is a great change after the constant chill during the battle.

Yes I have not given up hope of it being finished this year. All is going well and I don't see anything to stop them now that they are well away. Our Div. had 7000 casualties down there; which will give you an idea of our work. It is impossible for us ever to forget it.

I see by Fraser's *Herald*, G Cooper, the Padre, was down at the push. None of us came across him. He will be in one of the later Divisions probably. As for J Cooper getting a DCM, that is entirely out of the question now as most of the boys did as much as each other and it is difficult for them to fix on any single one for the

117

honour, and almost every one of them had their names taken for bravery under fire. When the shell burst in the DS, our lads who were not hit immediately set to work dressing the wounds of their comrades despite the fact that shell after shell, shrapnel was bursting over them and they were ordered to cover by an officer. Most of them had their clothes torn and bruises by shrapnel, but they dressed and carried every one of the wounded. Things like this were daily occurrences. Now Darling I must close.

Friday, 4 August 1916

Yes I fancy the service would be impressive. Isn't it awful and it is brought home to one more when they have to dig a hole in the field and drop our fallen comrades into it just as they are, sometimes with a blanket as a covering, and often nothing at all, and place the tiny cross over them? It is a cold cold grave, a soldier's, and better often that their folks at home don't know where and how they are buried.

We are still in rest, being reinforced as a Div. More than half our Ambulance are drafts. The old Tweseldown lot are getting scarce, and ever since we came out of action quite a number have had to be evacuated, their health having completely broken down with the reaction. Remember me telling you dearie about Bartlett, the chap whom we kept beside us in our DS whom we all thought was mortally wounded. He improved sufficient to be sent down the line. A letter came this week from a Hospital in England from himself, telling us he is getting on grand. We are proud, as he was a popular lad in the Ambulance. He will never be much use as his lung is practically destroyed, and he has six or seven shrapnel wounds besides.

What do you think, Jimmy Jack (Captain Jack RAMC) is coming to our Ambulance as an officer this next week. It will be quite a novelty for us Kirkie boys. Well lovey mine, I am going to give you another souvenir, a photo. J Fraser and I had them taken here the other night and they are a slight improvement on the last I had taken at ------. I cannot get that cynical sort of expression off in any of my photos.

I know lovey if I was home again, you would be all right and have better health, but please take great care of yourself till I do

118

1. William St Clair's shop in Kirkintilloch in 1910. William St Clair is second from the left.
2. William St Clair, Jane Edgar and her brother Duncan at Loch Ard near Aberfoyle in the Trossachs in 1913.

3. Jane Edgar, fiancée of William St Clair, in 1914.

4. Cooneyite house church in Kilsyth in 1906. The central figure at the table is William Irvine, founder of the sect, the bearded man to his left is George Walker, and the lady standing to his right with hands on the girl to the front is Mary Linn, mother of William St Clair.

5. William Irvine's mission in 1899 to convert Scotland. Second from left, William Gill, George Walker, John Hardie (wearing black hat), William Irvine, William Carroll, Irvine Weir.

Your King and Country Need You.

A CALL TO ARMS.

An addition of 100,000 men to his Majesty's Regular Army is immediately necessary in the present grave National Emergency.

Lord Kitchener is confident that this appeal will be at once responded to by all those who have the safety of our Empire at heart.

TERMS OF SERVICE.

General Service for a period of 3 years or until the war is concluded.

Age of Enlistment between 19 and 30.

HOW TO JOIN.

Full information can be obtained at any Post Office in the Kingdom or at any Military Depot.

God Save the King!

6. Kitchener's original recruiting poster calling for the First Hundred Thousand published in all the newspapers on 7 August 1914.

7. 27 Field Ambulance Column going through Church Crookham, Fleet, Hampshire, in late 1914. William St Clair is in front row, fourth from the left.

8. William St Clair and Peter Edgar, France 1915.

9. Imagined picture of the Battle of Loos with Piper Laidlaw on the parapet playing "All the blue bonnets are over the border". The illustrator shows no casualties, artillery is visible and the dashing officer does not wear a gas mask (*Illustrated London News* 4 December 1915).

10. William St Clair at Corbie, Somme August 1916: see letter of 4 August 1916.

11. William's brother, David St Clair, after enlistment in a highland regiment.

12. William's brother, Joseph in Kilsyth Academy F.C. football strip – 1916, aged 13. See page 188 *'War in the Imagination of Boys'*.

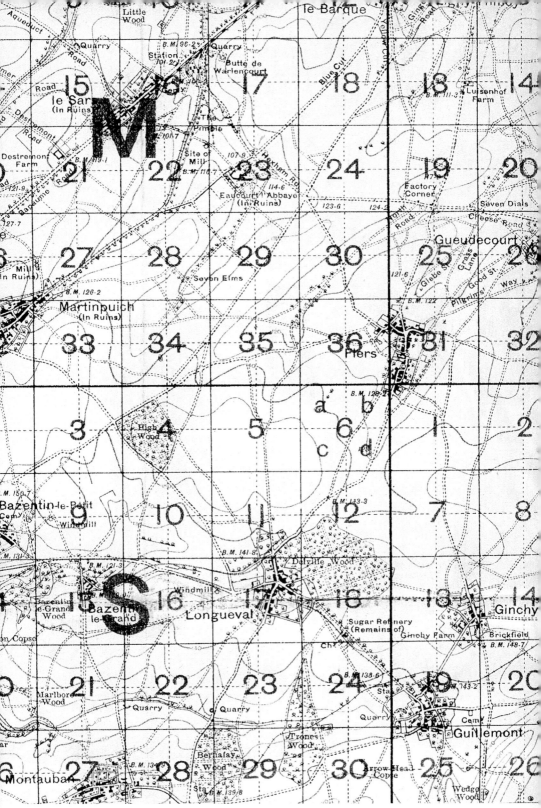

13. British Ordnance Map of 1917, showing Longueval, Delville Wood, Bazentin-le-Grand and Bazentin-le-Petit, and Butte de Warlencourt – Scale: the side of a numbered square is 1000 yards.

14. Battle of Bazentin Ridge. Men of 26 Brigade of the 9th Division returning from the trenches with 8/Black Watch piper after the attack on Longueval on 14 July 1916.

15. Battle of Guillemont. Wounded coming back from the capture of Guillemont and fresh troops going up. Chimpanzee valley near Montauban on 3 September 1916.

16. Somme: Battle of Guillemont. Stretcher bearers at Advanced Dressing Station at Guillemont. 3-6 September 1916.

17. Battle of Menin Road Ridge. Wounded man being carried to the Dressing Station near Zillebecke on 20 September 1917.

18. Artillery House from St Julien Pill Box, drawn by William, October 1917.

19. Early tank in action at St Julien, drawn by William, October 1917.

20. St Julien Pillbox, drawn by William, October 1917.

21. British stretcher-bearers carrying wounded man through the mud near Boesinghe during Battle of Passchendaele, 1 August 1917.

22. William on leave January 1918.

23. William's brother, John, Instructor at the Irish Command Gas School, 1918, Dublin .

24. 9th Division Christmas Card of December 1917 showing battle honours of Division represented as Christmas garland surrounded by holly.

25. 9th Division Christmas Card of December 1917 – greetings section – almost allegorical, showing Scottish soldiers with rifles and bayonets following a Christmas star.

26. Unit of the 9th Division on 13 December 1918, crossing the Rhine at Cologne by the Mulheim Bridge of Boats. In picture are the Royal Newfoundland Regiment, with left Capt. Arthur Raley and, right, Lt. Col. A.E. Bernard.

27. William's brother David in action with the Machine Gun Corps near Mosul in Iraq 1919 – mentioned in despatches.

28. The Reverend Captain Eustace Hill MC at Delville Wood in 1919, searching for and identifying the South African dead for burial, with Sister Flynn, whose brother Dudley Flynn was among the dead.

AUTHOR HERO'S PLUCK.

KIRKINTILLOCH MAN'S TRIUMPH.

HOW HE SCORED.

A STORY of talent and of rare personal grit lies behind the writing and production of a play by Mr. William St. Clair, of Kirkintilloch.

Mr. William St. Clair.

Mr. St. Clair, who is in business for himself in Kirkintilloch as a hairdresser, has been a most enthusiastic member of the local Players Club for years, and his play, "The Prayer," which was produced by the Kirkintilloch Players Club at the Festival of the Scottish Community Drama Association, got first place.

The play—his one and only—is based upon his personal war experiences while serving with the Royal Field Ambulance Corp in France, and, as he took one of the leading parts himself, much depended upon Mr. St. Clair for the success or failure of his production at the Festival.

To the great consternation of the other members of the cast, "Willie" took ill a few days before the Festival, and, being unable to attend the final rehearsals, it looked as if all the arduous nights of practice were to go for nothing.

On the night of the Festival, however, Mr. St. Clair decided to make a bold bid for it.

Accordingly, he was practically carried down to the hall by his friends, and, although far from well, he performed his part in a most brilliant manner, and, needless to say, he and his friends were delighted at the conclusion of the Festival to learn that the "team" had won premier honours.

More will be heard of this clever young writer, whose initial success will do much to encourage him to greater efforts.

29. Weekly Record Report of 25 January 1930 recounting winning performance of *The Prayer*.

30. Performance of *The Prayer* on 15 January 1930. Left to right: Captain Linn (Jim Meek), Gerry (Jock Nairn), Corporal Peake (A.C. Bain), Padre Hall (Bob Peter).

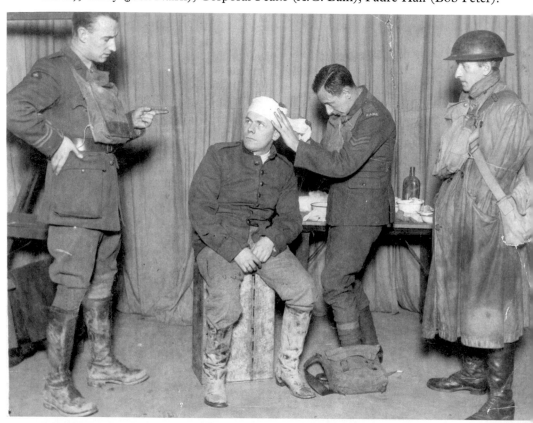

come home. How does Pete get on and what about his leave? I will be writing to him in a day or so. As to Sergeant Bagenal, yes he was badly wounded about the legs and I don't suppose he will be fit for soldiering again. Just before he went away he gave me another book. He was a very brave gentleman and had no fear.*

Tuesday, 15 August 1916

We are having a few wounded at present, just the usual daily toll, some days more and some days less, but never a day without them. One sometimes wonders what would be the ultimate outcome of all these precious fellows' sacrifices. Not till Mr Hun howls for mercy in his own country and they are finished as a nation will the country's duty be done to them. For it is to absolutely exterminate Germanism that men so gallantly give their lives, because to the lowest soldier it is known that that alone will do future generations good. We out here all want peace and have reason to want it more than any, but we do want and must have a peace that will prevent war for ages. We don't want to be called from our homes again, and the only way is to stick this till the Germans are 'nah-poohed'. Otherwise all the precious lives sacrificed will be in vain.

THESE ARE OUR IDEALS: ROBERT BRIDGES AND *THE SPIRIT OF MAN*

Willie describes in his letter of 4 August how Hope Bagenal was wounded and gave him a present of a book which had meant a great deal to him, and which Willie in his turn would treasure all his life, along with the copy of Keats Bagenal had given him earlier. The book was The Spirit of Man, *by Robert Bridges, the Poet Laureate and a Neo-Platonist. Bridges saw his poetry as part of the wider ideal of beauty and truth. On 22 November 1917, he gave an address to the Tredegar and District Co-operative Society, on 'The Necessity of Poetry' in which he set out his creed, saying that the basis of Poetry, Morals and Religion was the same, that is they*

---

* Bagenal was awarded a DCM.

spring from the universal primary emotions of Man's Spirit, which lead men naturally towards Beauty and Truth. The difficulty was not in relating Poetry with Morals and Religion, but in discriminating between them. According to Bridges, one could almost contend that 'Morals is that part of Poetry which deals with conduct, and Religion that part of it which deals with the idea of God.'[51]

In December 1914 Bridges agreed to a suggestion by his publisher Longman, who had just lost a son in the war, to compile an anthology of prose and verse which would bring some comfort to the bereaved.[52] Bridges believed strongly in the justice of the war and himself underwent military training at the age of 70. His son Edward[53] served with distinction on the Western Front, and his nephew Tom, a cavalry scout in the British Expeditionary Force, coming upon some Germans in August 1914, ordered his lieutenant, 'Now's your chance, Charles, get after them with your sword,' resulting in the first German killed by the BEF, and the first enemy casualty killed by the British Army in Western Europe for over 99 years – struck down by a sword.[54] In compiling his wartime anthology Bridges drew on the help and suggestions of a wide range of literary men such as W.B. Yeats, Gilbert Murray and Arthur Quiller Couch. Professor Walter Raleigh consulted his students, most of whom by 1915 had already lost friends and relatives in the war. One can say that to an extent the final selection in The Spirit of Man *was a collective national cultural enterprise.*

The Spirit of Man *was first published, with a royal dedication, in January 1916 and was frequently reprinted during the wartime years and beyond.[55] Although intended first for those who grieved at home, it soon became one of the books most often to be found at the front. The copy which Willie received from Bagenal was one of the luxury editions specially printed on thin India paper and bound in soft leather and, like the edition of Keats, obviously designed to fit a soldier's tunic pocket. Consolation, Bridges believed, required beauty as much as philosophy. Accordingly in some ways the book was a general anthology for wartime on the lines of Palgrave's* Golden Treasury *and the* Oxford Book of English Verse, *arranged by topic and not by historical period or by author so as to give the quality of timelessness. Some topics,*

120

notably love between the sexes and humour, were deliberately excluded. Also excluded were poems about the cleansing power of war of the kind which Bridges and Rupert Brooke had written at the time of the outbreak, and there was no Newbolt and no Kipling. The book offered extracts from the ancient classics and some from French and Russian literature, mostly well known, but also included unusual pieces such as the last testimony of Nayler the Quaker and the final evening of St Augustine and St Monica. Bridges took the opportunity of introducing the public to the work of Gerard Manley Hopkins, of whom he was the literary executor. While accessible to a wide readership, therefore, including soldiers like Willie, whose education had been limited, there was no populist condescension, and if there was any overtly intended propaganda purpose, it was well concealed.

Although the book claimed a universalism, it mainly consisted of older English literature. Among the authors most frequently quoted were Shakespeare, Milton, Keats and, above all, Shelley, from whom Bridges drew much of his own lyricism as well as Neo-Platonic ideas. The tone is one of sorrow and pride, without bitterness. 'The progress of mankind on the path of liberty and humanity,' Bridges wrote in the Preface, 'has been suddenly discredited by the apostasy of a great people'. For the long extract before the brief final commendation to a Christian immortality, Bridges insisted on a passage from Shelley on the need for forgiveness, a sentiment not common at the time of the book's publication, but one which, in later years, found a more ready audience.

As personal consolation, Bridges offered Christian and Platonic passages on triumphs over death and the immortality of the soul, which would comfort the bereaved and have soldiers going into battle think that death was not the end. Because Britain was fighting a just war, Bridges also took it upon himself to articulate what the ideals were that the country was fighting for. Just as at Gettysburg, Lincoln had introduced a moral dimension to the war and invented the ideals that have shaped Americans' idea of their own identity, so Bridges tried to do the same in the Spirit of Man. *After the burning of Louvain and the destruction of Ypres, Bridges assumed the civilised world knew that barbarism was at Britain's gates. But what were the particular aspects of British culture that should be held up as Britain's defining ideals?*

The defining ideals which Bridges put forward were to a large measure the ideals of the city of Ancient Athens, as set out in the funeral oration over the dead soldiers of the city, which Thucydides attributed to Pericles in his History of the Peloponnesian War. They consisted in democracy, freedom, the rule of law, sympathy for the poor, the excellence and beauty of arts and sciences and public institutions, patriotism. A particular ideal of Athens was not being a militarized society in time of peace, but relying on manliness – not on laborious military training. These were the values that had moulded the 'public school ethic' of Victorian England, and the same contrast that Pericles made between the militarized Sparta and the free Athens was cast during the war and for a long time after between militarized Prussia and Britain.[56] So important to the Athenians were these ideals that had their city been lost to the Persians during the Persian Wars, they had plans to go to Italy and implant their ideals there. Churchill voiced similar views during the Second World War, about keeping the British ideals alive in Canada and New Zealand, if Britain had been overrun. To the intellectually minded, reading The Spirit of Man during the war – soldier and civilian – it reinforced the righteousness of the cause, drawing on the founding documents of the national identiy, or certainly that of the elite.

There could be no mistaking the general message of The Spirit of Man, or its editor, and of the society which produced it and which admired it. The latter part of The Spirit of Man is an extended variation on funeral orations from Pericles Funeral Oration to Lincoln's Gettysburg address, extracts from which were also included. 'We can therefore be happy in our sorrows,' Bridges ended his Preface, speaking in the spirit of his age, 'happy even in the death of our beloved who fall in the fight; for they die nobly, as heroes and saints die, with hearts and hands unstained by hatred or wrong.' It was sentiments such as these last ones which Wilfred Owen, whose poems were not published till after the war,[57] was to call 'the old lie / dulce et decorum est pro patria mori.' *

---

* The line is from the Roman poet Horace and means that it is a delight and a duty to die for your country. 'Pro Patria' on war memorials is an explicit allusion to the line.

THE BUTTE OF WARLENCOURT

The 9th (Scottish) Division was withdrawn from the Somme battle area on 23 July 1916, having lost more than fifty per cent of its strength in the two weeks' fighting – 314 officers and 7303 other ranks.[58] After what the Divisional History called 'a reasonable interval to heal its wounds'[59] (two weeks), the Division took over from the French a sector of the front at Vimy Ridge, with Willie recording in his diary on 12 August 1916 that he had heard that it was a quiet part of the line, but 'won't be for long when the 9th get there'. Despite rumours recorded by Willie that the Division was to have to take the ridge before they left,[60] there were in fact no major hostilities at Vimy Ridge during the Division's six weeks there. When a German mine went off on 19 August 1916, burying German miners and 27 Brigade sappers, there was even an informal truce allowing stretcher bearers to bring in the wounded.[61] But then the blow fell. On 3 October, Willie recorded, 'We leave in a day or two and are going to take part in the greatest battle in history, so the Corps General said. Poor 9 Div. Few of the old men are left now and I am afraid this will finish them off.'

What the 9th Division was to be required to do was to return to the same area of the Somme where they had fought in July and take the Butte de Warlencourt – a large chalk mound which was a key German defensive position and natural vantage point. The British front line was now a few miles further forward than in July. To the rear was the hideous waste of three months of savage fighting and shelling – nothing but mud, detritus and the stench of the rotting corpses of men and horses. And at the front itself the water and the mud clogged and caked everything, and reduced all movement to a snail's pace. For the RAMC this meant that eight men were scarcely enough to carry a stretcher, where two would suffice in normal conditions.[62] According to the Divisional History the military operation was for the Division the most dismal of the war and was carried out at a rush and in spite of a strong protest from the Division's Commander, General Furse, to the Corps and Army Commanders. Capture of the Butte de Warlencourt was at an early stage given up as unrealizable, and more limited objectives set. Some meagre territorial gains were made, but in the fighting from 12 to 24 October 1916 the Division had 3,255 casualties. Attacks were made on 12, 18 and 19 October 1916, and then only on the strong representations of General Furse to the Corps Commanders was the Division not ordered into another battle arranged for 25 October 1916. During the period of these operations Willie worked in the Advanced Dressing Station at Bazentin le Petit.

Friday afternoon, 13 October 1916

I have just been relieved of duty in the dug-out where we have our Advanced Dressing St.* Some days ago it was a German munition dump and now we are using it as a Dressing St. This is going in a green envelope, but I don't think it will be possible for me to get it posted for some days as there is a big battle going on here and we are in it. I have eight hours off. We are working in shifts, could not possibly stand the strain any other way. I am in bed in a bunk that some of the Germans who lived here have made. I feel tired as we have been busy beyond powers of description, but I received your letter this forenoon telling me about you being so anxious for a letter and also that my Mother has been so disappointed because I have not written for some time. I feel so sorry but my God it has been utterly impossible these last few days. I cannot tell you all that has happened and how we have been tossed about, marched till our feet were like raw flesh for three days and three nights. I did not close an eye. The last stage of the journey I came in the motor Ambulance – my feet were so bad, but enough. If I am spared this trip again, and get home, my diary will give you all the news. Meantime I am in good health. But please you and my Mother don't talk to me about being in a huff. All our spare time at present is taken up trying to save the lives of the few of our Div. who are left along with the others in the Ambulance.

The parcel came at a most opportune moment, just as we arrived at the second stage of our march to this accursed place. We halted for a few hours rest at a town that you have heard about and there was nothing for us but a biscuit. I was put on guard for the night and the loaf and butter was more to me than I can say. The pies were mouldy and I had to put them away. I was

---

* Bazentin-Le-Petit Advanced Dressing Station.

so sorry but they had been on the road for some time. The sketch-book was welcome and is just what I wanted and the pencils. Thanks for everything. I wish I could get time to sketch some parts of this part of the line that is so historical now and is more desolate and shell-ridden than the very best artist could portray. We have shells every day. But the Germans made a good job of this dug-out and it is fairly safe, although in various places it was wrecked by our artillery before we captured it.[63] Outside some weeks ago there was a village. Now there is nothing but debris with not more than a yard between each shell-hole. One cannot describe it properly, it has to be seen – but our artillery has done its work to perfection and more than that, and all the country and villages here about are the same. All over the place, there are graves hastily dug, not dug but bodies just covered with earth, German and ours. Some are covered and some are not – dead horses and wrecked transport all over the place. The stench is worse than awful and we are treating 800 cases a day in this atmosphere. This is war they say to me. It seems more like hell, and worse than that. Still amid all this there is cheerfulness and joking. We could not stick it otherwise. One gets a cheery Jock cracking away and joking lying beside another who is dying. One dies and is buried just outside in a shell-hole and the other goes down the line, smiling to have been so lucky on the way to 'blighty'. It is the first question all of them ask, 'Do you think I will get home with this one?' 'You are sure to,' and off they go with a smile on their face that does one good to see.

There is one incident that has happened here that I will not forget. A certain Battalion (not Scotch) made a charge here some days ago. Our Div. relieved them, and we found they had left lots of wounded lying out in no man's land.[64] One of our Ambulance officers organized a party of stretcher bearers, mostly Jocks, who brought the poor fellows in. We got them all to dress. Most of them had been out there for five days and one chap in particular had seven days out, and days in the trench before we got him. It is difficult to believe it, but it is the fact they were all thin and worn and all their wounds were stinking awful, but they were alive. If you can imagine a man cast into hell and left there for five days and then brought back, it would give you an idea what sort of look these chaps had in their eyes, and the hundreds of striking incidents I have witnessed in this dug-out and the other I was in before this one, would take me all my eight hours to tell you.

Perhaps I will remember them when I come home. But it is an awful time and I wish to the Lord it was all over, and what is left of us home. But you will think this a doleful letter dear mine eh? I must close for the present, and never forget you and Mother little one that I love you both very dearly and never forget you even when our hands and brains are fully occupied with this work. Will continue next opportunity.

Sunday, 15 October 1916

In the dug-out on duty doing a quiet spell. Dearest Jane I have rather good news in a way this morning. They are going to give us green envelopes again soon, although the issue will only work out at one every five weeks. But I think I will manage to work more than that. It is raining this morning and the ground is very slippery and stretcher-bearing is doubly hard in weather like this. I expect we will be here for some time yet and there is heavier work in store for us during the next two days and after, I suppose more than we have had formerly. We are living in a constant boom of guns since we came here and Fritz pesters us every day with shrapnel etc but I would rather be on this side than beside Fritz, for our artillery does give them some souvenirs. The night before last, he made a counter-attack and what a sight it was to watch the display of fire-works, hundreds of guns firing incessantly and the heavens lit up with their flashes and also the starlights etc. More cases have just come in, so must stop for the moment.

Monday night, 16 October 1916 in the Dug-out

You see dearie I had to stop my letter owing to some patients coming in and this is the first spare minute since. The case that came in, or cases, I should say were very serious and we had to amputate a leg. The poor chaps were in a terrible state of wounds. Working just outside here, they accidentally struck a German bomb with a pick and three of them were badly wounded, one has since died. This place is infested with German bombs, grenades and shells which are a constant danger, and almost every day serious acci-

126

dents happen as a result of coming upon them unexpectedly. One has to be most particular where to step whenever we go outside the dug-out.

I was on duty all last night and have been on all this afternoon. It is coming on for 10.00 pm when we get relieved. I have just sent off a wee note to you and one to Mother, but cannot say much in them. You will understand when you get this one. I was outside this forenoon, a shell dropped the other side of the dug-out and caught a number of artillery chaps having their grub. The Allemand has been dropping them around here all day and the wood on our right was heaving with the heavy 'crumbs'. It was a fine clear day and one could see the shells bursting all along the now famous part of the line and the air fights were of hourly occurrence. It is all very exciting to watch but it is we in this dug-out that know the effect of it – a never-ending stream of wounded men, smashed in all ways, dying on our hands and dying before we get them, nothing but pure red British blood and gaping raw wounds. It is quite a different thing seeing a wounded man on a stretcher, with a blanket and seeing them as we see them, torn oh it makes one's heart bleed. God, how I wish it was all over and done with. But no the next few days has worse in store for us. One would like to forget most of the sights but cannot. Your letters that speak to me of your love and dreams of a peaceful happiness that is in store for you and I are very very refreshing and sweet, and you will never understand just how much they have meant to me since I came out here eighteen months ago. I love you very dearly little one and never for a moment forget that fact. I must close again and get a sleep and I feel tired. Will continue at the first opportunity. Goodnight little one and all my pure love to you.

18 October 1916 3.00 am

It is very wet tonight (or this morning) and all the cases we are getting in are wet and doubly miserable. The guns are not so noisy tonight, at least for the moment. But they never cease night or day and it will be a great change for us to get back to quietness again, but when that good time will come I cannot say. I don't expect it will be for a considerable time yet. I saw some 'Tanks' today – nuf said, but they are wonderful and so funny one cannot help smiling.*

I think I told you about one end of our dug-out being blown in some time before we came here. Well this last two days it has been cleared out to give us more room (we sleep at that end) and today two bodies were unearthed and their positions tell their own story. One was an infantry chap who had been wounded and was on a stretcher. The other, who was sitting beside a stretcher, was one of the RAMC. Both had been killed by the debris being blown on top of them. (Two more of the missing accounted for.) When one is reported missing, the mystery is generally cleared up in this way. The RAMC chap must have heard the shell that killed him and his patient coming, for his head was bent in the way we all usually do when a shell comes too close. So many incidents of this description happen here daily. I will not describe them, they are not cheery or good in a letter.

At present we are all finding it rather difficult to keep clean, there being no chance to wash clothes etc, and that is putting it mildly. We are miles away from any civilization, there being no civvies about this part of the line where one can send a washing. When I go to bed, I discard all my clothes as the blankets are rather 'crummy' and when they get on to a shirt, nothing short of burning the shirt will clean it. I have two shirts and one of them finished. I have stopped wearing pants, drawers I mean, and also semmits for obvious reasons. I must get you to send out some clothing later when we come out of this, as what I have is long since past being serviceable. My Father will give you the cash for them. As for writing paper and envelopes, we cannot get them while here. However, these things are only by the way. My health is of the very best and I am very strong, and when I see so many men maimed and shattered round about, I am very thankful to be as I am. The life here is certainly grim and often hard, but we are cheery and optimistic. But there go the guns again, hundreds of cannon all at once. We know what it means. In a few minutes there will be another attack by our Div. and then we will be hard at work with

* Willie's diary entry for 8 October 1916 records that 200 tanks had gone up in the last few days. It was illegal to keep a diary in case it fell into enemy hands, and this type of entry would be a particularly serious offence.

the wounded. Another success on the ------ front, the papers will say. Yes, but it is not easy for you to understand exactly what that phrase means. We here do.

Thursday, 19 October 1916 afternoon in bed

I stopped as the guns started banging in the early hours of yesterday morning. Since then we have been fearfully busy. I stopped writing and went outside the dug-out to see the effect of the bombardment. I cannot describe it to you. It only lasted about an hour, but you will perhaps have an idea what it was like when I tell you we could hardly keep our eyes open – the flashes were so brilliant and strong and numerous, and it was impossible to speak to be heard by the one next to you. Of course the infantry of our Div. went over the parapet and captured some trenches of importance, and we have had a very heavy spell of work with wounded of our own and also German. It rained all last night and today, and I have never seen men in such a mess of blood and mud as we have had in this forenoon, and they are still streaming in. Poor fellows, it would break the hearts of those at home if they saw them in the helpless plight we see them in just now. I am covered with muck and mud myself just working amongst them. And the fighting is still going on in our sector. Any who can crawl do so and the more serious are carried in here and some of the men who walk in are in ordinary times, even here, serious cases. They may all be cheery and talkative when they get further down the line, but not here where they are still in the danger zone, nothing but dull suffering of the most miserable kind is what we are witnessing here day and night, especially when the weather is so cold and wet and men have to lie out for hours, there being so many to be brought in.

The weather is getting very cold now, although we have not had snow. There is a rumour that we leave here this weekend, but nothing definite so far. I am doing billet orderly for three days – a decent job, and of course don't do any parades except the early morning one at 7.00 am. To be away from the SM is impossible, but in this job one is not troubled with him so much. He goes from bad to worse and bah how we ------ him. His chief pleasure is to make us suffer and, strange to say, the more brains a man has, the more he sits on him and some of our best medical orderlies have been sent to the very worst jobs to try and break their spirit. But, well, that is a task of enormous difficulty.

The leave is still going slowly. But it is always before us and at present, during weather like this, the Channel journey is anything but a pleasure. One of our chaps who came back yesterday told us it was awful – two nights ago and they had eight accidents of broken legs etc before they managed into Boulogne Harbour. It sometimes takes some of them three days to arrive here from England, and by the time they get to their unit they are glad in a way. I would not care what troubles or what sort of journey I got so long as I get home. My word but I wish they would just give me the chance. I will come bye and bye, and I am learning patience, nothing that I would do or say would make any difference. We must just wait on their pleasure. Ah there's the post and one for me.

Friday forenoon, 8 December 1916

I have been so busy these last two days that letter writing opportunities were scarce and I wanted to secure a green envelope, as I know the other sort are no good. However I have an envelope and will continue just as I get time today. Our Colonel is so energetic and must always have us busy at something. If you are idle he soon finds you a job that will keep you busy, so one has got to keep the eye skinned as he is always about.

I can tell you dearie that my knocking about has been an education I sorely required. Before the war I was so Puritan in some things, and had to suffer, making big things out of nothing in my mind. I am Puritan still but with more sense. However, we will have great talks about these things when I come home.

And even although this life has been at times stiff, it has had the effect of making me more of a man and a better husband for you, and better able to work for our mutual happiness. As regards going to Edinburgh right away, I think it a good idea, although going back home and staying the night in Monaville would do me alright, and there we would know where we were, and to get home now to me is the best holiday I can think about. I am open to any suggestions about where we will go dearie. So tell me just what you would like. I must take you to the King's or some place and I must live

130

with you at 58 and at Monaville. I feel I want to do so much in the few days we will have and I could fill a book with all I want. It will be so nice to be home. That will be pleasure indeed and the comfort will be glorious. I must have some long lies in bed, and some good fires. It is so damned cold here that to get near a fire gives one a great comfort. A nice bath every day I am at Monaville.

Chapter Nine

1917
ARRAS

'To the ordinary man incomprehensible-literally
a complete curtain of flame and death'

At the end of November 1916 the 9th Division marched at dusk
through the deserted city of Arras, en route to the trenches just
north and east of the city. On arrival, the 9th Division found their
new trenches dangerously shallow for men of normal stature,
having been previously occupied by the Thirty-fifth, a Bantam
division.[65] To avoid exposure to sniper fire, the trenches were
hurriedly deepened.[66] Otherwise, the Divisional History says, this
part of the line was very quiet, with only thirty casualties a week
among front-line battalions.[67] Willie was spared the worst of the
winter weather, going on leave in February. He was married in
Kirkintilloch, giving the Registrar 'France' as his 'Usual place of
residence', and was back in France a few days later.* For the
soldiers it was a period of training, especially in practising the
'rolling' or 'creeping' barrage, as it was later called, developed
largely by Major Alan Brooke, the future Chief of the Imperial
General Staff. This new system of artillery covering fire worked
by the targets of the artillery being moved steadily forward at
fixed times and intervals. The infantry followed closely behind,
synchronized to be on top of the dazed and disrupted defenders
before they could recover.

On Easter Monday 1917, after a titanic artillery bombardment
– 2,879 guns, one for each nine yards of front and 2,687,000

* See footnote p. 2.

*shells – British and Canadian forces launched simultaneous offen-
sives at Arras and Vimy Ridge. The bombardment worked as it had
not at the Somme the previous year, and, with a successful 'creeping
barrage', the British and Canadians achieved an initial military
success, with thousands of prisoners captured and large amounts
of ordnance. In one single attack the Canadians took Vimy Ridge,
for which the French had bled to death in their thousands in 1915.
There was rejoicing right along the front at the prospect of a speedy
British victory. But the initial success was not exploited, through
lack of adequate back-up and because of the advent of driving
winter blizzards, Arras having had its coldest January and February
since 1839.[68] The offensive was called off on 15 April. 'Attack',
however, was the watchword, and the Division took part in two
further offensives on 3 May and 5 June, before marching in the
middle of June to a six-week stay at rest camps at Ruellecourt
where the Division had rested between the offensives. These subsequent attacks did not match the success of 9 April and the attack
of 3 May was a costly failure. The Divisional History stated that at
Arras, the Division experienced in almost equal measure the elation
of triumph and the depression of defeat, and that with over 5,000
casualties[69] suffered during the months of April and May chiefly
among the infantry, the men were sorely in need of a rest.'[70]*

Wednesday, 11 April 1917 Night 7.30 pm

As you will probably know by reading the papers we have been
busy lately, and so writing has been entirely out of the question. I
am in bed at present but go on duty at 10 tonight till 6 tomorrow
morning. We are working eight-hour shifts, as much as possible
and everybody on duty if a big rush of wounded come in. We take
every advantage of getting a rest by officers' orders, as these are
strange times and one never knows when we shall have to stick it
without sleep for a considerable time.

Easter Monday at 5.30 am our battle started and our Div. have
given Fritz some of his dues since then, but I shall tell you about
all that later on. It has been a great victory and we are all so proud
of it.

We have had rotten weather and just now it is snowing heavily
and the country is covered. The weather has been in the Germans'

favour, but even that has not saved him about here, where he has his best troops, Prussian and Bavarians too. They seem to be demoralised. Prisoners by the thousand have been taken. I would like to tell you all about it but have not the time. Of course as usual we have their wounded to look after as well as our own, and they seem surprised at the kindness and consideration shown them, and no wonder after what they have done. But we are British, and every wounded man gets the same attention. I wish the weather would clear up and let us get on with it. We have lost some of our Ambulance again unfortunately wounded and killed, but in the meantime I don't know how many compared with other battles. The casualties have been few and the things accomplished great. I am well and strong now, was not so well Sunday and Monday with a bad cold that I cannot shake off properly, but I am taking all possible care of myself dearie. So don't you annoy yourself about me. Compared to what is around us, I have reason to thank God and do so when working with those poor shattered chaps. That is the best cure for petty troubles.

Saturday afternoon , 15 April 1917

We are a bit slack with work for the first time since Monday morning when the battle started, and so I will make good the time and get some word through to you. I have no doubt you will under-stand the reason why you have not had a letter this week by reading the papers. Our Div. began the battle on Monday morning and absolutely chased the Germans, and capturing something like 2000 prisoners before nightfall on Monday night. It was a great perfor-mance and one that brings great credit. The fighting has been going on all week, and of course at times we have lost heavily and conse-quently there has been plenty of work for us, but taking into consideration the things accomplished, the casualties have been comparatively slight.

It is not finished yet, although for the present there is a lull, and then the Jocks are at them again. The weather has been dreadful and all in favour of the Germans. It has been like midwinter all week with a very high wind blowing, and heavy snowstorms, which has made the sufferings of the wounded more intense. The Germans we have had through our hands have been of the best type physically, pure Prussians and Bavarians, all big heavy chaps, but they were absolutely whacked on Monday. To describe the artillery fire is an impossible task. It was perfect and to the ordinary man incomprehensible – literally a complete curtain of flame and death and no wonder the Hun was glad to get into our lines for safety. We as usual have been using those who are in hand for carrying stretchers. One gets a specimen of the brute amongst them now and then, dirty rascals these look, and capable of doing all that is reported of them.

It is wonderful the effect that a victory such as we had on Monday has on the spirits of everybody. Even the very badly wounded were quieter and more content because they knew that their sufferings were being revenged by their comrades who had not been hit. The 27th Amb men attached to battalions went over the parapet with the first wave at 5.30 am on Monday morning, carrying their stretchers. So far as I know at present, three were killed and some wounded. I saw two of them just before they died and it brings it home very forcibly to see amongst the many suffering men your own comrade with his red crosses on his arm, and the knowledge that his wounds are fatal is a thing he knows perfectly well, but if you ask him how he is 'Not too bad thanks'. It makes one feel like tearing the heart out of his next neighbour who is a German and perhaps the man who did it. But even with them one cannot but be kind. It is the law of our Corps and all wounded are treated alike.

I shall endeavour to send back that form in this letter if I get time to fill it up. I suppose I shall have to sign it also. Let me know if it is alright when you receive it dear. I shall keep your sketch of roses till later on. It is very good and if you had painted it would have been great. I am in perfect health now dearest. The cold I had at the beginning of the week is away in the meantime. The weather is fine today but it changes so very suddenly these days. One cannot say much in its favour. I have been working as a dresser in the Main Dressing Station again, with the usual heart-breaking sights. Have not heard how J. Cochrane is or if he was in it. His Reg. are out from the battle line at present.

Later Sunday Night, 16 April 1917
Midnight

We are very quiet tonight. I am on duty till morning. In the meantime, our wounded are few. It has been a great week, a week of wonderful fighting and great achievements. What will happen during this next week no one knows, but we all feel confident that the Hun is beginning to pay the price. I was quietly pleased to receive your letter of Monday and Sunday tonight when I came on duty. Your letters do me more good than I can possibly express dearie. By the way our SM was wounded early this morning and is now down the line.

It is very amusing to read that part in your letter about that company saying how and what should be done re the war. God what would be their opinion if they were here these days. All I can say is that the effect is the same on everyone. That we are a great nation and must not give in by one iota till the full penalty has been extracted and that is the opinion of the men who have fought and suffered for two long years and hate the war more than anyone. Everyone wants to be in at the death now that we have waited so long but how long it will take to completely finish them off the Lord knows. It may take as long as the war has lasted and it may surprise the most sanguine. I sincerely hope so for I am wearying wearying to get back to you my darling.

Thursday, 19 April 1917

We are back to our usual way of working, although we have not moved yet. Any day may bring a repetition of our last week's work. I have been busy as we all have. This year looks as if it was going to be a stunner. Today was the first day we have had bread for some considerable time – biscuits and bully for breakfast, Maconochie* in for dinner and biscuits for tea, bah, but it gets sickening. Your parcel coming in between kept me right for a meal or two. It is generally the way in the Army, the more one has to do the less there

---

* 'Maconochie' was a type of goulash made of soup and meat and vegetables and came in tins, named after the makers of it. So common was it, that the Military Medal was called the 'Maconochie Medal'.

136

is to eat. In your letter of yesterday, I see you enclosed John's photo. He sent me one on some days ago and so I will return you your one. It is very good indeed and he is looking fit and well. As to my corresponding with Kate Jeffrey, well it is difficult for me to find time to keep you and 58 sufficiently well posted.

I will enclose both of your drawings in this letter dearie. Your last one of the roses is very cleverly done and thank you for allowing me to see them. I have not heard any news of J. Cochrane since the battle and don't know whether he was in it or not. Some local men we know were killed but a number of them again got safely through.

Sunday 22 April 1917

Oh by the way Kate Jeffrey came to the Dressing Station the day before we left to see me, and it was the Colonel that brought her to where I was working. I was speaking to her for a few moments. Captain Jack showed her round the place. She is looking well. I don't suppose she will know we are away from there as the order just came in an hour after she had gone and we were away first thing in the morning. We don't know where we are for but may get near Pete before long. The weather has been excellent today. I hope it continues so.

Yes everyone seems to be fairly confident that the war is on the wane. Wouldn't it be great if it finished this summer? The fighting that is going on here is awful. To read about it in the papers does not convey half an idea what it means and to be in a Scotch Div. means that where it is hottest you are sure to be. According to the papers even the wounded can't get to England owing to U Boats – no more 'blighty' wounds now – hard luck, it was most soldiers' only hope, to get a wound that would take them home for a few weeks. We had some horrible cases last battle. Yes as you say, one does get a little sick at times, but we are well used to it now and a good thing too.

Friday, 27 April 1917 Night

We arrived at this city today to start an advanced Main Dressing Station. We came up in cars from a small village where we went to a week ago after the battle to allow the various battalions to be brought up to strength, and they sorely required it. During our stay in the village we had lots of marching and training and good weather, and, so far as I am concerned, I feel ever so much the better of it. Things have been very hot in this part this last week and last night we received a quick order to come here today. It was a long journey and our cars took us the journey, which was a great boon.

By the way dearie, did I ever tell you what our postman always says when he brings me a letter, no matter how many are about. It is always, 'St Clair your tonic', and that's exactly what they always are to me.

Well dearest, we are going to be busy again, and I cannot say just the arrangements as yet. I have not seen much of this place as yet, although it is a city that is before the world at present and fairly well knocked about – the usual ruins and debris, and our billets in an old shell-shattered house with not a single pane of glass. Oh yes it is very dirty. Since we arrived today Fritz has sent a fair number of shrapnel shells round about, but so far not just in our quarters. Formerly, or before the war, this building was an Institution for deaf and dumb children, and here and there, in the parts that have not suffered from the shells, one sees the Greek grammar books, French and also English grammars and histories scattered about with the little sun hats, cots and articles of clothing of the little scholars, and also amongst everything bombs (Mills), hand grenades and ammunition, all over the place. That makes one wary of what we disturb amongst the debris. However, we cleared a lot of it out this afternoon. It is much too dangerous to be lying about a place.

The fighting about here has been very fierce this last week, in fact has been since it started a few weeks ago and most probably will be till the war is finished. Looking out of the window of this billet, one can see some hundred yards across our old front line and the battlefield where our Div. again made history the first day of the battle. Fritz is further off now but still kicking very hard, and incidentally being very badly kicked. I shall continue later. I must go and secure my one blanket. I shall require it in this sanatorium tonight. However, being 'an old soldier' will make shift to keep myself warm.

Sunday 28 April 1917

I was not able to finish my letter last night. Today we have been doing navvy's work getting the place into order. I slept fairly well in our 'open work' billet last night, at least till the guns let loose just before dawn this morning. To describe the sort of bombardments we give the Germans these days is quite impossible. One would think it was worked by a handle being turned for hours and thousands of shells fired every turn of the handle. We have had quite a few back this forenoon in the city. I have visited the cathedral of this place*. It is an awful sight to see such a grand historical building in ruins – absolutely ruined beyond repair. One has to keep the eyes skinned while walking about the place, as parts of the roof are being kept up by the frailest support. Some of the streets are in fairly good condition, the narrow streets especially having escaped the shelling and in some of them, the French people continue (and have done since the war started) to do business in a small scale, but one can see the sallow paleness in their faces that is caused by their having lived in cellars almost three years. The worst is over for them now and it is comparatively safe to be about and in a week or two, may be quite free from German shells – let us hope so, although to do it is costing Britain her manhood.

* Arras.

Chapter Ten

The Damned Clergy

The following letter of 8 May 1917 is extraordinarily full of incident, as well as revealing Willie's own inner thoughts as the war begins to appear never-ending. First there is the family bereavement of John Cochrane's death and Willie's visit to the grave, meeting Jane's cousin Kate Jeffrey (John Cochrane was engaged to Kate's sister, Helen). Willie then tells of other casualties among his friends who had been through all the Divisional battles and escaped till that time. The odds caught up with everyone was the depressing message he must have given to Jane. Willie then suggests that the war had almost got a life of its own and had taken control of men's lives to which it was totally indifferent. He wrote that the whole thing was much too gigantic for them, in fact anybody to give an opinion about. To see the bombardment before their last battle, or in fact any of their bombardments, one wondered how it was possible for it to go on for long, but still it went on and seemingly no difference. He then hinted at atrocities or some such thing, 'There are some things about this battle I dare not mention in a letter, but we shall never forget them or those responsible.' Finally there is a note of despair that the war is pointless and that the belligerents are out of control.

Having given Jane his despairing thoughts on the war, Willie then described the dereliction of duty of two clergymen, during a night of explosions caused by the blowing up of an ammunition dump. Against the horrific backdrop, the scene is of two padres seeking safety while a wounded soldier cries out for their comfort. This sight confirmed Willie' worst prejudices about the established clergy, who were literally 'damned' according to the doctrines of Willie's family's religious sect'.[71] *This scene is referred to in Willie's play* The Prayer *in 1930, in which the padres are cursed as 'damned'. But in tracing Willie's inner development during the war, one has to read this incident with his equally powerful account of the extraordinary behaviour of another padre in a pillbox at St Julien near Passchendaele, which provides the main scene in the play.**

Tuesday, 8 May 1917

Since I wrote to you last, we have had quite a series of events. In fact since we came here, it has been one eventful incident after another and many of them too tragic for me to give to you. I was extremely sorry to hear about John Cochrane's death. I had heard it the day before your letter came. Since I came back from leave, I have tried to meet him but luck did not favour me. He, as I said in a former letter, was enquiring at this place for me just before we came up and just before he went to the trenches for the last time.

Yesterday morning after I came off duty (being on night duty in the Dressing Room) Fraser and I went down to number 41 CCS on a car going there. I intended to take a sketch of the grave, but, when I arrived there, found that the grave was not properly finished. The cemetery is just outside the Hospital in the fields. It is situated in quite a nice quiet locality but it is heart-rending to see how full it is already. I had not much difficulty finding the grave, receiving all particulars from the book or register – Row A Plot 4 and Grave No. 12. He is buried beside 100s of his comrades and ours, and although I have seen death continuously for the last two years, and been in similar places often, I felt a gripping at my throat, as I stood at John Cochrane's grave for I was personally acquainted with the full circumstances and suffering those at home dear to him were undergoing just then. We saluted him and came away, Fraser and I both with different feelings, he thinking of his brother Willie's grave in another part of the country and I of John, Helen and you all at home, and the barbaric cruelty of this awful war. For while

* See letter of 12 November 1917.

we were standing by the grave the stream of dead were still being carried in and laid by many many open graves and this is one Hospital only. God knows how things will total up when it is over and the numbering complete.

We made for the main road to pick up an Ambulance car or lorry to take us back to this place, and just as we were turning to go up the road a bit a lorry stopped and I saw Kate Jeffrey get out of it along with a friend. I knew at once she was on her way to where we had just left. I went over and she told me she would get full particulars from the nurse who attended John and that her friend had brought her camera to take a photograph of the grave, and also see about placing a suitable cross there. We had to hurry back as none of us had a pass and a moment may alter the position of a unit these days. However, we had not been missed. I suppose you will get full particulars from Kate, but I was glad that I had the chance of visiting the grave, for we may never be near enough again.

Well, we had just arrived here the last letter I wrote you, and looking back over the last week, it seems ages, for we have had another battle and what affects us most is the loss of so many we knew. One day and night cost our Ambulance seventeen in casualties and two of them killed outright and both of them were old lads who joined up with us, both Scotchmen and very popular in the Ambulance. Our chief medical officer was killed and our Colonel is now A.D.M.S. in his place, and many of our chums in the infantry went west also this time. A wee chap Shaw from Kirkie was killed, also Arnott, also from Kirkie, these two since ever we came to the country have always come to see us whenever possible and they had been through all the Div. battles and escaped till this time. God but it is cruel and awful. There are some things about this battle I dare not mention in a letter, but we shall never forget them or those responsible.

We had a terrible night here the other night while on duty. An Ammunition Dump just beside us was set off – thousands of shells were set a-going. We carried on our work for some time till one terrific explosion, which nearly brought the building about our ears and sent some whole shells into our Dressing Room, (without exploding thank goodness) forced us to take all our wounded into the cellars of this building where all our men had already rushed to for safety. For four hours explosion after explosion kept us from showing our faces. Quite a number of men were wounded as a result, and of course we had to dress them all in the cellars. It was a dreadful experience and every moment we fully expected to be absolutely buried, as the building is very much shattered and rickety and the cellars nothing very special. Our Staff Sergeant was wounded on the face inside this building, had his chin cleft open by one of the pieces of shell. Every explosion sent 1000s of pieces of shell and many whole shells all over the place. It absolutely rained metal for four hours. None of us are ever likely to forget that night I assure you. Till well on the following afternoon the explosions occurred at frequent intervals and the Hun kept sending over his shells just to keep the fun going. Luckily the gas ones did not catch on or we . . .

The weather has been splendid but last night and today we have had heavy rains and thunderstorms. I received your very fine parcel the day before yesterday – thanks very much dearie, oh yes the bread is always quite good and soft. Oh yes do please send me a couple of socks as I have just the pair I am wearing. I intended asking you some time ago but it escaped my memory while I was writing to you. I am very sorry to hear that Dunk is not so well. He must look after himself. I wrote to Pete the other day there. I was overdue him a letter. By the way I had a letter from Mima today. She does write a very beautiful letter indeed.

You ask me, 'Do I think the war will finish this year?' We have given up giving our opinion long ago about that, because the whole thing is much too gigantic for us, in fact anybody to give an opinion. To see the bombardment before our last battle, or in fact any of our bombardments, one wonders how it is possible for it to go on for long, but still it goes on and seemingly no difference. The bombardment the other night was a wonderful sight indeed. I cannot describe it, so I will not try. One has to see these things to believe them. They awe one. The answer to your question is yes dearie.

How are you keeping yourself dearie mine? You tell me you are longing for me. Yes and I am longing for you. Longing does not truly explain it. I wish oh how I do always wish it was all over and we were together for good. Two years today we arrived in this country, two years of this, and as the days go past, it grows in

143

intensity and fierceness and what for, eh? God but the nations are fools, fools.

There is one incident that left an indelible impression on me. I think I will tell you. It will perhaps show you why I take a certain attitude to a certain class of profession. It was the night of the explosions. We were all clustered in the cellars as I told you before. The particular cellar I was in was where we had our wounded and we were doing what we could under the circumstances for those who were coming in. The place was full up, being quite a small place. We had some very bad cases. One in particular, a poor chap who had an abdominal and also a chest wound. The poor chap was dying, but like a true Scot was fighting for life. 'Oh dear, oh dear, give me a drink,' which of course we daren't do. 'Ah but I am just about beat,' he would say. 'I cannot stick it any more.' We had work to do of course but some of us always managed to sit and mop the poor chap's sweating brow and reassure him while the whole place was trembling and ready to tumble down on us by the terrific concussion of the explosions. And sitting two yards away close against the safest part of the cellar with their pipes in their mouth sat two chaplains talking about various people they both knew and different other subjects, but all piffle and not once did either of them take any notice of this poor fellow, or try to give him any of the comfort they are supposed to be able to give, and incidentally are paid for giving. They continued their conversation, and I dare say will continue it after the war and preach many a stirring sermon and tell many a sad tale that will bring tears to the eyes of their hearers and dwell at length on their many and varied experiences while in France amongst the poor wounded soldiers. But this one I don't think they will tell, nor will they think I am sure that eyes, that will know them anywhere, watched them for a proof of, not their Christianity only, but just of ordinary decency, and found them conspicuous by their absence. How two or three of us cursed them in good soldierly language. If they had heard us, I am sure they would have lifted their divine and pious faces and prayed for us. Their uniform saves them many a straight word, which of course will keep. Of course there are exceptions yes . . . eh, but one sees many strange things out here.

Thursday, 17 May 1917

As I have secured another green envelope, I can get on with a letter. We are back at the rest area now, and out of the line for a little while. We were brought down in the train and have been doing some shifting about before we settled at this isolated farm where we have had rotten weather – rain every day. We were all glad to get away from that place. I assure you it was not comfortable in more ways than one. We are living in an old barn now, quite comfortable, there being plenty of straw, although the pigs are much too numerous about here for it to be pleasant, and if the weather would just pick up we would have nothing to grumble about. Sorry to hear about W. Knox. It must have been in the part where we were. I do hope he turns up all right, even although it is on the other side. Thanks for sending the photo of Dave. I think it is excellent and would like to keep it. Can you not get another one? Has he to go at the beginning of the month? I hope not. Things are getting to such a dreadful pass.

I am afraid dearie it is quite impossible for me to get news from those who carried J. Cochrane, as they are in a different Div and there are so many similar cases such as his. It would be difficult for them to remember. I may find out through a lucky stroke though. As to Bill Knox, you see we do not know the Battalion he is in. There are so many Royal Scots. If it is the 11th or 12th Battalion, I may get news. Yes it was one of the wounded Argylls that told me about young Arnott. He said that Shaw and Arnott were killed on the same day. I shall make further enquiries and make sure.

I had a long letter from Pete today and am delighted to hear he is doing well although everyone all along the line have their fair share of work. We have got a new CO now, quite a stranger, our old CO having been promoted ADMS in place of Colonel Symons killed. What changes this new one will make, I don't know. So far we have not had a chance to find out what he is like, but I believe he will be all right.

Monday, 22 May 1917

Thanks very much for the socks, which arrived two days ago, and also the parcel that has just arrived in excellent condition. I am sorry dear it is not possible for me to get a sketch of J. Cochrane's grave as we are away from there now and as I said, in the rest area. Of course we are running a Hospital here for sick. I could not sketch it while there simply because it was only a heap of stones and earth. They were busy levelling it off and I dare say by now the cross will be up and the grave better set off. Kate Jeffrey assured me she would have it photographed. It will be easy for her as she is only a few miles away from it. I may not be ever near it again. We never know what direction we are going.

Sunday evening, 27 May 1917

We have had a very lazy day today. The sun has been shining and very hot. I just went outside the tent and did a little watercolour, which you will see some day. The Div. band came here and played over some beautiful selections for the benefit of the patients. It was grand, and to hear the old favourites from the Quaker Girl and lots of old favourite musical comedies you and I used to go to.

Thank you for the photo of Dave.* You will have a better chance of getting one. I do sincerely hope that neither John or Dave have to come out to this awful country at present. I would never have a moment's peace for I know just exactly what the dangers are. One is quite sufficient. So far there are no changes made since the new CO came. When we go up there it may be different, although I don't expect it will affect me darling. We are so fully fed up, we do not worry ourselves much whether he does or not. We are sick up to the eyes of the whole damn business absolutely. Over two years in this country does that very effectively. However I do not want to talk about that here. We live one day at a time. Tomorrow can look after itself so far as what it will bring us. To be in the green fresh country, as we are now, and to see the ploughed fields and all the glorious beauty of nature at this time of the year is beautiful and peaceful and grand, but one does long so very very much to be back home to our own dear country with its greater and more magnificent beauties and to our more than dear loved ones there.

PS Cannot find Bill Knox's Battalion, sorry to hear there is no news of him yet. I dare say it will come all right. It takes some

---

* Willie's brother.

considerable time for news of prisoners to get through. Remember me to Helen Jeffrey.

Monday, 4 June 1917

You gave me a little dressing down in your letters of today about being careless. It makes little difference up here dearie whether one is or not. One has work to do even although shells fly about and it is just as well to carry on, as, attempting to dodge them, many a man has dodged right into it instead of away from it. Don't for a moment think I will be careless dear. I love you and want to come back to you too much for to be foolish. It is all a game of luck and one must take the chances. We lost a comrade before our eyes yesterday, and no one else was hit. Poor chap, he had the shell to himself, as if it was meant for him. Do you think for a moment darling we delight in a place like this? No, but we would be useless men, if we allowed ourselves to think too much about it. If one is working outside and shells dropping at a safe distance away, no one takes any apparent notice, but all our ears and senses are on the alert for the next one, and so the day goes on. Just had a bit of a digression at this stage of my letter, a German aeroplane just over-head deliberately firing his machine gun on this road and flying as near the ground as ever I saw an aeroplane. For cool deliberate cheek or daring he is the limit, and despite the fact that about half a dozen of our machine guns, beside anti-aircraft guns, were firing like ------, the sod got away. Oh no no one on this front believes the stories of how we have Fritz beaten in the air. We know different.

Tuesday, 5 June 1917

Just going to post my letter but I forgot to mention about that point of your letter where you mention you would like so much to be out here. I thank heaven there is no possibility of such a thing, and even although you were, you would not ever have the chance of seeing me. Yes I do hear there were some women out here now working up from the base, but my wife will never have my sanction to take on the job even although it was possible. So put it out of your mind forever dearie. I know why you would like to be here dearie. But it

147

would be an impossible position. I would not have you where Kate Jeffrey is for all the cash in the world. And I know what I am talking about.

Afternoon, 8 July 1917

Yes it is very sad about B. Knox. B. Peters had word yesterday from home. We fully expected the news all along, although we could not be certain. We know that particular part of the line very well and there are many more in the same position as Bill. It does not make any difference to them, but very bad for their folks to know the truth. Ah yes Dave has clicked for the Reg. they don't as a rule keep long out of the thick of it. Unless he volunteers, they cannot send him into the trenches until he is nineteen and surely he will not be such a damned fool after all he has been told. John is doing well, I am pleased to hear, and he is sure to get his commission. We, any of us, could get one for the asking now, especially those who have been out for some time, but we have seen too much of it now. John I fancy will stand a good chance of securing a home job, if he watches the ropes properly. I sincerely hope he does, for I don't care to think of any of them coming out here. He is a deal smarter, and has more brains than the average officer.

Saturday, 21 July 1917

I am afraid the little hope the Knoxes are clinging to is very feeble. It is very hard lines. I am awfully sorry dearie to hear your Father is not keeping up to the mark. One does not grow any younger living in days like these, and the end of the war will rejuvenate him and many another Father in the country.

Chapter Eleven

Passchendaele and St Julien

'I could not possibly hope to make you understand that hell of hells.'

Haig launched his Flanders Offensive on 31 July 1917, convinced he could take the ridges overlooking the British positions and then recapture the vital Channel ports of Ostend, Zeebrugge and Antwerp. Britain was suffering from the German submarine blockade and Admiral Jellicoe was persuaded by Haig to tell the Cabinet, 'If the Army cannot get the Belgian ports, the Navy cannot hold the Channel and the war is as good as lost'.[72] Haig's generals did not believe what Jellicoe had said, but Jellicoe's advice persuaded the Cabinet to sanction the Offensive. Three months later it was called off, the British having suffered 244,897 casualties.[73] Nothing of any military significance was gained, apart from the infliction of an even more appalling toll on the Germans, who lost around 400,000 dead and wounded.[74] Soon after the Offensive began, the situation had become a hopeless stalemate, with Haig's two most senior officers, Generals Plumer and Gough, urging him to call it off.[75] But Haig persisted, even if it meant ambulance trains being unloaded in London at night,[76] to avoid civilian disquiet over casualties.[77] General von Kuhl, the German Chief of Staff on the Flanders Front, later described the slaughter in Flanders over these months as 'the greatest martyrdom of the World War'.[78]

Lloyd George never forgave himself for authorizing the Flanders Offensive. After the war he chose the Flanders Offensive or 'Passchendaele', as it was always known to the British soldiers, as his battle-ground to accuse the generals, and Haig in particular, of almost criminal incompetence in the prosecution of the war. Haig never visited the front[79] and, Lloyd George suggested, from the

149

accounts of those who had, that if Haig had searched the whole line from the Belgian coast to the Swiss border, there was no worse terrain to mount an offensive than that at Passchendaele.[80] Lloyd George then accused Haig of not calling off the Offensive, when it was clear that to carry on with it was to reinforce failure on a colossal scale. This attack did much to create the public image of Great War generals being out of touch with reality, while safely ensconced in their châteaux.

The Battle of Passchendaele began for the 9th Division when they attacked from the crest of the Frezenberg Ridge on 20 September 1917. It was their first major attack since June, having been in rest camps, and then in August in a comparatively quiet part of the line at Trescault-Havrincourt-Hermies. But training had been intense in how to neutralize the Germans' newest defensive devices, namely the forward network of mutually supporting concrete pillboxes, devised by Colonel von Lossberg, the Chief of Staff of General Sixt von Arnim, Commander of the German Fourth Army. Placed in front of six rows of trenches, these veritable fortresses were so formidable that it was not until 16 August 1917 that the British found a way of attacking them that offered a reasonable prospect of success.[81] The attack on 20 September was reasonably successful, even with 2,376 casualties[82] including the Brigadier-General of Willie's 27 Brigade, F. A. Maxwell, VC, CSI, DSO, killed.[83] It showed that carefully co-ordinated infantry sections could overcome the pillboxes.

On 12 October the 9th Division attacked again, just north-east of St Julien, which lay between Ypres and the village of Passchendaele. The conditions could not have been worse. About midnight on 11 October torrential rains came down, swamping terrain that had long lost any means of drainage. Men drowned even before they got to the assembly points on the morning of 12 October. There they met with a barrage of gas and HE[84] shells, and all had to wear respirators for hours on end. The attacking battalions of 26 and 27 Brigades, who were attacking on a 1500-yard front, lost their way in the featureless terrain. Some ran into their own barrage; others could not keep up with the barrage, or got pinned down by fire from the pillboxes. Communication was lost with forward units. Even the pigeons proved useless in the gas and winds.[85] Messenger dogs broke loose after their handlers became casualties.[86] *Flares were pointless, and telephone cables could not be laid. Guns were clogged and did not work, and could only be brought to the front by light railway, since the horses could not leave the roads. Except on the extreme right, the two Brigades had gained no more than a hundred yards before being ground to a halt. The men were utterly exhausted and on the night of 13/14 October 26 and 27 Brigades were relieved by the South African Brigade, which had taken the place of 28 Brigade after it was effectively wiped out at Loos.*[87]

The fortnight which the 9th Division spent at St Julien nearly overwhelmed the medical services. A special Gas Hospital had to be opened, so pervasive was the use of gas.[88] *A normal detail could not have brought anyone through the swamp. If someone was hit, the chances were also that he would fall off the duckboards and drown, unless rescued immediately.*[89] *To cope with these extreme conditions, 300 South African Infantry were allocated to assist the bearers. The humanitarian work never stopped. The bearers also collected the men's socks to send back for washing, rubbed their feet with whale oil to guard against trench foot, and issued clean socks. Apart from the odd captured pillbox, there was no shelter in the forward areas, and 'elephant' tents were taken up to serve as makeshift stops for bearers and patients. All this work at St Julien, according to the War Diary of 27 Field Ambulance, was done under very heavy shell fire.*[90] *The two-week period from 12 to 25 October 1917 took the Division's casualties at Passchendaele over 5,000.*[91] *The Brigadier-General later wrote of the soldiers' horror of the place, describing St Julien as a place of 'evil memory', and how the soldiers cursed and spat on the ground as they left it. Describing the road to St Julien, he wrote, 'But St Julien! Many a time one has walked down that road, and one's stick would come out of the mud a dull red wherever one liked to put it in.*[92]

Saturday, 4 August 1917 Evening

Today is the third anniversary of the war and this month completes my three years away from home. We little thought it would just last so long, few did then. However we are still alive and well despite everything, which is something to be very thankful for, and also dearie our love for each other is as always, deep, faithful and lasting. The only thing I am sorry for now is that we did not get married before I left home then. There again, we denied ourselves, but we have sealed that compact also now, and when the war is over start together again for the period of our lives in this world. The months are flying, although one at times feels an awful drag. August, another few months and I shall be warning you to prepare for a sturdy husband coming home to you. I wish it could be just now, but we must look ahead to the time when our turn comes. It will pass and quickly, and it shall be of all the former leaves, the best.

It is no news to hear that some are making money out of this war dearie. Many are. We are not, but we are by no means any the worse of that. You do not know just what I know about who are profiting by it. At times when one is inclined to grouse, it sticks in the neck and makes one wild at the unfairness, especially as one has lost as a consequence of joining early. But after all, what is the use of worrying? Let those of us who are not profiting by it get back home again, and I guess there will be some fun. Isn't it very strange, the nearer you are to the danger, the less pay? The real fighting man is the least paid of all – funny, and also damnable, but the army way nevertheless. Aye aye, one would get quite a lot to worry about and get miserable over, but what's the use dearie mine?

Tuesday 14 August 1917

Yes I heard a few days ago about Charlie Stuart. What dreadful bad luck it is, and I feel so sorry for them. He was such a success as an officer. It is too awful for words and makes me feel very grateful indeed that life has been spared me all these years out here. Please convey my deepest sympathy to them dear if you get a chance. We Scotchmen have enough to make us hate the name of German for generations to come. I trust that it is possible to make them pay the toll for precious lives lost, before the war finishes.

2 September 1917

Well dearie you know we are out of the line at present, but have had to shift our quarters twice and that of course spoils part of the rest. We, at least a detachment of the Ambulance, have taken over

152

a Hospital to work while we are out, and the result is we find ourselves with a great deal more to do here than what we had most of our long spell in the line. So there you have our rest as it has worked out this time. It does not matter. I would just as soon be occupied at this work as being dogged about by my old friend the SM. He is not on our staff here and that makes up for a lot. He of course has put the tin hat on my Paris leave as I dare say you will have deduced. Bob, Peter and I had passes in at the same time, and while he was on leave, had hopes of going together but he cut mine out whenever he came back with the excuse that I had extended leave when you were ill dear. Only such a nature as his could have said it. That still sticks in his neck, the few days extra I had then. However there may be still a chance of getting to Paris despite his objections. I do not care now whether I go or not other than I do not like unfair treatment.

These are busy days in France at present and such a Div. as ours cannot hope to have it easy while there is so much tough work on hand. If it brings the day nearer my getting back home to you, by ever so little, I do not mind going through it with a good will. I shall be on the look out for Jim Smith's boy, and if he has my address, as you say, there should be little difficulty, but that we shall meet soon. I have a Seaforth Highlander working with me here and this morning, and at every opportunity in conversation, he yarns about his little chap at home who is three years of age and of course he is the most amusing little chap in the country as well as the best kid breathing. I like to listen to him talking about the kid and you can imagine dearie mine how I envy him. I should dearly love to be able to talk so of our little chap. Wouldn't that just be glorious dear? This is another of our 'hopes' for the future.

The air is getting much colder now out here and we are having a lot of rain besides mostly at night-time; the winter is not very far off now. I do hope that we shall be able to push the Boche well back over his old line into new country, because the desolation of these old battlefields is the most depressing feature of our life out here during the winter months. To describe them is quite impossible – ruin, desolation and all around wherever you look, grim remembrances of life and death struggles oft repeated. Things are shaping well, but if he is allowed to settle down again, the war is just where it was. To describe my feeling of home sickness and utter

153

fed-upness at the whole thing, I can't, it is horrible and detestable and I would to God it was over never to return in any generation.

Tuesday, 4 September 1917

We had very cold weather but yesterday and today it has been really good, very hot today, and we are quite comfortable in our shorts although at 5.30 am they feel just to the cool side. This place we are at is nice when the sun shines (everything is) but freezing when it doesn't and like the last place nothing but ruins. And of course there are no civilians about. It is some considerable time since we were anywhere near civilization. I keep in most excellent health but am very sick of the whole business and am just counting the days as they go by, one less to do and one day nearer home and you. Monotony is a thousand times worse for us than danger. So long as one's mind is fully taken up, the time passes better. At least I think so. Our next place will perhaps give us plenty to think about.

We had some great air 'stunts' here these days – looping the loop etc is a daily performance and of course old Fritz pays us a visit every fine day and, except for the falling shrapnel and dud shells, is not much more than amusement for us. So Ralph Laurie is killed, poor chap. Yes dearest we have everything to be thankful for, being alive and kicking and well despite our three years of it.

Sunday, 30 September 1917

This is a very beautiful day and we are away back from the line in a nice village in a rest area. It is all so peaceful and clean. We are camped just behind the church, which is a fair size and very nice inside, a good pipe organ and all the other things, images etc that the French Roman Catholics are so fond to see in their churches. They really take a keen interest in their religion. The first day we arrived here I walked inside the church and what struck me most of all was the terrible destruction that has been caused by the Huns in these places. It is only when you see one in good condition that you are able to judge the terrible havoc made of those more famous cathedrals which we have been oftener beside than those behind like this one. There is nothing very grand about this one, but the harmony of colour and plaster images painted in all colours is very

154

pleasing to the eye. Our march to here was a very hard one and we slept by the roadside and off again in the morning long before it was daylight. But we don't trouble about the marches a moment longer than they last.

Tuesday, 9 October 1917

We have just been told we have nothing to do this forenoon but get ourselves dry after a very miserable march in a severe storm last night. Every man was soaked to the skin and, when we arrived here, found our billet partly flooded and anything but 'airtight'. We all felt very miserable, our pack feeling doubly heavy with the wet and all I had to eat before getting down to bed was one of the famous biscuits. But my usual good fortune saved the situation. Our postman had been sent on here in the morning and had our mail ready for us when we arrived, and again your parcel saved a very hungry situation. It was a perfect God-send dearest and the chaps I invited to share with me thought the same. By a strange coincidence, when I am at the last stage and as a rule after a long march when our rations are of the biscuit type, the parcel turns up. It was a bitterly cold wet night and the heavy marching had made us sweat, and of course, later on, we felt very shivery. Having no blankets, we got our wet things off and lay close with all the coats etc overlapping and passed a decent few hours till the cold of the morning made us very glad to get up again. But that is just a few lines, describing one of our many marches these days. I expect we will not be long here for we work the line this time and will probably go up tomorrow. I sincerely hope the weather clears up for it is dreadful during wet weather.

Tuesday night, 16 October Midnight

I dare say you will have an idea why you have not had many letters from me for some time. We have been in action, and are still. It has been one of the worst weeks in all our lives. I have been a stretcher-bearer this time. I have received all your letters dearie and was a bit amused the other night when I read where you wished to goodness Pete was beside me. As he had been in those famous pillboxes, he would be no better with us in the meantime I assure you. For I am

155

writing this in the pillbox I have been carrying wounded from for the last week to the pillbox further down, and, as we were so unfortunate as to have it wet, it made the track unimaginable.

Our losses in the Ambulance have been heavier than usual. One squad had a shell all to themselves as they were carrying a case and three were killed and the other one wounded and the patient had the good luck to escape being re-hit. I fancy I know where Pete is and it is much quieter than here where he left evidently. The fact that we have had to go for days soaked to the skin has given us all bad colds and we shall welcome as never before the day we get out of this hole. War, to describe what is before our eyes daily, is beyond the powers of man; so what is the use trying? Old Fritz is landing heavies all around this old pillbox which has been able to resist direct hits easily. His gas shells give us a lot of trouble especially at night time, and we have always to be on the alert. Hope to be able to tell you I am well out of this by next letter dearie.

Leave is still going very slowly and, if it does not improve soon, I am afraid Nov. won't see me home. But cheer on we will hope for the best. By the way we carried a little chap Richmond down the other night.* He was wounded in the leg. He had a draper's shop at the Cross. We were glad we found him. It made it ever so much quicker for him to get away, for we did a double carry to keep him from being delayed at the next Post. I hope he turns up in Blighty alright.

Saturday

I am very pleased to be able to tell you we are out of that dreadful place now. I had fifteen days there, much longer than any of us expected at first. I will not try to describe to you lovey what it has been like, for to tell you the truth I could not possibly hope to make you understand that hell of hells. It has been the worst time of our experience, even of those bearers who have been in every stunt. At the post I was at twenty-five of us went up and three privates and two NCOs came down when we were relieved. All the others were wounded, gassed or went down sick. In fact we had a gas shell

* Many years later Richmond later gave Willie two half sovereigns as a token of gratitude, which is described in the Introduction.

dropped right at the door of our dug-out about the second day and we all got a sniff of it, but not sufficient to knock us out. Yes my throat was bad. In fact I have not been able to speak for the last eight days and often felt like giving in, but managed to stick on to the last day, and of course have the personal satisfaction of knowing I did stick it. Till last night I had not slept for five nights and felt tired to death and my throat was swollen and very painful, but this morning and today I have been very much better and in fact have been able to carry on cutting the boys' hair. We were all like wild men but look our old selves again. This is a very bracing place near the sea and we are billeted in a farm barn and expect to feel the benefit of the next few days' rest.

I received all your letters and also the parcel dearie but could not possibly write sooner, but I sent a Field Post Card every day, which I hope you got. We did not always manage to get them sent down for post. Had a bath and a change this afternoon and oh but it was glorious to get rid of the dirt and lice. Those pillboxes are absolutely alive with lice. I could narrate many very sad tales, almost beyond belief and tales of men suffering untold sufferings and all the horrors of those fifteen days but it would only sadden you all and make you more anxious. I have one or two incidents to tell when I can collect myself properly. I want to get this short note off tonight, with all my love. Your ain Willie.

A MAN OF THE FIRST WATER

The War Diary[93] of 27 Field Ambulance enables us to plot on a map the route of Willie's 'double carry' of Richmond.[94] We can also find on the map the 'St Julien Pillbox', which was the scene of the incident in the following letter on which Willie based his 1930 play The Prayer. *These War Diaries of the participating units are the indispensable building blocks for any reconstruction of a military event on the British sector of the Western Front. But for the reconstruction of the experiences of the men who took part in the events, one has to look beyond the War Diaries. There is perhaps no letter in Willie's correspondence with Jane during the Great War that is so revealing of his inner struggles as his letter of 12 November 1917, which describes the extraordinary display of compassion of an army padre, proof that Willie's previous contempt for the clergy was based on bigotry.*

The padre Willie described in his letter was Captain Eustace Hill of the South African or 'Springbok' Brigade, which had replaced 28 Brigade of the 9th Division after its disaster at Loos. Willie always thought of him as a South African, but in fact his father was an English Major-General[95] in the Indian Army, and he had been educated at Lancing and Christ Church, Oxford. Most of his adult life, however, was spent in South Africa in pastoral work as Chaplain to the Railway Mission in Grahamstown or as a master and later Headmaster of St. John's College Johannesburg. Twice before the Great War, he had served as an Army Chaplain, first as the Chaplain to Lord Methuen's column during the Boer War and later as Chaplain to the Forces during the suppression of the Zulu Rebellion that broke out in Natal and Zululand in 1906. Although he was on their enemy's side, the Zulus knew Eustace Hill as 'The man whose face has looked on God'.[96]

In 1914 Hill became a Chaplain again in the South African Forces, first in the Luderitz Bay area of German South West Africa and then on the Western Front, winning a Military Cross for his selfless devotion to the wounded during the Somme battles. Attempting to bring in a wounded Captain during the Battle of the Butte de Warlencourt, he was caught in a torrent of machine-gun bullets and as a result of his wounds lost his right arm. But as soon as he had recovered, he was back again, as always making a point of being first over the parapet with the infantry. In March 1918 he was captured by the Germans, when the South African Brigade was virtually wiped out at Marrières Wood holding up the German onslaught. Emaciated by hunger when eventually freed at the end of 1918, Hill was nevertheless again back in 1919 at the old battle-fields of Longueval and Delville Wood, identifying and burying the dead of his Brigade and erecting makeshift memorials and crosses.[97]

Hill's attitude to the war and his views on the Germans reflected a certainty of conviction typical of a class of late Victorian padres. They hated the carnage of the war. Hill wrote on 24 July 1916 that there seemed no Geneva Convention or relic of humanity left in war. It was utterly damnable and should be a method only heathens should use for settling disputes. He sometimes hoped that Germany

158

alone would be made to bear the entire guilt for the war. He even hoped that the war would go on and on, until men loathed it and determined forever to give it up as an un-Christian damnable method of settling disputes. In his words, 'We must force this down the Prussian throat until he spews his whole being up and turns with disgust from his filth.' On the other hand Hill's faith in God and an after-life gave him the uplift to go on. He wrote that he felt great spiritual elevation in the war and rejoiced at being able to prove God's protecting love, and the fact that 'the path of duty is that of safety here[on earth] or salvation beyond'. He kept returning to the suffering of the wounded and lamenting the absence of pity and chivalry. It was all just killing. But Hill had no doubt that the killing had to go on in order to build a better world, and was convinced that, but for 'the hope of a better state to be evolved from the war, the gloom would be hellish.'

These attitudes of Hill were the main reason for padres being enlisted in the Army. General Haig had laid down the policy quite clearly, that the padres were there to preach to the soldiers the official line, which was that the war was being fought for the emancipation of mankind from German tyranny and barbarism. If any padre was not prepared to preach that line he was to be sent home immediately.[98] This propaganda role of the padres meant that their job could not be described as purely humanitarian. The ideal padre, as far as the Army was concerned was one like Hill, who not only preached the official line but was in the thick of the battles urging the men on by his saintly example. Part of Hill's counselling to the soldiers was that they should never carry white handkerchiefs in case they were tempted to wave them to the enemy in surrender. A soldier in the South African Brigade, who had been wounded in the Neuve Eglise region, also reported in April 1918 how, when the battle was going badly and all the officers had become casualties, he suddenly heard their one-armed padre yelling at his side, 'Hold on men – for God's sake hold on, you can only lose your bodies once but your souls are going to last for ever.'

Monday, 12 November 1917

I wonder if Dave will come out here. I hope that I get home before he comes at any rate. I have many things to say to him that would save him lots of trouble. Poor Dave I hate to think of him in the firing line and in battle as I have seen so many others. We have had a lot of rain lately but the conditions here do not make it so bad. Today's weather has been very fine.

Things do not look over-bright these days. If we could give some of the British doggedness to different nations the war would have been finished long ago. God knows when it is going to finish. It seems that we will have to do lots of jobs besides our own. If leave would go more quickly, it would not be so bad. However hope still reigns. I have expected to see D. Smith lately, but like me, it is nigh impossible for him to get a pass for anywhere. I may knock up against him before we go from here. Yes, as you say, those two young fellows would much better remain as they are.

I think I said in one of my letters that there was one incident that I wanted to mention, which I particularly noticed last time in the line. Months ago I wrote to you and described a scene in a dug-out during a very trying and dangerous time when two ministers failed miserably in my opinion not only to do their duty but even to show common sympathy. This time I again noticed another minister who was a <u>man</u> any soldier would be proud to salute. He has been with us or the Div. years now and I have often heard about his daring, trying to succour the wounded not when they came into the Dressing St but on the battlefield where they lay just where they had been hit. He has risked his life as often as any man in the Div, and risked it so fearlessly that we used to wonder why it was he was not killed. No man's land made absolutely no difference to him. He went out right in the face of the Boche and took comfort to the men waiting there till opportunity made it possible for us to get them safely in. Even the Boche admired his courage, for many times they could have killed him but did not fire.

However, his wonderful charm against the bullets was broken last Oct, during one of our battles. While carrying on as I have described, he got a very bad bullet wound in the arm. We did not think when we saw him in the Advanced Dressing St that it would cause him to lose his arm, but it did unfortunately.[99] He went to Blighty, had his arm amputated and came out here again this summer, and in our late actions has been carrying on his wonderful work. No matter what the existing conditions, he roughs it with the very best, and one of his sleeves dangling empty. One night in

160

the pillbox we had some frightful wounds to deal with – one in particular, leg smashed to a pulp and of course it had to be amputated. The chap stood it well despite the fact that surgery, so far up as we were, was only done where it was the last chance and absolutely necessary, and appliances were very few and also the fact of the great shock he suffered. We carried all the other cases down but this one, so that he could rest and perhaps survive. This minister never left his side, stood there while the other officers had their grub in the other compartment of the pillbox, stood with bent head whispering to the soldier and drawing his hand over his brow soothing the man to sleep because the doctor mentioned that, if he could sleep, it would help his chances.

I stood and watched him and admired a man of the first water. Other wounded were coming in, slight cases which we soon disposed of, and still that silent figure in the gloom of the pillbox with bent head and his hand moving lightly over the poor fellow's forehead and his own empty sleeve dangling at his side. The wounded man slept and he mentioned to us to be as quiet as possible. We watched and it was plain to anyone that the poor fellow was dying. The Doc. came in, shook his head, told the Padre and went out. He took up his place as before till the last moment and long after, then turned about and asked us to join in the prayer.

I would like to picture before you that scene dearie – we bowing our heads at the jobs we were at the moment, the one-armed tall and strong-faced man in officer's uniform, and the motionless form on the stretcher. He prayed as I have heard very few pray – simple, straight and like a soldier, brief, and we all whisper after him the one prayer we all know. He took all the particulars of the man, address of mother etc etc and wrote slowly with the left hand notes which I am sure will be the great treasure of that dead soldier's mother. I could not help from muttering splendid, looking at him all the time, and also remembered the other night and the other Padres that made me so mad on that occasion and determined to write to you about this one as I had written to you about the others. No there certainly are exceptions always. Every time we go into action men die like this soldier did. I have watched them scores of times, but I have only this <u>once</u> seen <u>such</u> faithful <u>attendance</u> come from a chaplain, and he comes from South Africa.

161

Monday afternoon, (probably 19 November 1917)

I am glad that I have managed to get a chance to write just now to send you my very best wishes for the 24th and many happy returns of the day. It is not possible for me to send you a present. That must wait until I come home on leave. We are all very tired these days, having been on the march these last three days, and more in front of us. My feet are not troubling me very much as yet, but I shall be jolly pleased when we settle down again for a little. Being on the treck in the winter is not just the best experience one would wish for.

Friday, 23 November 1917

We have finished marching in the meantime at any rate but have not got properly settled down yet here. We arrived last night after being on the march for days. Needless to say we were jolly glad to get it over, although personally I enjoy the change. It keeps one very fit and this time my feet did not trouble me. They seldom do if my boots fit me properly.

And so you have got my suit ready dearie. It will be a great change for me to get into mufti again. By the way dear is my overcoat in good condition? Have no fear my clothes will not be too tight for me, because all those who have gone home on leave and worn civies say that it is quite the reverse – three years takes all superfluous material off one. I see by the papers they are rationing you all at home, now things are getting very difficult to get – and all the more reason why you must not send foodstuffs out to me lovey.

8 December 1917

Circumstances have prevented me writing lately. We had a very sudden move from our rest billets and find ourselves amongst the wounded again after a bit of knocking about en route to here. This time we are doing Dressing St, and I am working in the Dressing Room. So you need not worry dear. The times are very exciting nevertheless in this district, which of course I am not allowed to speak about. I have received all your letters dearest and receiving

162

them after a day's travelling is an excellent tonic indeed. I had your lucid description of the baptism in last night's letter.

9 December 1917, Evening

You see dearie I did not get very far on with my letter. It is difficult to get sufficient time to settle down and finish a letter at one sitting. We are having wretched weather, cold and wet, and the mud is awful, but we are very used to that now. So Mother was asking what our arrangements are for my leave. I think a quiet rest is what I feel in need of. I can't see any possibility of getting home during the New Year time. Just at present leave is so erratic, and after the New Year will suit me just as well, and you also dear eh? I am wearying very much on it dearest, but I cannot help it on one single day, and will get away whenever my turn comes. Soldiers have to be prepared for little disappointments and, as a general rule, always get them, and I suppose soldiers' wives prepare for the same thing.

Friday, 4 January 1918

Well I cannot say I have been over happy lately and do not feel like writing a cheery letter simply because of my leave taking so long to come round. If it continued as it was doing a fortnight ago, I should have been at home with you now but it has been reduced again. Oh but it does sicken one. After all the talk about the great improvements that were made about Tommy's leave, having been out here since near the beginning does not weigh one iota; in fact we are inclined to think all the favours are given to those who had to be dragged out. I know it is rotten for you to be disappointed like myself, but even our very dearest and most sympathetic do not realize how very helpless we are about our leave and how impossible it is for any of us to hasten it by a single day.

We have been in the wilds for the last five weeks in the severest weather and look like being all winter. It just requires the one rumour that leave is reduced to make us all as miserable as can be, can go to bed beside the rats and sleep it off. Lost the last of our first chums in the Argylls three days ago, killed, Peter Bell. Comes from Kirkie and has been in every battle the Div. has been in and survived till the other days Fritz tried (but didn't) to take part of

163

their trench. There used to be about thirty of us who used to meet shortly after we came out. Peter is the last except ourselves. If one could only speak what one thinks about it. Few at home care much about these lives except those of their family, but we care and, in many cases, as much as their family do and will not forget when it is all over. Tommy knows better than anyone how very indifferent the people are at home now that they have got used to us all being away. I firmly believe, if they would see themselves at home, it would not last so very long.

I wish you all happiness this year dearie and hope with you for this to finish before it flickers out. I can't say when I shall be home. I am still hoping it will be before the month is out. God knows but don't you go and get miserable about it. It makes it all the worse for me to keep my mouth shut. As to having the same luck as last year, well must just chance that as well and put up with it. It will be rotten if it happens for this one as well won't it? It is evident you can not be sure yourself. I should have liked to have seen Dunk in his swank uniform. He is doing well in the air raid line eh? I can't say I ever get used to them. Every day and night is about the average and still one feels uncomfortable especially at night. He has dropped about 20 bombs 200 yards from where I am writing in the last hour. The more you get the less you like them is my experience. They are worst to put up with than shells I think.

15 January 1918, Tuesday Night

Do you know dearie it makes me feel very miserable indeed knowing you are daily expecting me and I cannot help things on any so far as the leave is concerned. I should not have said anything about when I expected my turn would come round. But there is hardly a man in the BEF who can keep from speaking about it and reckoning up the days according to the rate of leave at the time, fully expecting that everything would go on smoothly (which it never does) until at least he gets his leave. But there you are, anything may alter the rate of leave. Things like that, no matter how much you hiss about them, the folks at home never seem to understand. We are the most helpless of mortals on the face of the earth so far as hastening on our leave and also this to us, it means much more than it does to even our very dearest at home. I would rather sacrifice a right hand than one leave if I had a choice. Just at present I can think about nothing else dear and keep all my ears open for any news of warrants and tick them off and say one less before me, but this last 10 days only one of ours has gone. So you may imagine how we who are near are feeling about it.

We are having dreadful weather still, although it has changed from severe frost, the worst since I came out, to heavy rain and wind and the state of things with the mud is deplorable. What a beautiful countryside it looks around. It only requires us to let our minds dwell on our beautiful surroundings for a day or so to go rank staring mad or 'dopey' as we put it. We have lots of cases these days. These are pitiful cases – two chaps just allowing their melancholia to get the better of them, just giving in to their feelings and 'dopey' is the result.

Chapter Twelve

March/April 1918
The Kaiser's Battle

'It is costing the enemy terrible losses for every inch of ground he gets'

If there was one spark of hope in Willie's gloomy letters at the end of 1917, it was that he was in line for leave. When it came, Jane took dangerously ill with peritonitis and would have died had she not been operated on in time. By then in the war, many at home were becoming ill as a result of malnutrition caused by the German submarine blockade, or just from the cumulative stress of the war, which seemed to be going on for ever. The military situation for Britain on every front seemed to have become desperate. Even as Haig was slogging it out at Passchendaele, he was forced to send British divisions to help the Italians, on whom Austro-German forces had inflicted a catastrophic defeat at Caporetto. But worse still was the news from the east, where the Russians ceased to be an ally and were now out of the war.

On 3 March 1918 the Kaiser was drinking champagne to celebrate the Russo-German peace which was being signed at Brest-Litovsk. Russia had to give up all claims to the Baltic provinces, Poland, White Russia (Belarus), Finland, Bessarabia, the Ukraine and the Caucasus. The price the Bolsheviks were paying amounted to one third of Russia's 1914 population and arable land and nine-tenths of her coalfields.[100] The victory of the Germans in the east freed three thousand German guns and one million men for deployment in the west. Ludendorff, the German Commander-in-Chief, was planning a knock-out blow against the allies in the west, before the United States of America could begin to make a serious contribution. There were to be a series of complex thrusts in France aimed at dividing and then smashing the British and French armies. New methods of attack had been devised, relying on stealth, surprise bombardment, infiltration and gas. The code name given to this defining battle in the west was Kaiserschlacht, 'the Kaiser's Battle'.[101]

After the Brest-Litovsk peace, everyone knew a big German offensive in the west was inevitable. On Monday 18 March 1918, Churchill, who was then a Minister but with direct experience of the front, having served five months in 1916 with the 9th Division, was sent by Lloyd George to meet Haig and report. They agreed that the main threat was not in Flanders, but on a fifty-mile stretch of the front which the British had just taken over from the French. Here, just north of the Oise River, fifty-seven British divisions faced 110 German divisions. Haig was expecting an attack daily. Churchill then went and spent the next two days inspecting the defences of the 9th Division. On Wednesday evening General Tudor, commanding the 9th Division, told Churchill, 'It is certainly coming now. Trench raids this evening have identified no less than eight enemy battalions on a single half-mile of front'. At 4 am Churchill awoke in the silence, and then at 4.40 am, he heard mines going off, sapped beneath British positions. Churchill wrote later, 'Exactly as a pianist runs his hands across the keyboard from treble to bass, there rose in less than one minute the most tremendous cannonade I shall ever hear'. All communications were cut, gas spread over the artillery parks and machine-gun nests, and a flame of the bombardment lit Churchill's cabin. He went out on to the duckboards and met Tudor. The general said, 'This is it.' A few minutes after 6.00 am, 500,000 Germans emerged from dense fog outnumbering the defenders four to one.[102]

Churchill drove by car to Peronne shortly before the road was cut, and then returned to London. The following day contact between the British and French had been broken. Back in London, Churchill was asked by a desperate Lloyd George whether the Expeditionary Force could be kept intact now that its intricate trench system had been overrun and the soldiers were reeling back. Churchill answered, 'Every offensive loses its force as it proceeds. It is like throwing a bucket of water over the floor. It first rushes forward, then soaks forward, and finally stops altogether until another bucket can be brought. After thirty or forty miles there will certainly come a considerable breathing space, when the front can be reconstituted if every effort is made.'

Churchill's analysis of the military situation turned out to be correct. The Germans, even with overwhelming odds in their favour, could not keep up their offensive for more than a few weeks before running out of reserves, ammunition and fodder. There just was not the back-up to exploit their initial breakthrough. The hoped-for knock-out blow in the west petered out. But there was no inevitability about this result, despite the German supply problems so far from their railheads, where the transport of munitions by horse required huge amounts of fodder.[103] Without the skilfully executed fighting retreat of the British – the most difficult of military manoeuvres – the outcome might have been disaster. The 9th Division fought from 21 to 27 March, retreating over the Somme area, which had cost so many lives in 1916. It was in action again from 4 April to 26 April stemming a German offensive in Flanders at the Lys. In these two periods in the Kaiser's Battle, the Division suffered 8,985 casualties. The South African Brigade* suffered such serious casualties, especially on 24 March at Marrieres Wood, when they fought until they were overwhelmed by death or capture,[104] that the Brigade could not be reconstituted. This was the same Brigade that in 1916 had fought at the Somme, with 121 officers and 3,032 other ranks on the first day and 29 officers and 751 other ranks at roll call on 21 July 1916. Churchill in the World Crisis described the South African Brigade, waiting for the start of the Kaiser's Battle, as 'Serene as Leonidas and his men before the Battle of Thermopylae'.[105]

During most of the Great War, the soldiers were seldom kept informed properly by the military authorities but rather were given highly misleading accounts of the military situation. This was not designed primarily to keep military secrets, in case they fell into enemy hands, but in a mistaken belief that news should be upbeat for morale purposes. The New Armies especially disliked being treated this way. This misleading and somewhat paternalistic approach to news dissemination was carried on by the Army until

---

* One battalion of the South African Brigade, being largely of Scottish extraction, wore kilts of the Murray of Atholl tartan.

the 'Kaiser's Battle'. General Haig on 11 April, however, was forced to admit the gravity of the situation, and made an appeal to the Army to fight to the last man, with 'Backs to the Wall'. According to the Divisional History, from then on the official communiqués gained significantly in reliability. It said that men who had fought in a battle like Loos 'were exasperated to find it reported in the Press as a great British victory'. 'British Official', formerly the hall-mark of truth, had become a dubious phrase, and the practice of soothing the timid by toning down reverses was more than counterbalanced by a loss of faith in the veracity of the British Government. The change of approach, according to the Divisional History, unquestionably led to a raising of morale in the Army.[106]

Sunday afternoon, 14 April 1918

We out here are living continuously in a state of excitement and have had many experiences thrust on us just lately. All the old style of warfare has vanished meantime and we are at grips every other day with a very powerful and clever foe. We in this Ambulance know it is certainly costing many lives to stem the rush. But we also know it is costing the enemy terrible losses for every inch of ground he gets.[107] All this is keeping us very busy. We are hoping that this stir will finish the war very soon.

Monday, 22 April 1918

I did not manage to get your letter written last night, but must get one off before tomorrow's mail. I received your very welcome letter of Wednesday 17th and was very glad to get it lovey for I have been very tired and weary of all this fighting and the constant work among blood, and through time the strain does tell on even the best of us, and we get weary and wish it was all finished. I had a short letter from Davy today but no news other than that he is well and is feeling the terrible heat.

This place where we are at present was, before the severe fighting started, a fairly big hospital. They have moved further back now to safer quarters and we are using it as a Dressing St. There is a very big military cemetery of ours just beside us and Willie Fraser is buried in it. We all visited it first day we were here and Jock managed to get some flowers planted. The night before last Fritz came over as usual and dropped one of his bombs right at the foot of Willie's grave, but luckily did not disturb it, only splintered the little cross a bit. It makes one very wild, this sort of thing, for he must know that it is an Hospital and that is twice we have had our Dressing St. bombed since the retreat commenced.

Saturday 27 April 1918 Night

I was delighted to have your letters yesterday with further good news as to how you are getting on. You seem to be picking up your strength splendidly lovey and no one is better pleased to hear it than myself. No, as you remark dear, I shall not forget that awful night at Belle's, although I was hardly prepared for the terrible stunning news the Dr. imparted to me in the morning like a thunderbolt. It was that standing or rather pacing up and down where you saw me as you passed to the operating theatre dear waiting until you were safely through your operation that I shall never forget. It was the worst trial of my life, and I have had a few trying moments since I came back from leave. And then that night at Monaville. God but I was afraid to look the facts square in the face, things were so critical, but that is all over now and you are recovering your strength, thank God, and I expect you will have better strength than you ever had before.

I had a nice letter from Pete the other day and he managed to give me an idea where he is – not where you said dear, but not far from it I believe. I am still hoping to see him especially these days when we are being moved about so much. We are some distance from Pete North, but I dare say the papers will tell you that, as I see they do not hide our whereabouts nor that it is the most critical position in the line at present, and God but we know that, and what it means – battles are almost daily occurrences and such grim death struggles.

I have been on all sorts of jobs since the retreat started on 22 March, stretcher-bearing, dressing, and once or twice doing a little bit of sprinting to keep from spending the remainder of my soldiering in Germany. We had a tight fit not many days ago. At present I am dressing in the Dressing St. and to tell you the truth darling, the sights are more trying to me now than ever before. Not one of us are the same so far as that goes. Lately it has been too constant and one gets so very tired of the whole thing. Within the last two days the Ambulance have had bad luck and old Fritz captured six of the Ambulance lads, and we are all anxious to hear how they have fared. I trust they get safely over it. At times he is not so particular as one would wish even with the Red Cross men. We shall all be pleased when we are shifted out of this dangerous sector. But times are much too stirring to give troops a rest. Perhaps they will improve before long.

It is surprising how the civil population stick on to the last moment. To see them wheeling barrows etc, men women and children during the retreat, was rotten, but to see some of them knocked out as we had to today was enough to make one curse. One case was a boy like oor Pete, younger I should think, and I am sure he had five bad wounds, and did not make much ado about them as many soldiers would have done. Poor wee chap I felt very sorry for him, to see him so badly hit, and that wee, he only took up half the stretcher. His elder brother had a bad one in the mouth. They should not be allowed near the line at all, but will not go so long as they are able to make a franc out of Tommy.

As to my health dear, I am fine and strong, just tired, and feel so with the whole damn business, day after day, the same bloody game. But then I must not write to you in this strain. At times one must get just a little of the facts into one's letters. If it would finish this year, my word but we would be smiling eh dearie? I will see such a mighty difference in you next time I come home. Of course you know all leave has been stopped and we are not hopeful of it opening again. I was very lucky as only two got leave after I went, and no one has gone since I came back. My lucky star never fails me seemingly.

PAINTING AMONG THE APPLE BLOSSOMS

After the desperate battles during the German onslaught in March and April 1918, the 9th Division left the line on 26 April 1918, having lost the majority of its strength as casualties, although there was comfort in that half of the casualties were prisoners.[108] *The Division stayed out of the line until 24 May 1918. Nowhere else in Willie's letters is there such an exuberance about the beauty of nature, which is captured in his best picture of the war – his 'Tents among the Apple Trees' – a picture that veritably radiates vibrancy. At the same time the soldiers had a stream in which to bathe. It was a type of scene that left almost as much of an impression on the soldiers' minds as the battles themselves, given their intense sense of relief at their own survival. Edmund Blunden, in the poem* The Guard's Mistake, *talked of such a scene, with 'cherry clusters beckoning every arm', and a 'stream wrinkling by with playful foam', but the main idea being the same as Willie's, that the 'surrounding pastoral' could make you 'forget' until, as always in the Army, the gruff voice of the sergeant-major calls you away.*

During the Great War Willie painted and drew pictures as often as he could. For serving soldiers who were artists, the act of painting was often as important as the images they created. For some it was a bridge to the pre-war world, or a creative outlet amid the death and destruction all around. For others there was a determination to make an accurate record as a counter to the imagined heroics of the illustrators – such as S. Begg's illustration of the Battle of Loos. But for most, painting's greatest solace was as a transport and escape from the tedium, hardships and danger of a soldier's existence. Willie painted portraits, landscapes, ruined buildings like the Cathedral at Arras and ordinary scenes of soldiers such as the inside of the Advanced Dressing Station at Bazentin le Petit during the Battle of the Somme or a French estaminet occupied by soldiers. The pictures form a historical record as well as showing what Willie thought interesting and important. The picture of the Advanced Dressing Station at Bazentin le Petit shows wounded Scottish soldiers in their kilts and aprons sitting waiting to be treated along with wounded Germans in their field grey uniforms. Black and white sketches of the swamps of Passchendaele drawn in the St Julien Pillbox show an early tank. His 'Roll of Honour' for Christmas 1917 is both a picture and an act of piety to be shared with the survivors of Passchendaele. It is very different to the Divisional Christmas card of that year which is upbeat and heroic. There is no pathos on the Divisional

172

Christmas card. War is camouflaged and familiarized. The Division's battle honours are wrapped round a garland of holly and men with rifles and bayonets follow the Christmas Star.

14 May 1918

We are still in good quarters and well back. We are feeling the benefit of the change and hope that it is a long time yet before we have to go up among the muck etc again. I have been sent with one section of the Ambulance on a detachment, and as we are away from H.Q. and most of the officers, we are able to get on with what little work we have and rest after. This is quite a delightful little place, well in the country, and there is a clear stream at the bottom of the field where we can have a daily bath weather permitting. It has been very wet these last two days, which spoils the whole aspect of things, but is much nicer today and looks like good weather ahead.

I received a letter from you just before we were sent on here, but have had none since coming here as yet. Wed 8th was the last, and to hear that you had been able to take a short walk was just splendid dear. How I wish I could just be there to give you my strong arm to lean on.

16 May 1918

We are indeed in a nice quiet place looking after a few Div. sick. The weather has been perfect these last three days and I have taken full advantage of the stream today. It is very hot but a bit sultry. I hope we are not going to have thunder. I have done another little picture of our tent which you shall see in due course dearie. Our rest is gradually working in.

I suppose this temporary lull for our now very famous Div. could not be expected to last long. One of the disadvantages of a fighting reputation is that it has got to be kept up and, believe me, we get every opportunity going so far as being up against it is concerned. But all this dear is 'shop', and while I am here, I wish to forget all about it at least as much as possible. I could be quite supremely happy with just you here lovey mine. The apple trees are in full blossom and look beautiful, and all the countryside, not yet defaced by the ravages of war, looks full of vitality and, in the perfect sunshine, is a tonic from nature to all of us after our late experiences, which we appreciate to the full.

Friday night, 17 May 1918

And so Fergus has been home. I was a little surprised to hear that he had been talking to you about how ill he was. Poor Jock generally put his foot in it. It was not through illness that he left the Ambulance, although that was the means adopted to get him away. But you need not mention this. He had a little trouble with the officers, but say nothing about that wifie. Anyone may be as unlucky any day.

7 June 1918

We are still in the line, but it is fairly quiet and some nights we get a decent sleep, but old Fritz is a great nuisance at night time with his bombing planes. Saw one of the most thrilling air fights before dark last night I have yet seen. It was splendid and we had the pleasure of seeing the German beaten again. There is no doubt of the fact that our air service is superior to his now, although at night time he does make us anxious to a great degree when he comes over. It must be ever so much worse for his men over there with our night planes. It is gradually telling on some of our lads now, even the old ones who have been with us from the beginning, I think them in particular. The chap who sleeps beside me cannot rest at night time, and whenever a plane comes over he is up and away to some hole and I don't see him until the morning. He says his nerve absolutely can't stand it <u>now</u> and to sleep above ground where we are is impossible for him. I have not yet got to that stage thank goodness, but I feel d------ sorry for him and some others who were not always so windy. I think the powers would do well to give men who have been fortunate enough to escape for over 3 years a bit of a turn at home. But that is hardly within the range of possibility with the enemy so much on the offensive as he still is.

Saturday night

I received your post card today which is quite interesting. You are living in a very nice place judging from the photo, and very near the sea front. The weather here is still good, but we have slight trouble in the Ambulance at present. There is an epidemic of sickness of a slight but peculiar kind that is spreading very rapidly just like influenza,[109] but it is making us very short-handed. We have thirty of our unit down with it already, and it appears to be affecting all the units of our Div. Living in cellars continuously with gas always about, I dare say, is the cause. It is quite a mild thing and I dare say will clear off in a day or so.

Monday, 8 July 1918

I am very pleased to say that we have had word about our comrades who were posted missing since the Kemmel battle, and up-to-date five out of the six are reported prisoners in Germany. We are all very pleased, as they were good lads and well, it might have been ourselves. Their folks at home have had a long anxious time waiting on news and, I am sure, afraid of it coming too in case it was the worst. Three of them are young married men. It must be like getting one back from the dead to get news of their safety at home.*

My word they are giving us a severe test – years of this damned lustreless game at the best time of our manhood. But surely we shall be permitted to make up a little some day. I could so easily get quite miserable in this letter dear and I don't want to. That would not brighten your holiday any. You mention 'Fair Week'. My word it sounds like an echo of something away in the past to us exiles. We almost forget what it means.

---

* See letter of 27 April 1918.

Chapter Thirteen

'The Knighthood' of the Air

In a letter of 12 June 1917 Willie describes a German aeroplane being shot down and the pilot jumping out of the burning aeroplane. He wrote that the German airman 'had seen too much to be allowed to escape.' Although he admitted to Jane that it was a gruesome sight, he nevertheless introduced the topic by saying he had seen an exciting fight in the air. In fact throughout the war Willie retained a fascination for air combat, which he must have transmitted to Young Willie, his eldest son, who became a pilot in the Royal Air Force at the beginning of the Second World War. Several reasons made these fights in the air of interest to the soldiers. First these aeroplanes were at the cutting edge of technology, with France, Britain and Germany in a competition to leapfrog each other's designs. Secondly, the air war was one bit of the war which could be seen by the soldiers and this was especially true in the trenches where all you saw was the strip of sky above your head, except if there was an air battle going on. Thirdly, airmen were already national heroes at the outbreak of war because of their conquest of a new frontier of human endeavour. The air war added to an already existing glamour. Finally there was the idea that the battles in the air were paradoxically more like war of old, with combat between heroes and codes of chivalry. Lloyd George referred to the airmen as the 'knighthood of the war'.[110]

'They skim like armed swallows, hanging over the trenches full of armed men, wrecking convoys, scattering infantry,

176

attacking battalions on the march . . . They are the knight-hood of the war, without fear and without reproach. They recall the legends of chivalry, not merely the daring of their exploits, but the nobility of their spirit, and amongst the multitude of heroes, let us think of the chivalry of the air.'

In fact to survive the dogfights, the aces had to be cold-blooded technicians in the art of destroying the other man, like the British ace Edward 'Mick' Mannock with seventy-three 'kills', although blind in one eye. He loathed the idea of aerial combat as sport and the public school ethos that went with the idea. There was no room for chivalry if you wanted to stay alive. He hated the Germans and wanted to kill as many of them as he could. On Mannock's death in July 1918, Ira 'Taffy' Jones, who idolized the ruthless Mannock as a modern hero, sought to avenge the death of his friend. He also shunned the notion of sportsmanship, and had no time for the 'Eton and Sandhurst' type, who condemned his shooting of 'Huns hanging in parachutes' as bad form. By that stage in the war Jones' attitudes were typical, with few of the public school type left alive. Convinced socialists like Mannock were now officers, and the War Office had put a stop to the RFC taking too many public school boys. The age of chivalry in the air, if it had ever existed, was by this stage in the war, dead, although for years after the war the myth persisted. This meant that, up against the aces, new pilots stood little chance. By June 1917 the RFC had thirty-two training establishments, but training time was wholly inadequate, with most new pilots having only fifteen to twenty hours' flight time.[111] The result was that the average life of a scout pilot over Arras in May 1917, was three weeks.[112]

The dogfighting life was not only very dangerous – with more than fifty per cent of British pilots becoming casualties [113] – but it soon mentally and physically affected the ace for the worse. Once the pilots got to the front the stress manifested itself in stomach ulcers, insomnia, nightmares, and the terror of being' flamed', i.e. shot down in flames as Willie described. The British authorities would not countenance parachutes in case they diminished the pilots' fighting ardour,[114] and pilots like Mannock carried a revolver to shoot themselves if their plane caught fire. Even the successful participants – of whatever class or nation – in the

repetitive and unrelenting stress of aerial fighting, all came eventu-
ally to display its characteristic physionomy: 'skeletal hands,
sharpened noses, tight-drawn cheek bones, the bared teeth of a
rictus smile and fixed, narrowed gaze of men in a state of controlled
fear'.[115]

Until 1918 the main function of the aeroplane was reconnais-
sance, especially to give directions to the artillery. In order to do
this, some degree of air control was necessary, and hence the battles
in the air were to keep spotter planes out of your area. A lesser
purpose was ground attack against concentrations of troops, and
other targets. In 1918 British aeroplane production alone was
running at over thirty thousand per year,[116] *and they were used*
increasingly for ground attack, but even with air superiority they
were never a decisive weapon. Some passages by Willie are given
below, because they are a clear commentary on this facet of the
Great War, showing reconnaissance, dogfights and ground attack
with conventional and gas weaponry .

Tuesday, 25 May 1915

Last night we had a great aviation display here. After tea we get to
expect some fun and last night we were not disappointed. Pete and
I secured a window in this building (which has formerly been a
school) where we could see comfortably. Five aeroplanes passed
over us and in a few minutes they were over the enemy's trenches
and then the fun started. Shells by the score were fired at them. We
watched spellbound (for this is very exciting to see) expecting every
second to see some of them being hit. Shells burst over, under and
all round them, they dipped, circled and did everything known to
aviators, and never a one was hit. Of course they were dropping
bombs and viewing the German position and literally tormenting
the life out of the Germans. It was just splendid and grand.
Sometimes they disappeared in the smoke of the bursting shells and
we held our breath till it cleared away and there they were, seemingly quite regardless of their danger, flying as if for their own
pleasure. We knew this scouting of the aeroplanes was for some
purpose and we were right, for they had just got safely back (away
behind us by the way) when the thunder started. Pete and I sat on
the windows till we could not keep our eyes open with sleep and

watched. I could hardly hear Pete for the terrible noise when he said, 'My word Bill what would they say at home if they heard this?' What a terrible artillery duel, and the rattle of the machine guns, and lull in the noise and the rap tap tap of the rifles, and the whole sky lit up like daylight by the fire balls and star shells.

Friday, 16 July 1915

We had a German aeroplane just over our camp this forenoon. It came very close and our men fired scores of shells at it, but it got away. One of our aeroplanes tried to get between it and the German lines, but the German went higher and higher and then what planing at an awful rate high over our man. It was very exciting to see this. How cheaply those men hold their lives, but it is very difficult to bring them down. They fly so high.

24 August 1915

An aeroplane fell here last night and the aviator was dying when we left. Their St. is just over the field and we have daily displays of superb aviation.

28 November 1915

It is a beautiful frosty morning and Sunday. Dear me, how difficult it is to realize that here at the present moment. Some German aeroplanes are overhead and our machine guns are having a rip at them. Of course we all disappear when the whistle goes as we don't want them to give us a 'straffing'. They are sure to do it if they see some men clustered about a dug-out.

Sunday, 7 May 1916

The weather is inclined to rain today and it is dull and of course we have not the usual air excitement, although yesterday the sky was cloudy and we could hear just overhead the spit spit of machine guns – two aeroplanes hard at it, and when the cloud broke up a little, we had a glimpse of the fight in the blue.

Wednesday, 28 March 1917

Bang! 'Mr Allemand' is dropping one or two on the main road today. By the way one of our aeroplanes came down just in the next field today in flames. The airman landed very cleverly and quite unhurt. We saw about thirty go over the lines at once today. It was like a flock of birds, a beautiful sight. So far the big thing has not started on this front, but ------ and that of course is where the censor makes us shut up.

(Don't know the proper date)
Sunday, 12 June 1917 Night

. . . sitting curled up in this dug-out with the various 'little things' occurring just outside to keep one wondering where the next one is going to land and hoping that the concrete above will do its duty faithfully if it gets a sudden shock.

However, we have done not so badly, although Fritz has made all our faces go a trifle white dropping an occasional one too close to us when we were outside to be at all comfortable. Last night we were all wakened at 12.00 am and had to get our gas helmets on 'toot sweet', because of gas shells. The shells are awful things and put the wind up everybody. We dare not be a minute without our helmets on us.

Saw a great air fight the other night. Our planes set fire to a German just overhead. It was a trifle gruesome all the same to see one of the German airmen jump out of the blazing plane and drop to earth before our eyes. War is a very horrid thing all the same and better him than one of our chaps. He had seen too much to be allowed to escape.

Chapter Fourteen

1918

'The Black Day of the German Army' and the Defeat of Germany

'Oh hang it all, I wish Fritz would retreat in trains instead
of running, so that the war would finish sooner
and let me home.'

The 9th Division took over a sector of the line at Meteren on 24
May 1918, where it stayed for three months, capturing the Meteren
Ridge on 19 July 1918 in a well-co-ordinated surprise attack on the
German trenches in broad daylight – referred to by Willie in the
following letter as a successful stunt – with the soldiers going over
the parapet to attack 'like a pack of hounds' according to the
Official History of the War. The night before this tactical success
of the British, the French Army aided by five large American
Divisions, 25,000 strong in their battle order, drove back the
German vanguards which had crossed the Marne three days before
in a final German thrust to capture Paris, the battle being called by
the French 'the Second Marne'.[117]

In July Ludendorff still thought that the German Army retained
some initiative, but its position was precarious. His infantry were
worn out and supplying his horse-drawn artillery with fodder and
ammunition was proving a nightmare. Meanwhile the British
and French had concentrated an unprecedented force of tanks –
530 British and 70 French – for an attack on 8 August in front of
Amiens. The attack, when it came, was the start of the road to
victory, even if only six of the 400 tanks that took part in the attack

were functioning four days later.* But in that period most of the old Somme battlefields had been retaken and by the end of August the German Army had been pushed back to the outworks of the Hindenburg line from where the Allies had been pushed by the offensive in March 1918. Ludendorff called 8 August 1918 'The Black Day of the German Army'.

The three months' offensive by the British after 8 August until the Germans sued for an Armistice at the beginning of November 1918 was marked by a series of Allied successes including the breaking of the Hindenburg Line. Communication was much better with some use of battlefield radio for the first time. The Allies had air superiority and aeroplanes engaged in ground attack. Also the Allies set themselves a number of limited objectives, which amounted to a rolling offensive. The 9th Division took the Hoegenacker Ridge on 18 August, and then had about a month out of the line. In the line again east of Ypres from 22 September, the Division attacked on 28 to 30 September, and then on 1, 14, 20, 22, and 25 October 1918. The rate and depth of the advances was unprecedented. In the course of the war, certain key military positions had acquired Scottish names and were shown as such on the Ordnance Survey maps of the war. The first objective of the 9th and 29th Divisions on 28 September, for example, included the 'Glasgow Spur' and the storming of 'Stirling Castle', which was the name given to the south end of the Passchendaele Ridge.[118]

Although the tactics and strategy adopted by General Haig in the last three months of the war brought complete victory over the German Army, the victory had been sealed by the Allied policy of attrition in the 'wearing-out battles' of 1916 and 1917 – the Somme and Passchendaele. The truth was that the German Army could not win a war of attrition. It did not have the manpower to replace the casualties lost in these battles, and in the Kaiser's Battle. The German Army was running out of materiel, just as the British and American war economies were producing guns and tanks and aeroplanes in ever increasing numbers. Finally the influenza epidemic had killed and weakened large numbers of soldiers.

By contrast the Allies had American aid in prospect – men and materiel. They also had unlimited manpower in their colonial

* Strachan at page 143.

182

empires. The German 'War Manual' [119] claimed that it was an unacceptable method of European War to bring uncivilized troops on to European battlefields where they might behave in a barbaric manner, by for example not respecting women and prisoners. The Germans circulated horror tales of Gurkhas slitting throats to drink blood, in an attempt to shame the French and British not to use Colonial troops. On 4 October 1914 ninety-three of the German Empire's leading intellectuals, artists and scientists published in all the German newspapers and abroad an 'Appeal to the Cultured World', denying any atrocities by the German Army in Belgium and contrasted German innocence with the conduct of Britain and France, who were presenting to the world the 'shameful spectacle of Mongols and Negroes being driven against the white race'.[120]

From the end of 1915 to the end of the war General Haig had command of the Expeditionary Force. Before the Great War he had worked out the policy of attrition, which, executed properly, would eventually deliver a British victory. He had concluded that the only method to defeat the German Army, if it was on the defensive, was to wear it down until it ran out of reserves. He brought cages of German prisoners to Lloyd George to show their poor physical condition, suggesting that the Germans were now scraping the barrel for proper manpower. His optimism was often premature, but his prediction was eventually vindicated. Later Haig was virulently attacked by Lloyd George,[121] and in the post-Second World War play and film Oh What a Lovely War he was again caricatured on the blithe assumption that other methods of warfare might have offered a much easier route to victory. However, Haig had been innovative, enthusiastically embracing gas, tanks, aeroplanes and radio, in an attempt to gain advantages that might lessen the dependence on attrition. But none of these weapons proved decisive. Despite the setbacks, however, Haig clung to his belief that he was God's chosen instrument to defeat the Germans [122] and after the war he was given the estate of Bemersyde on the River Tweed, paid for by the public subscription of a grateful nation. He was buried in 1928 in Dryburgh Abbey alongside Sir Walter Scott, whose poetry and novels had done so much to revive medieval notions of chivalry in the imagination of nineteenth century Europe.

183

Monday, 22 July 1918

I have just come down from the line today, having been sent up a few days ago in a hurry for a stunt (that was very successful). I had no kit of any description and could not of course write.

Our Div. gave old Fritz a bit of a stir up on Friday morning and we had almost as many wounded Germans to attend to as our own. Most of them are (like ourselves) very fed up. The news all round is brighter and one hopes that it will all help to finish it off soon. If we could just hope for it finishing this year, what a brightness it would bring into our lives right away. Then our innings would start and not before time.

Sunday, 5 August 1918

The situation out here has been very critical for a long time now but things are much better now I believe and we are beginning to think that the German is having his last fling. One cannot be certain of course, a day makes a big change in everything and often on the whole outlook. In our good moments we think that it shall surely finish this year and we like to think so. I think Davie must be in the fighting area in the East now according to Joe's letter received yesterday. He is seeing around a bit. So long as he keeps his health, the experience will do him lots of good.

Thursday night, 22 August 1918

I have two of your letters to answer now and both of them splendid letters too. I received that grand fat one tonight when I arrived back at this billet about an hour ago after a fairly hard day's work at ADS and it is splendid. The other I received the day of our stunt (which was very successful*) when we were very busy indeed and how much I enjoyed it is more than I can put in writing. I am sitting in my corner of this billet writing before our lights go out, and the heat, well it is almost unbearable. Today has been dreadful. The exertion of changing one's mind was sufficient to bring the sweat pouring out and tonight it is so close that it is dropping drip by drip

---

* The capture of the Hoegenacker Ridge.

from my face as I write – phew we shall have thunder before long I fancy. I hope it is cooler on Saturday, the day we pull out of this part after a stay of three months. It will be a great change to be down again. I wonder how long they will give us this time.

By gum Davie is seeing this old globe of ours quickly. I wish they had taken our Div. out there for a spell. He should have collected some very interesting little experiences by the time he gets home. It would be a great education for a youngster like him. I shall be very pleased to meet Kate Smith's boy. I dare say I shall meet him when we get out. What Battalion is he in, do you know? As far as the Paris leave, that is completely knocked on the head meantime. However I am not troubling much over that trifle. I wonder where Pete has shifted to. I think I know, and I dare say we shall all have a turn down there before long. Isn't old Fritz fairly getting it in the neck these days? We captured lots the other day. And well they looked pleased to be out of it to say the least. Oh I hope dear that the end of it all is near now. It is so terribly sickening and sad. Victories mean more than most folks at home imagine or ever will in waste of good valuable life.

I was very pleased to hear Mary visited Kilsyth and enjoyed her visit. I wish I had been there too, dear. Ach, but I am wishing that every minute of the day. I feel just as lonely now as I did four years ago when I first left. I am sure you must feel ever so far away, the force of this heart longing I have for you. Does it not convey my message to you at times when there is no letter to hand dearie? I am sure it must. There is one of the loveliest rottenest full moons anyone would wish to see (or wish anywhere but shining so brightly, showing aeroplanes, everything like daylight) shining tonight and it of course augurs a restless night. I dare say many of the farmers at home will be rubbing their hands and saying, 'What a splendid harvest moon etc'. We of course have our own special way of expressing our appreciation of such a beauty as is shining tonight. I must close now pet. Time is up. We shall be preparing for our move tomorrow, but I will try and get time to continue my letter. There you are three blasts of the whistle already, which means enemy aircraft over. He is up to time tonight – the sod.

185

Friday

We are getting a fine Divisional mark to wear on our tunics sleeves, a lovely wee thistle (white metal) on a blue background of cloth, and we are all very proud of it of course, especially old originals who were formed with the Div. four years ago. Have not heard from Pete just lately and am looking forward to one from him soon. It is exactly two years and three months since I saw him. It seems strange that we have not had the luck to meet. However, we are always keeping our eyes skinned for the chance when we do get near enough each other.

Friday, 6 September 1918

I was greatly pleased to have your letter of Sunday yesterday, and yes I received the postcard the day before with Milroy's address. It is not possible for me to see him at present as his Battalion is lying a considerable distance from where we are, but, now that I know his address, I shall look out for him. We are still out, but we in this Hospital are being kept very busy indeed, but we do not mind that in the least. We are in good quarters and feed well at present, and the work is not uncongenial and great advantage, as I said before, is we have not the SM flashing around all day long as he usually does when we are working an Ambulance Hospital of our own. It has rained quite a lot lately but during the night mostly, the days being very warm. By the way Bob Peter went to Paris for seven days yesterday morning. So far there is no word of mine. He (the SM) has acted so badly with mine in delaying it and sending in passes for new chaps before their turn that most of the boys are a bit disgusted at his attitude. However such is life and well I don't really care.

Thursday evening, 13 September 1918

We have been marching these last two days and have just finished our distance for today. My feet of course are a trifle sore as yesterday's was in very heavy rain and a full day's trek. Well dearie I just want to give you a note to keep you from worrying, can't say whether we will be able to get them posted or not, but I hear we stay at this place or farm till the day after tomorrow and have another march somewhere. Of course we have finished our 'rest'.

Sunday night, 23 September 1918

Ach I am so tired of being away and the atmosphere of our unit is worse now than ever. We who came out with it are pretty much in the background now. So we keep aloof and are allowed to do so. It is a weary life this with so much in it that goes against the grain, perpetual discipline that any Tom, Dick or Harry can work against you if they feel inclined and if they are just out of the ranks. I do not say it is unbearable, but oh my word, what a glorious day it will be when we are free and need take nothing from any man, unless we want to, when one can think, speak and act for oneself and not be at the beck and call of any NCO whether he is a fool or otherwise. It has always been hateful to me, but well, we bound ourselves to it on our own without force. But the years are getting numerous and I am heartily sick of it. There is one thing another year should bring us very near home again, I think so. What's the use of despairing eh dear? No not now after so long. One often is inclined to get very tired at the last lap, but that is silly. So we will just carry on as usual and live in hope that soon it will be over and we shall be permitted to take up our lives where we left off four years ago.

Sunday, 29 September 1918

Our stunt started yesterday and we have had great success, more than we expected, and still it goes on of course. We had a hit again – four of our Ambulance lads were killed last night and three wounded the day before. It is very sad about the chaps who were killed. One of them is one who joined up with us. He was only three days off leave and is the fifth son his mother has given; five killed in one family. Isn't it dreadful? We have lots to thank God for when we compare our lot to that family dear. The other one is our tailor who was up with a Battalion for the first time. So far I have not had to go up this stunt, still being with Headquarters. So you need not worry about me dearie, and there is just the possibility that when I do go up, the worst may be over because the Boche is being forced out of positions here that he has held since the beginning of the war and when he is properly on the run our job is not so dangerous. We are kept very busy at this Hospital owing to so many of the Ambulance being further up. We have all three or four men's work to do, but we do not grumble about that. Every day brings changes now and one does not have the faintest idea where one is going to be sent before a day is out. The results are glorious these days and you have no idea how much heart it gives one, hoping and believing that every day helps on the end of the whole dreadful business.

Monday, 30 September 1918 Night

I was delighted with your letter of Wednesday 25th received today. We are at present up to the neck in work preparing to go up into the line tomorrow. The order came very suddenly today. It is a big battle and the rotten weather conditions have made it well nigh impossible to properly clear the wounded from the field, and so we have all got to go up and work. It has rained continuously since last night and only those who know this country can understand what that means during a battle such as is raging here. We have been hard hit again. Two of the boys were killed yesterday and, worse than anything to us, one of the two is James Brown of Canal Street, the Kirkie lad I told you about some time ago who joined us three months ago. Poor Jimmie he had made himself well liked with the boys and now he is dead. We feel this casualty very much, we Kirkie chaps. Please do not say anything to any outsiders or his people dear until it is confirmed. He proved himself a very brave soldier since he has been with us.

WAR IN THE IMAGINATION OF BOYS

In the following letter Willie explodes in anger at his younger brother, Joe. The reason for this outburst was that Joe had been caught volunteering for the Army, although only sixteen. At the time he volunteered very few at home expected the war to end so soon, especially a war that had defied all previous predictions. Willie was furious because he thought Joe had let down Jane's sister's husband, Bob Dickson, who had got Joe an apprenticeship as a draughtsman in the Lion Foundry in Glasgow where he was a manager. By risking his life in the Army, Joe was also giving his mother unnecessary worry and throwing away chances that the men at the front would envy him for. Willie was all for dragging others kicking and screaming into the Army, but never thought that his younger brothers should have to go, being very protective of them.

If the scale of the numbers of Kitchener's volunteers confounded the pre-war pacifists, who doubted that a country could be mobilized in the way it was, volunteering was perhaps more understandable at the beginning of the war, when a taste for adventure and ignorance of the nature of modern warfare was mixed with patriotism. By 1918 the truth about the risks of service on the Western Front had reached most homes, even if they did not appreciate the nature of the horrors. The fact that volunteers came forward throughout the war in considerable numbers showed just what reserves of patriotism Britain had.[123] Although throughout the war schools in Britain stepped up the teaching of martial poetry,[124] and innumerable 'Boys Own' style books were circulated, emphasizing British gallantry, fighting prowess, and spirit of sacrifice[125] – with war glamourized and portrayed as an exciting game – Joe, Willie's brother, had no illusions about the war. He had absorbed what war meant from Willie's letters, which were read to the family. He knew the risks of service in France. We can see this in his school essay book. At the beginning of 1916 aged thirteen – a few months after the Battle of Loos – he was marked 'Good' for the following imagined account of 'My experience as a Private in the Army':*

When war was declared I resolved to join the army. I left my work and joined the Black Watch or the Gallant 'Forty Twa'. I was put to training down in England. After six months strenuous training we left Southampton. We were going where fate might lead. It was France. Day after day we came nearer and soon we got use to shell fire. It was a bright night in September when our battalion were ordered up to the trenches. We

---

* This essay is copied as it was written including mistakes.

prepared for the open plain that lay beyond. Countless numbers of areaplanes seemed to be over us. At certain intervals the sky would become lit up with these wonderful german star shells. We arrived in the trenches more or less worn-out. These horrible places where hundreds have died for their liberty, were nearly two feet deep with mud. We knew by this time that something dreadful was going to take place in the morrow.

An intense bombardment was going on further down the line. Some of our younger chaps seemed to lose their heads. I was glad when the dawn came, but now I saw very pointedly the desolation around us, for we were near a large village which had been blown to atoms. We were told that we were to charge at a certain time. Now and again we saw an areoplane being brought down. At last the word came and 'Charge' sounded right down the line. Up and over the parapets, no time for hesitating, and now out and get revenge, but 'Oh! The horror, the felling, the agonised groan of a comrade, the sight in front of us, Germans slaughtered and hundred holding up their hands, 'Mercy, camarades', they say, Men raving mad on the barb wire, that terrible ordeal which they came through. Hundreds, nay thousands lying dead and wounded with that terrible stain of their khaki. Who invented War? No, we had seen war in its truest form and also the awful consequences of war. I was running on when I heard the words, 'Gas, Gas'. Although I had my respirator on, I hadn't it fix right and now I was gassed. Oh! The sensation which went through me. I fell and I knew no more.

When I came round I thought I was still fighting the Germans and my first thought was to go for the orderly that lay beside me. 'Where am I ' he answered me. At last it dawn me that was in hospital through gas poisoning, and that I had came through the Battle of Loos.

I am home in England but I haven't got over the gas yet. I am progressing favourably.

Joe's surviving essay book has essays on the Royal Navy and other aspects of the war set by the teacher during the war. All the descriptions are graphic, showing that even at the schoolboy level, the censors could not really keep the horrors of the war from the people. The greatest shock evinced is at the German sinking of neutral merchant shipping. In 1916 he wrote, 'In order to carry out their frightfulness, as we call it, the Germans have to use all the treacherous devices they can get. They attack merchant ships of the non-combatant class which is against all the modes of warfare.'

Wednesday, 9 October 1918 Night

I received your grand letter of the 2nd and also your note today informing me about Pete. I also had one from Pete along with yours today. At first it was a great shock to me. But as Pete tells me he is feeling quite good again, I think it is the best thing that could have happened to him for it has taken him out of some very severe fighting his Div have had in their sector just lately.* I was getting very anxious about him, knowing what was going on. I dare say he will be kept at the base a considerable time and may get to Blighty; which would be the goods, as he would probably escape the winter out here and may, with his long service out here, check for a staff job. If he does not get over, he is going to try and get back to this unit beside me when he is drafted up the line again, and that would be glorious, for we would be together again. Yes as you say dear it would be a boon to get some sort of coucy [*presumably* 'cushy'] wound and get a turn home for a change. I assure you the prospect of the winter is not cheery, but I believe we shall not require to do another out here.

We have been very busy these days doing mostly spade work. This city [Ypres] is war famous, but what a sight it is – no one could possibly describe the absolute ruin of it and he still shells it. However I fancy it will not be long until he is forced back out of range. I am in very good health darling and early prospect of the war being finished is bucking us up great. Bob Peter is on this detachment along with me (the Ambulance are back working a sick Hospital). Can't say how long we shall be away from them. Bob Peter will be home Tuesday or Wednesday and will be calling of course and can give you all the news as to how I get on.

My word but I am dreadfully angry with Joe. I feel I could give

---

* Pete was gassed, which was reported at the time in the *Kirkintilloch Herald*.

him a hiding he would remember for acting as he is doing. If he does not act honourably by Mr Dickson, I shall never forgive him after all that has been done for him. Let him be careful or he will be the sorry man. My word to think that a kid like him should give Mother so much worry these days, when after the chances she has given him. And we who are away would give anything to be in his shoes. If he wants to go, let him do so. <u>He will soon be cured of that</u>, but surely he can do it in a more manly way. I am very cut up about the way he is acting to Mr Dickson. I am going to write a note to Pete now as I shall not be in bed until 3.00 am, being on Guard tonight. It is a very eerie job in such a place as this.

22 October 1918

I am sorry I have not been able to write so often lately, but you must know it is because we have had very exceptional times lately. This has been a big advance and of course it keeps us always on the move following the infantry. Stunts have been more numerous this last month than ever before and we are over thirty miles from our starting point. We are in a newly captured village working a post for wounded in the school room. I am in the very best of health. So you must not worry about me. There is no doubt about it, advancing is much more interesting than what we have had in the last four years. Our good old Div. have licked Fritz hollow up here and made quite a name again. Will give you more news later. I have no more word about my month's leave, can't expect it just yet while things are as they are with us.

Thursday night, 4 November 1918

We are working a very large hospital dearie and, except for the air raids, quite safe. Of course this is supposed to be our rest. It is a change certainly from our last experience, but there is a great deal to do. I received your papers yesterday and also the letter of Friday last giving me an account of your visit to 58. I should just have loved to have been able to pop in and find Mother and you nodding. I think I would love to come now for good darling I am so tired. The prospect of this winter does not by any means cheer us up. Every one makes us feel the strain more. If leave would only

192

go a little quicker, it would not be so bad. It has been increased now to fourteen days, which is a great deal better. The prospect of fourteen days with you lovey mine is a great stimulant indeed. I don't know how it is but I feel very inclined to mope and get more sick and fed up every day. It is not a good way to be in, for it makes everything so much harder. I dare say I should be able to shake the feeling off and keep smiling again.

Friday night

Just received your letter of Sunday last and very refreshing it was to me. I hope you have received my letter alright. I wrote when we came out at first opportunity. I am wearying very very much dearie, as I dare say you know, and will wait counting the days till my leave comes round. Your advice to look on the bright side etc is certainly the best; if one does otherwise, misery is the result. I forgot in my last two letters to mention that Captain Jack got the Military Cross, and very pleased we from Caurnie are, for he has worked very conscientiously since ever he came to the Ambulance.

8 November 1918

You will be thinking I am getting lazy with letters, but we have had a big Div. inspection by the King of the Belgians and his Queen,* and we had lots of parades and practice for the march past and polishing kit which has kept us very busy. It was a very wet day, but a very stirring sight all the same.

I was very sorry to hear about T. Money's death. What a dreadful blow to Sal. I am very sorry for her indeed and please convey my sympathy to her next time you see her. Yes as you say Pete is certainly having lots of lady visitors at base. I hope he is allowed to remain there for a long time yet. I had a long letter from him the other day and wrote him all my news. He wanted to know all about

* According to the Divisional History, on 5 November 1918 the whole Division was reviewed by HM the King of the Belgians. After the ceremony HM the Queen of the Belgians requested General Tudor to cut from his sleeve the divisional sign (a silver thistle on a blue background); he did so, and then she pinned it on her breast. Ever after that the GOC wore only one badge (see *Ewing* at page 383).

this month's leave etc. By the way, is there any word of Dave getting leave soon? The war is pretty well finished now, but I dare say it will be some time before we all get home, but so long as they get the fighting finished, we can stick it until we are able to get home.

So far there is no more word about my month but we are out of the line dearie and it would be much better to have the month's leave when the Div. are in action, but if I had my way I would be home now dearie. I weary so much to be with you again. Keep cheery dearest and keep looking forward to it. It will come surely and you know what glorious times you and I will have then. We are having very wet weather these days. One good thing about that is that it keeps old Fritz from booming at night. I am in very good health dear; in fact the best. I hope you are taking great care of yourself when this 'flu' is so prevalent. I get quite anxious when I read about it in the papers dearie mine.

Willie's Final Diary Entry of the War

Armistice night or rather the night of 10 November 1918 about 11 o'clock, we received official news that the Armistice was a certainty and will not try to describe that night of riotous joy. Nothing could hold us. We all went mad for one full night. This was naturally the preliminary to what seems to me the greatest moment of the war, the event which brought the fact home to us that it was over and marked our success beyond our dreams, the moment when we had the order the Div. will commence to march to the Rhine on the 17th. One could not at first realize what this meant, what this portended, the enemy beaten completely, the allies advancing right up to his most important strategic military barrier, the river which has figured so often in history and which now marks the final stage in the greatest war of all time, in whose bloody embrace all nations were locked with a power that tended at one time during those awful years to crush them.

Epilogue

In terms of the Armistice the Germans were to withdraw all their forces over the Rhine and allied troops were to advance and occupy the German west bank of the Rhine. They were also to cross the Rhine and occupy bridgeheads at Coblenz, Mainz and Cologne. The British Army was to occupy the Cologne bridgehead. It was decided in the days after the Armistice that the 9th (Scottish) Division would have the 'honour' of being the only New Army division to march via Waterloo to the Rhine and establish the British bridgehead. Willie's 9th Division began the march to the Rhine on 14 November 1918.[126] They arrived on 9 and 10 December and crossed by the Muhlheim Bridge of Boats at Cologne on 13 December 1918, with bagpipes playing 'All the blue bonnets are over the border' – the same tune that the most famous bagpiper of the war, Piper Laidlaw VC of the KOSB had played marching up and down the parapet at Loos.

Willie served in the British Army of Occupation of the Rhineland until his discharge in May 1919. The Army of Occupation stayed until 1929. Apart from the desperation to get home, life was easy with all sorts of entertainments laid on for the soldiers, including in his case a visit to the Cologne Opera to see Wagner's The Valkyrie. *He was deeply impressed with this aspect of German culture and wrote to Jane, 'It is quite beyond my powers of description to tell you how wonderful it was. I have never heard such beautiful music and singing, and the whole thing was superb and whacks home productions hollow. I will enclose you my Guide,*

195

which you must keep for me. The piece was from the 'Nibelung's Ring' by Wagner.'

On a grimmer note, Willie was an eye-witness to the starvation of the German population which was inflicted on them as a deliberate act of policy by the Allies in order to force them to accept the peace terms – a policy which, according to Winston Churchill threw away the moral victory of the war and helped pave the way for Hitler. The starvation was caused by the continuation of the wartime Naval Blockade, bringing death to hundreds of thousands of Germans. On 3 March 1919 Winston Churchill, who by then was Secretary of State for War, told Parliament that his officers had reported that Germany was on the verge of complete social and national collapse through hunger and malnutrition. Germany was like a 'besieged town'. Lloyd George told the Allied Conference at Spa in March that the British troops were indignant about the Allied refusal to revictual Germany and that General Plumer had advised him that he could not be responsible for his troops if children were allowed to wander about the streets half-starved.

Willie wrote in his diary, 'There is no doubt whatever but that the German is suffering from the Blockade. I have seen kids wait for hours on the off-chance of getting from a soldier what he usually throws in the swill, and also men have been forced to beg for permission to lift what we would give to pigs.' He talked of restaurants accepting scraps on the plates as payment for cooking rations because food was unobtainable. Against the blind working of the official policy he mentioned individual acts of kindness to the Germans by the British soldiers, 'The Iron Cross I have is a real one given to me by the German who won it while fighting against our own Div at Kemmel Hill April 1918. I gave him a small luxury for his sick mother, and protested when he offered me his medal in payment. "The medal is useless to me," he said, "Germany is finished".'

Appendix

The Prayer, *which draws on a real incident described to Jane in a letter,* * *was completed in 1929 and was voted best new one act play in Scotland in 1930. It was the first attempt in Scotland to portray life in the trenches in a totally realistic manner.*[127] *This realistic approach had also not been tried in the English theatre until R.C. Sherriff's play* Journey's End, *which was performed in the previous year. Audiences had never been shown before on the English stage, according to Sherriff, 'how men really lived in the trenches, how they talked and how they behaved.'*[128] *Both plays employ the same motif of the soldier dying, just when he thought he was safe – in the case of Sherriff's soldier because he thought he had caught a 'blighty', and, in the case of Willie's soldier, because he was going on leave the following day and would miss the forthcoming battle. This motif of hope dashed is now common in literature on war. Paul Fussell, in his book* The Great War and Modern Memory *suggests that the motif is a virtual allegory of political and social cognition in our time.*[129] *In 1931* The Prayer *was performed at the 27 Field Ambulance Veterans' Association Annual Reunion. One veteran later wrote to Willie that he could almost feel the smell of the blood and dirt from the trenches as he watched.*

* See letter of 12 November 1917.

The Prayer
by
W. St Clair

CHARACTERS

Corporal Peake RAMC — An Englishman.
Private Jeffrey RAMC — A young Soldier.
Private Jock Shaw, Argylls. — A Scotchman.
Captain Linn, RAMC — A Doctor.
Private Dick MacAlister, RAMC — A Scotchman
Padre Hall. — Of the South African Brigade.

Jerry. — A German Soldier.
1st Stretcher-Bearer. — A Cockney.
2nd Stretcher-Bearer.

THE SCENE

The Scene is the interior of a captured German pillbox at St Julien, France, during a lull in the battle of Passchendaele, October 1917. It is being used as an Aid Post by a Field Ambulance of the RAMC attached to a Scottish Division. There is an opening back right, opening to battle country, but during the action of the play this opening is covered with an Army blanket. The door is built into the wall to show the thickness of the pillbox with the blanket on the inside. Inside this opening going right is another section of

198

the pillbox used by officers. Down left is a small collapsible table which is covered with white gauze. On it there are three small enamelled bowls, one holding gauze dressings, one cotton wool swabs, the other instruments, forceps etc. A small pile of bandages, a roll of cotton wool, a bottle labelled 'Eusol', a primus stove, a small sterilizer, a hurricane lamp, safety pins etc. An enamelled pail and small basin underneath table, an ammunition box above table. Back centre, a wooden erection to hold three or four stretcher cases.

Back, right, centre a wooden erection to hold three or four stretcher cases.

Centre – a pair of trestles three feet high where the wounded are dressed. A hurricane lamp above.

Down right, a form, an old Army biscuit tin, blankets and a spare stretcher up back, left.

As the curtain goes up Captain Linn, Corporal Peake, and Jeffrey are busy at the trestles dressing a wounded German soldier who appears to be unconscious. Captain Linn (centre) is bandaging the German's head. Peake with the bowl of dressings and a bandage in his hand, left of stretcher, Jeffrey is right, looking on.

There is a pause as they finish the dressing.

Captain Linn:	He is not seriously wounded, although he looks worn out, poor chap.
Peake:	He hasn't spoken a word since he was brought in here, sir.
Captain Linn:	*(To Jeffrey)* Go into the mess and bring a little brandy.
Jeffrey:	Right Sir. *(Goes out door to left)*
Captain Linn:	*(Feeling pulse)* He must have been wounded some time ago.
	He has lost a lot of blood, but I think he will be all right directly.

Peake:	The bearers said he crawled into our lines tonight sir. Must have lost his way. They say he was a sniper.
Captain Linn:	Ah, well, it makes no difference to us what he was; he is wounded.
Peake:	Yes, sir.
	Jeffrey comes in with brandy. Peake lifts up the German's head, while Linn gives the wounded man little sips of brandy which revive him immediately.
Captain Linn:	That's better.
Peake:	Don't know, sir.
	The German has revived and looks around, then at officer.
CaptainLinn:	Do you understand English?
German:	A little.
Captain Linn:	Feeling better?
German:	Yah, dank you.
Captain Linn:	Good. Are you married?
German:	Yah.
Captain Linn:	Which part of Germany do you come from? *(no answer)*.
Captain Linn:	How long have you been in this part of the line? *(no answer)*.
Captain Linn:	Which regiment do you belong to?
German:	*(In fairly good English)* I am a soldier of the German Army.
Captain Linn:	He doesn't give much away.
Peake:	No sir, but he is to be admired for that.
Captain Linn:	Yes, he answers like a soldier. *(To German)* You'll be alright my man. *(To Peake)* See that he is made comfortable Corporal, until we can get him down, and get him something to eat. I'll be in the Mess if you want me.

Linn goes out door to Officer's quarters. Jeffrey and Peake put blanket over German and tuck it in below him. Then lift off trestles and slip stretcher into erection at back of pillbox.

Peake: There you are Jerry, and I hope your fellows are as good to our chaps over there.

German: Dank you.

Peake: That's alright old sport, you've got guts. I'll say that for you, Jerry or no Jerry.

Peake: *(To Jeffrey)* Get some tea and some Rootie.

Jeffrey: Where will I get it Corporal?

Peake: *(Looking at Jeffrey with a scowl)* Why, at the Trocadero of course. Where the hell do you think you are? Get it next door, he ordered it.

Jeffrey goes out. Peake goes to table to arrange his dressings, etc. Jeffrey comes back with mug of tea and piece of bread, gives it to German, the starts to clean up dirty dressings etc. from floor, into biscuit tin.

Jeffrey: Well, Corporal, this is the first quiet spell we've had since I came up here.

Peake: Yes, we've been kept busy enough lately, considering there's a stunt on.

Jeffrey: I hope we have a quiet night tonight.

Peake: Why?

Jeffrey: *(Tensely)* Oh, it's just terrible for me to see all this suffering. I'm not used to it yet.

Peake: *(Coldly)* You'll soon get used to it, don't fret. You haven't seen anything yet; you'll get lots of practice when the stunt starts.

Jeffrey: Oh I know. It's horrible.

Peake: *(Looking at him)* You're young yet. Take it from me, you're very lucky clicking a job here for a start. Get that into your nut.

201

Jeffrey:	I'm not grumbling Corporal, but I would like to write a letter to home. I haven't written since I came up here and this is my first experience up the line.
Peake:	I see you want to tell the tale to the folks back home, eh? Don't bother, they wouldn't believe you. Send a field post card and try to get a little sleep when you get the chance sonny; you'll need it before long.
	Jeffrey takes biscuit tin with dirty dressings and puts it under form right, then takes writing pad out of his haversack, sits on form and starts to write when Dick MacAllister comes in with full marching kit, valise, haversack, tin hat, etc. He is a rough-looking soldier, with a strong Scottish accent. His boots and puttees are covered with mud, and he looks dirty, coming centre and slipping off valise.
Dick:	*(Brightly)* Hallo Peake, how goes it?
Peake:	Hallo Dick, where did you spring from?
Dick:	*(putting valise and haversack etc. in corner left)* Been attached to the Royal Scots: word sent up from Headquarters to report here.
Peake:	What's up?
Dick	*(Cheerily)* Well, I'm next on the list for leave. My warrant must be in or they widna bring me doon here.
Peake:	No. I don't think it's through yet Dick but I heard that the next batch arrives t-morrow.
Dick:	Good stuff: Ma word, but A feel like twa men and a boy at the prospect of gaun hame tae see the wife and wee Jock. Ye see, I hiv'na seen him yet. Man alive, it fair keeps me aff ma sleep thinkin' aboot it. Ay, an' tae get anither guid snoak o' the air o' Bonnie Scotland maks ma hart loup. Man, Peake, it's a peety ye're no' a Scotsman. *(Giving Peake a slap on the back)*

202

Peake:	*(Sarcastically)* Oh yes, but we can't all be kings you know.
Dick:	Ay, that's quite true, mair's the peety. *(Going and sitting on trestles)* Ma luck's in this time fur yince. There's gauntae be anither stunt, so when ye're uptae the neck in it ye can think o' me hivin the time o' ma life at hame.
Peake:	Oh yes! Rub it in! There's going to be a stunt alright because we have orders to prepare for a rush.
Dick:	*(Thoughtfully)* Weel, it'll be hell getting' the wounded over this country. The Royals are lyin' in shell holes up there and there's nae roads. *(Brightly)* Hooever am no worryin' this trip. A'll be oot o' it fur a change.
Peake:	Oh yes, I'm all right chum. By the way Dick, have you heard the latest?
Dick:	Naw, whit is it? *(Eagerly)* Serg. Major evacuated?
Peake:	No damn fear. I wish he was the b------.
Dick:	*(Cutting in)* Noo noo, Corporal, mind ye're stripes.
Peake:	Well, Padre Hall's back to the Division.
Dick:	Whit! Already! Surely no?
Peake:	Yes.
Dick:	When?
Peake:	Last night.
Dick:	Imph! By heavens ye're in fur a cushie time from noo on, I don't think. But what aboot his wound?
Peake:	Yes, he seems to have recovered from that wound he got on the Somme very quickly.
Dick:	My God, Peake, he canna be back already. His airm was completely busted in that stunt.

Peake:	Yes, I know, but he's back minus that busted arm. By the Lord Harry he's some man and no mistake.
Dick:	You bet your life he is, but A wid feel a damned sich mair comfortable if he wis still in Blighty. He'll nose oot a' the hottest corners in the line and whit's worse drag us wi' him, whit a life! I can see the shell wi' ma number on it getting' nearer and nearer. A hope naethin' happens to that leave warrant.
Peake:	*(Laughing)* Maybe it's because he's back you've been ordered to report here, Dick.
Dick:	Oh ay! It's a' damned richt fur you tae laugh that's got a job inside this pillbox, with four or five feet o' concrete aroon ye. Bit tae gang oot there wi' Padre Hall again mak's ma bluid rin cauld. A'm getting windy.
Peake:	Maybe you are Dick, we're all getting windy, but you'll be the first to volunteer if he wants anything special done.
Dick:	*(Angrily)* A'm damned shair A don't. A've had enough o' that. Naw, naw, nae mair fur this chicken. Heavens, when he got wounded that nicht at the Somme A had a 'hellifa' job getttin' him tae oor trench and whit did a get? Packed back again tae bring in the ithers.
Peake:	Well, you asked for it. You volunteered to go with him, you wanted a 'Blighty'.
Dick:	Ay, a ken; sometimes A think A'm daft. I wis oot there six times that nicht an the man that got the blighty had only been in the country a week. Ay! An' anither thing, wha got the medal? No me, naw, bit the Officer's servant, wha never had his nose ootside the bloody dug-out. Ach, it fairs scunners* me.

* disgusts.

204

Peake:	Yes, I know Dick, that was one of the many shameful things that has happened in this war. But I also know you'll be the first man to go again if there's a stiff job.
Dick:	Oh shut up. Dae the boys ken the Padre's back?
Peake:	I should think they do. He went straight up last night, heard there were some wounded in no-man's-land, got a couple of squads together and went right over. They got four chaps of another Division who had been out there for days. Old MacPherson got a regular beauty in the leg that should keep him at home for a bit.
Dick:	Some blighters hiv a' the luck. I suppose when A get yin I'll get it a' tae masel. Whaur's the Padre noo?
Peake:	He is away up again. Two of the Argylls got hit last night, out after a sniper, and when the bearers went for them they could only find the Serg. But he was dead. The other one must have crawled into a shell-hole, for they couldn't find him, so the Padre's away to have a look for him.
Dick:	Bully for him. However, A'm gaun tae dodge Padre Hall this trip. By the way, Peake, that's a nice wee rockery you hiv ootside the pillbox, bit it's dangerous.
Peake:	What do you mean?
Dick:	That dump o' German shells, jist ootside the door there. If Jerry lands wan amang thae shells in their nice wee baskets it's 'Ta-ta Bella' fur everybody inside this pillbox.
Peake:	Yes, we know that, but nobody here has had time to shift them.
	Jeffrey, who has been writing and following the conversation between Dick and Peake closely, suddenly asks:

Jeffrey:	Excuse me, but who is this Padre Hall you've been speaking about?
	Dick, turning suddenly, and noticing him for the first time.
Dick:	Hally Sonny*, when did you come up?
Jeffrey:	Last week, with the last reinforcement.
Dick:	*(To Peake)* Whaur did ye get this bit laddie? *(indicating Jeffrey)*
Peake:	He was sent up from Headquarters. He's young, but a good worker.
Dick:	It's weel seen he's a 'rookie', askin' a question like that. *(To Jeffrey)* Padre Hall's the bravest man in the British Army, pit that in yer pipe and smoke it. Ay, and I'll gie ye a tip, if ye want tae see yer mammy again keep oot o' his road.
	Dick takes his knife out of the top of his puttee and starts scraping the mud off his puttees and boots.
Peake:	Yes, Jeffrey, the Padre came to the Division along with the South African Brigade and has earned the VC many times, although he hasn't got one yet.
Dick:	*(interrupting)* Naw! He wid hae a better chance o' getting' yin if he was doon at the base.
Peake:	*(laughs)* You get Dick to tell you a few of his exploits with the Padre. It will be good material for your letter. Next to the Padre Dick has brought more men out of no-man's-land than any man in the Medical Corp.
Dick:	That's all rot. I go whaur A'm sent, and if A could get oot o' it, ye widna see ma heels fur stoor.†

* Holy Sunday.
† dust.

Peake:	Bunkum.
Dick:	Honest Peake, I'm as windy as onybody, bit I can hide it better than some. That's a' the difference between courage and funk.
Jeffrey:	Is it that with this Padre?
Dick:	Naw, he's different frae the rest o' us. He never seems tae think o' the danger. It's his duty tae minister tae the wounded and he does it nae maitter whaur they are. But it's just rotten luck tae be in his road when he's on dangerous the jobs.
	Jeffrey, very interested in Dick:
Jeffrey:	Are all the Padres like him?
Dick:	*(Scowling at Jeffrey)* Whit! No A'm bloody shair they're no'.
Peake:	*(who is resting on haversack beside table, smoking)* No, there are very few like this one. Why, at the Arras stunt we met two in the dug-out . . .
Dick:	*(interrupting)* That's whaur ye'll get maist o' them.
Peake:	*(continuing)* that should have been kicked. Remember them, Dick?
Dick:	I should think A dae. A can see the twa o' them sittin' in the safest pairt o' the dug-out, gassin' aboot their freens, and us up tae the elbows in bluid. Ay! And a Jock deein' at their side and damn the notice did they tak'. A hope A meet yon twa in civil life.
Peake:	I suppose there are good and bad in every trade. The two at Arras were two damned bad specimens.
Dick:	Padres! Huh! A'm no' struck on them as a class, but Padre Hall, he's different. Ye simply canna explain the man. There's something aboot him, yince ye ken him, that mak's ye want tae go through hell fur him.

207

Peake:	Yes, he simply roves about the front trenches as cool as if he were visiting the West End of London. Lord knows how he has escaped so long with his life.
Dick:	God knows. Why, when we were doon on the Somme, he wis oot in no-man's-land almost every nicht.
Peake:	You see, sonny, down there quite a lot of chaps were lying out for some time. The Division would take a bit of line here and lose a bit there, and naturally all the wounded couldn't be cleared at once.
Dick:	Ay, and whit's mair we hadna enough stretcher-bearers on the job onyway.
Peake:	That's right Dick, and by the way, Jeffrey when you get to doing a little bit of stretcher-bearing up to the knees in mud, you'll know what work is. Dick and I had a real taste of that at Loos before those who sneer at the RAMC came up.
Dick:	That's the damned thing aboot it. We don't get the credit fur being sojers at a'. Poultice Wallers, ay! Ye don't get the men who have seen anything saying that aboot a Field Ambulance, they <u>ken.</u> It's the blooming 'nyaffs'* that hiv been dragged intae the Army by the scruff o' the neck that say it. A've seen some o' thae same smert Alicks daein' a wee bit o' oor work when they were attached tae us. They were'nae long at it till they were wishin' they were back wi' their battalions. It fair maks ye seek. Tak it from me, sonny, it tak's a man to be a stretcher-bearer wi a Scottish Division.
Jeffrey:	But how did the Padre lose his arm?

* a trifle; a thing of no value.

Dick:	That wis at the last Somme 'do' in October. Oor Div. took ower from a London Div. The first nicht we were in, word got aboot that there were lots o' wounded in no-man's-land. The Padre slips ower and crawls aroon' the shell holes and locates the cases. When he gets back he explains the position tae oor Officer, who gets a couple o' squads thegither. The Padre scrounges a' the grub he can lay his hands on, and ower we go. That nicht we got a guid lot o' them in. Hoo we managed it, God only kens, the muck wis that bad. We were three nichts at the same job.
Peake:	Yes, and I'll never forget the smell of that lot, Dick, when we were dressing them. God's truth, they were awful.
Dick:	Ay! I fancy ye wid need yer gas helmet on dressing yon bunch.
Jeffrey:	And did the Padre go out every night?
Dick:	Go oot every nicht! He did mair than that; he stayed oot there. He went oot wan nicht, got intae a shell hole beside a chap an' stayed there wi' him a' nicht and a' the next day and when we got ower tae him at nicht, the wounded man wis just ready tae snuff it. We did oor best tae get him in, but a shell landed amongst us, killing the wounded man and Wilson who wis working wi' me. The Padre got his airm completely busted and, well, that's the sort o' man Padre Hall is.
Peake:	Yes, but Dick hasn't told you how he brought the unconscious Padre in all on his ownio.
Jeffrey:	Yes, it seems to me that you are just as good a soldier as this Padre Hall.
Dick:	Here, wee Fella, dinna let me hear ye say that again, or I'll bust yer jaw fur ye.
	Noise of voices outside the pillbox.

First Stretcher-Bearer	Watch whaur ye're gaun there.
	Groan from stretcher case.
Second Stretcher-Bearer	It's all damned right for you at the back, but I canny see whaur A'm gaun. 'Stretcher Case!' Lift the blinkin' blanket.
	Dick and Jeffrey rush to opening and draw back outside blanket which gives a glimpse of the country outside and two stretcher-bearers carrying a wounded man come right into the pillbox. They are up to the eyes in mud and look absolutely exhausted. Dick and Jeffrey prepare the trestles on which the two bearers place the stretcher. Peake is busy at the table and puts some fresh Eusol out of the bottle into one of the small bowls. Over the wounded man is a blanket. First stretcher-bearer when the case is on the trestles:
First Stretcher-Bearer	There ye are noo Jock, the worst o' it's by for you.
Jock:	Thank ye.
	The two bearers go and sit on form and light cigarettes, too tired to take any further interest in the case. Peake and Dick get busy and slip blanket off wounded man, who is a Private of the Argylls, very dirty, muddy and pale with exhaustion. A dressing is on his left leg below the knee, the dressing is bloody and dirty. Peake looking at leg turns to Jeffrey.
Peake:	Go in and tell Captain Linn to come.
	Jeffrey goes out and goes right to Officers' quarters.
Peake:	*(Examining the leg wound)* Is this the only one Jock?
Jock:	Dae ye no think it's damned plenty! It's sair enough onyway.
Peake:	Yes, it's quite an nice one Jock.

Jock:	Ma airm's gettin' stiff. Hae a luk at it.
	Peake slits up sleeves of tunic, disclosing a flesh wound in the forearm. Dick is giving Peake a hand.
Dick:	These are twa beauties you've got, Jock.
Jock:	Ay! They're no bad. Dae ye think I'll get tae 'Blighty' wi'them?
Peake:	Of course you will, you'll not stop until you get beside the Nurses in England.
Jock:	That's cheery, but I'd raither gang tae Glesca if it's a' the same tae you. Ye see, I belang tae Kilsyth and Glesca wid be nearer hame.
	Captain Linn comes in and goes straight to the stretcher, sees Dick.
Captain Linn:	Hallo, MacAllister, what are you doing here?
Dick:	Had a note sent from Headquarters for me to report here sir. I handed it into the Mess as I came in.
Captain Linn:	Oh, yes. I remember your leave-warrant should be here tomorrow.
	Dick smiles broadly.
Captain Linn:	*(to Jock)* Well, where are you hit Jock?
Jock:	*(cheerily)* Leg and arm, sir.
Captain Linn:	*(examining wounds)* Oh, they are not too bad.
Jock:	Wull I get hame wi' them, sir?
Captain Linn:	I wouldn't mind having your chance of that, Jock. The bone in your leg is fractured.
Jock:	Thank God fur that. *(everyone laughs)* I've waited long enough fur it onyway. I've been wi' the Division since ever they cam' oot.
Captain Linn:	Bully for you Jock, you've done your wee bit.
Jock:	*(turning to MacAllister)* Hae ye a fag aboot ye? Ay, I the only yin left of six o'us that jined the Argylls in 1914.

211

MacAllister gives Jock a cigarette and lights it for him. Jeffrey goes to table and hands dressings etc., as they are required.

Captain Linn: *(looking at wounds closely)* When were you wounded?

Jock: Last night, sir.

Captain Linn: How did it happen?

Jock: Well ye see sir, there's a sniper up there that's been playing wee Hell lately, so the Serg. And I went oot last night tae see whit could be dune. We think we got him sir, but his pals must have spotted us fur we got a bomb richt on us.

Captain Linn: Yes, and what about the sergeant?

Jock: He is killed Sir. I crawled into a shell-hole and lay there. I must of fainted or something fur when I cam tae, it wis broad day licht, I put ma field dressin on ma leg and lay whaur a wis, fur I didnae ken which wis oor trenches and which wis theirs.

Captain Linn: How did you get in?

Jock: Well, when it got dark, I let oot a yell tae let oor chaps ken whaur a wis.

Captain Linn: Who found you?

Jock: It wis yon Minister wi the wan airm. I got the fricht o ma life when I saw him slippin' intae the shell-hole. He gied me a drink oot o' his watter bottle. Yon's guid stuff fur a Minister tae hae Sir. He stayed wi' me for a wee while and then went back fur the stretcher-bearers.

Captain Linn: That must have been Padre Hall.

Jock: Ay, that's the yin. He's a game yin yon Sir.

Noise of shell bursting outside the pillbox. He left us up the trench a bit and said he wud be doon later on.

Another bang. Peake and Linn busy with splint on Jock's leg. Peake with a grip of the foot applies extension.

Jock: Here you, that's sair.* Heavens, this is worse than getting' the damned thing.

Linn and Peake only smile. Dick hands bandages etc. to Linn. Another shell burst.

Jock: *(Cocking up his head at shell burst.)* By the way, sir, will I hae tae bide here long?

Captain Linn: Why?

Jock: Well, I widna mind getting' doon a wee bit faurer† before I get ony mair. *Another bang. The outside blanket is lifted and Padre Hall, a tallish, thin, pale-looking man with an empty sleeve(left) comes in and looks into Officers' Quarters.*

Voice outside. Hallo Padre, come right in and get some grub.

Padre Hall: I'll be in a minute. I want to have a look at a patient.

At the sound of the voices, Dick looks up with a start, then smiles to Peake.

Captain Linn: *(to Jock)* Here comes your Padre.

Padre Hall comes right into pill-box. Tin hat, haversack, top boots. He is covered with mud.

Captain Linn: Hallo Padre, how goes it?

Padre Hall Linn, have you an Argyll here?

Captain Linn: Yes, here he is, all ready for 'Blighty'.

(Padre Hall comes centre and holds out his hand to Jock)

Padre: Well Jock, how do you feel now? Better, eh?

Jock: You bet your life sir.

(Padre seeing Dick for first time.)

* Sore.
† Further.

213

Padre:	Hallo Dick.
	Dick salutes, the two look at each other as they shake hands. Captain Linn goes and washes his hands at basin on table. Peake and Jeffrey get Jock fixes with blanket. Hall and Dick on right of trestles. Two sretcher-bearers go outside.
Padre:	Glad to see you again Dick.
Dick:	Same to you, Sir. *(Nodding at empty sleeve)*
	Sorry sir. *(Bang outside)*
Padre:	Yes, but I have one left. How's the Missus? Have you been home since I saw you?
Dick:	She's champion sir. I am going on leave tomorrow; just waiting on my pass coming through.
Padre:	Splendid. I hope you have a good time.
	Stretcher-bearer rushes into pillbox and shouts: 'These shells out there are on fire!!' Dick gives a start and explains to Hall:
Dick:	It is a dump of old German shells in baskets just outside the pillbox sir. That last shell must have set them alight.
	Padre Hall goes outside, the others in the pillbox start speaking to each other.
Captain Linn:	Get Jock fixed up.
	Linn goes out, Padre comes to inside of door and shouts:
Padre:	Get a blanket someone and lend a hand out here. We must get this out or we will be blown up.
	Dick glances at Peake who is busy with Jeffrey lifting Jock off the trestles. Dick snatches up blanket from form and rushes out. Jock's stretcher is put at back beside the German.
Jock:	A see you've got a Jerry here.
Peake:	Yes, Jock, and he's an old friend of yours.

Jock:	A freen o' mine! Don't be funny Corporal.
Peake:	You two have met before. Why man, this is the sniper you were out after when you got wounded.
Jock:	Whit's that! My God Corporal, let me get at him. *(To German)* So it was you that killed the Serg, eh? A wish A could get ma hauns on ye!
Peake:	But look here Jock, you can't blame him; it's all in the game, and after all you would have killed him.
Jock:	But I thocht A had killed him.
Jerry:	*(Who has followed the conversation keenly)* It was my friend you killed; there were two of us.
Peake:	There you are Jock, he's just in the same boat as you are. He had his duty to do, he and his pal, so had you and the Serg. You killed his pal and he killed the Serg, and now you're both here wounded. *C'est la Guerre*, Jock.
Jock:	*(Cooled down.)* Ay, that's so, Corporal. But it's a damned funny war, when you think on it. *(To Jerry.)* Are you fellows no' aboot fed up wi' this war yet?
Jerry:	Yes, we are very much fed up.
Jock:	So are we, and whit are we a' fechtin' fur onyway? Can ye answer me that yin, Jerry?
Jerry:	I cannot tell you.
Peake:	No, I don't think anybody can tell you that, Jock.
Jock:	Ma God, if it wisna see tragic, it wid be comical. Look here Jerry, you and I are oot o' it onyway and A think we're a' lot o'goats. Wull ye hae a fag?
Jerry:	Thank you, Kamerad.
	(Peake gives them a light, looks on and smiles. Noise of voices outside. Padre, Linn and Dick's voices.)

Jock:	Yes sir, Jerry's been trying to hit it since ever I arrived here.
	There is a bang of shells bursting close to pillbox; everyone in the pillbox starts, quiet for a moment, and then Hall and Linn's voices in agitation trembling then quiet.
Captain Linn:	*(At door of pillbox)* Peake!
	Peake rushes to the door.
Peake:	Yes sir. *He meets Linn and Hall carrying in the wounded form of Dick.*
Captain Linn:	Get a stretcher quickly. MacAllister is hit.
	Jeffrey and Peake rush for spare stretcher and open it. Padre and Linn put Dick carefully on to the stretcher. Jeffrey and Peake lift it on to tressels. Dick groans.
Peake:	Is he badly hit, Sir?
Captain Linn:	I'm afraid so. What damnable bad luck.
	Linn is busy with the wound, side away from audience. Dick is conscious, but seems in great pain.
Captain Linn:	How do you feel, MacAllister?
Dick:	Bad, Sir. The pain's terrible.
	Linn is feverishly padding the wound but has a very worried look.
	He knows it is hopeless. Peake and Jeffrey help with dressings.
Padre:	Stick it, Dick, my boy.
Dick:	Aye, I'll stick it. But I've seen too much tae be gulled, sir. I'm afraid A've got it bad.
Padre:	God bless you my son.
Dick:	*(Weakly)* You and me hiv had some narrow squeaks, Padre. A've got mine noo.
Padre:	But we have saved lots of lives and that's something that God will most assuredly bless you for.

Dick:	A doot A'm past gettin' ony blessin' noo, Sir. It's the wife and wee Jock ye'll hiv tae look efter. *(Dreamily)* Dae ye ken, Padre, A've – never seen wee Jock. A suppose he's a wee divert.* If a had just got hame tae see – him – before this happened.
Padre:	Don't give in like this, Dick. You'll see them soon when you get over this.
Dick:	Ay. But it'll no' be on this side, A'm thinkin' Padre, a feel am din fur. *(to Linn.)* Whit dae you think aboot it, is it bad, sir?
Linn:	Yes, MacAlister, it's very serious, I'm afraid it's –

He looks to Padre who asks a question with his eyes. Linn shakes his head. Dick sees this and realizes he is mortally wounded.

Dick:	Oh! God.

Padre stoops down and whispers a few words to Dick who collects himself with an effort.

Dick:	Whit's a' this war aboot onyway? *(very weakly)*
	Padre --- a want ye tae promise me something---
Padre:	Yes, my Son.
Dick:	If --- you ever get hame, wull ye go and see the wife---
Padre:	I certainly will.
Dick:	*(who is dying)*
	Tell her everything and --- say that she's tae bring up wee Jock --- tae be a man --- but --- tae learn him to hate the very name o' war --- like poison --- a'm gettin' cauld, Padre. *(Pause)* Gie me ma pocket-book. *(Very weakly)*

---

* An amusing person.

	The Padre takes pocket-book out of tunic pocket. Dick feels inside and takes out photograph of his wife and child, lifts it slowly so that he can see it, looks as it for a second. It slips out of his hand. His hand drops.
Peake:	*(strung up).* Oh God, surely he's not —-
Captain Linn:	He's dead.
	Peake turns to his table to hide his emotion. Jeffrey, who has been watching everything puts his hands to his face and goes right. Linn turns away a little. The Padre behind stretcher, looks at Dick affectionately, then raises his head and starts to pray. Everyone in the Pill-box bow their heads the moment they hear the Padre's voice. The German who has been watching everything lifts his hand to the salute. The two stratcher-bearers come in, realize the position and stand at the door and bow their heads.
Padre:	*(very slowly)* 'Our Father, Thy will be done, but grant O God that the generations that come after us, see to it that these sacrifices are not in vain, Amen.'

SLOW CURTAIN

References

Abbreviations used in Reference Notes

'*Churchill*'   *The World Crisis 1916–1918, Part 2,* by Winston Churchill, 1927, Thornton Butterworth, London.

'*Croft*'   *Three Years with The 9th (Scottish) Division,* by William Croft, 1919, John Murray, London.

'*De Groot*'   *Douglas Haig, 1861–1928,* by Gerard J. De Groot,1988, Unwin Hyman, London.

'*Ewing*'   *History of the 9th (Scottish) Division,* by John Ewing, 1921, John Murray, London.

'*Gilbert*'   *The First World War,* by Martin Gilbert, 1994, Weidenfeld & Nicolson, London.

'*Keegan*'   *The First World War,* by John Keegan,1998, Hutchinson, London.

'*Magnusson*'   *The Clachan and the Slate – The Story of the Edinburgh Academy,* by Magnus Magnussson, 1974, Collins, London.

'*Manchester*'   *The Last Lion,* by William Manchester, 1983, Michael Joseph, London.

'*Morrow*'   *The Great War in the Air,* by John Morrow, Jr.,1993, Airlife.

'*OHW*'   *History of the Great War based on Official Documents, Military Operations France and Belgium, 1915, Vol II,* by Brigadier-General J.E. Edmonds, 1928, Macmillan and Co., London.

'Strachan'   *European Armies and the Conduct of War,* by Hew Strachan, 1984, George Allen & Unwin, London.

'Winter'   *The Great War and the British People*, by J.M. Winter, 1986, Macmillan, London.

[1] See *Wearing Spurs,* by John Reith, *1966,* Hutchinson, London, at page 222.

[2] By the time conscription was introduced in January 1916 the number of volunteers was 2,466,719. This figure was surpassed by the Indian Army in the Second World War with 2,581,726 volunteers.

[3] There is a lot of published material on the Medical Services during the war, including several categories of Official History. Articles during the war were published in the *Royal Army Medical Journal*. Practical advice for training was also given in a *Memorandum on the Treatment of Injuries in the War*, published by HMSO in 1915, and a *Manual of Injuries and Diseases of War*, published by HMSO in 1918, which was based on experience gained in France.

[4] See *Keegan* at page 191.

[5] Early drafts for *Fields and Battlefields* were given to Willie (St Clair Papers).

[6] *Fields and Battlefields* was published by Constable in June 1918 in London. A separate edition was published by Robert McBride and Co. in New York as part of the British propaganda effort in the United States (St Clair Papers).

[7] *On a Louis XVI Coin taken by a Friend*

> How hast thou been hot-handled and transferred
> By waiting coach door after midnight brawl
> Or flung to peasant from a chateau wall
> What gathering secret curses hast thou heard
> In patriots palm what hatred hast incurred –
> Or clutched with bon-bons in a Valence shawl
> By ruined Marquise fugitive from all –
> What various passion has thy crowned head stirred
> Or lain preserved from traffic, tumult, lust,
> For twilight years amid broken beads and dust
> Why hast thou stirred to evil dreams again –
> The dreams, the tears, the cannon on the plain
> As once to the ears of Danton the same tune
> In galloping caleche through old Béthune.

[8] See *OHW* at pages 393–394.

[9] See *OHW* at pages 151–157.

[10] See *OHW* at pages 170–171.

[11] See Frank Richards' account of the battle in *Old Soldiers Never Die* (published in 1933 by Angus & Robertson in Sidney and by Faber & Faber in London), in which he claims that the Germans taunted the British before the battle that they knew gas was going to be released on 25 September 1915.

[12] Haig died in 1928 as Field Marshal Earl Haig.

[13] See *OHW* at page 179.

[14] The Divisional History says: 'there is no evidence that it (the gas) affected the enemy in the least' (see *Ewing* at page 59).

[15] 26 Brigade consisted of 8/Black Watch, 7/Seaforths, 8/Gordons and 5/Camerons.

[16] 28 Brigade consisted of 6/KOSB, 9/Scottish Rifles, 10/Highland Light Infantry and 11/Highland Light Infantry.

[17] 27 Brigade consisted of 11/Royal Scots, 12/Royal Scots, 6/Royal Scots Fusiliers and 10/Argyll and Sutherland Highlanders.

[18] Fosse 8 was a mining structure of some height giving commanding views. The Dump was a slag-heap made from mining waste.

[19] See *OHW* at page 237.

[20] See *OHW* at page 238.

[21] The Official History reads:- 'On the higher ground astride the Vermelles-Hulloch road and facing Loos, the slight breeze was from the south-west and south, but here about the La Bassee canal it was more from the south-east. Its changeful fits during the period of the gas discharge carried the cloud of gas and smoke against the waiting battalions, and seriously affected them. By 6.30 am it had actually drifted behind the British trenches, so that the attack of the 28th Brigade, with numbers reduced by gas casualties and completely unprotected by smoke, was begun under very adverse conditions. To add to these grave disadvantages, the German artillery placed a barrage on the British front trench; and some of the cylinders were hit, and burst with fatal effect to those waiting near by for the signal to assault.'(see OHW at page 240)

[22] Maj.-Gen.G.H. Thesiger.

[23] Brig.-Gen. C.D.Bruce.

[24] This figure is from the *OHW* at page 392 where there is a breakdown of its composition. The figures include the casualties of the Indian Corps.

[25] According to military historian and Conservative MP, the late Alan Clark, twelve battalions of 21 and 24 Divisions, or just under 10,000 men, took part in the main attack which lasted about two and a half hours and suffered casualties of 385 officers and 7,861 men (see *The Donkeys,* by Alan Clark, 1961, Hutchinson, London). Clark's

221

casualty figures are almost identical to those in the *OHW,* but he suggests wrongly that the casualties are for twelve battalions, whereas they are actually for the twenty-four battalions of the two divisions. This mistake accordingly grossly inflates key figures on which he places great store in his book. More bizarrely, Clark's figures are quoted by the eminent historian, Sir Martin Gilbert, as the British casualties at Loos, which goes in the other direction to Clark, and grossly underestimates casualties in this battle (See *Gilbert* at page 201).

[26] See *The History of the Great War based on Official Documents, Medical Services General History, 1921–1924, Vol II,* by Major-General WG MacPherson, HMSO, at pages 463 and 464.

[27] See *OHW* at page 334. For a German account, see J Forstner, *Das Reserve Infantrie Regiment 15,*1929, Berlin, pages 226–232.

[28] The *War Diary* of 27 Field Ambulance for that time reads;- 'Lieutenant Hancock in the dug-outs at Guy's had an enormous amount of work to do in very unfavourable conditions the trenches being very heavy and slippery and the going being bad. All the bearers worked hard and well and without relief for 24 to 36 hours.' (WO 95/1758).

[29] See *Ewing* at pages 64 and 73.

[30] See *The Unending Vigil-A History of the Commonwealth War Graves Commission,* by Philip Longworth, 1967 (revised 1985), Leo Cooper in association with Secker & Warburg.

[31] For an account of this attack, see *Gilbert,* at page 217, and *Ewing,* at page 72.

[32] See *Strachan* at page 138.

[33]   **THERE'S A LITTLE MAID A-DREAMING.**

> There's a little maid a-dreaming,
> And I know she dreams of me,
> When the silver moon is gleaming
> Far across the Irish Sea.
> Oh, I wonder if a smile she wears,
> And I wish that it could be
> That my lips might press a kiss on hers
> In the dream she dreams of me.
> There's a little maid a-praying
> And I know she prays for me,
> When the mountain top is greying
> And the wind sobs drearily.
> Oh, I know it is a prayer divine,
> And as simple as can be,
> And I wish my name no fairer shrine
> Than the prayer she prays for me.

There's a little maid a-waiting
And I know she waits for me,
And a faith that's unabating
And a heart's sweet constancy.
Oh, the day goes creeping into night,
But I know a dawn there'll be
When dreams come true and prayers unite,
And she waits no more for me.

E.NORMAN TORRY
(Musical Rights Reserved)

[34] See *Ewing* at page 394.

[35] Britain meant England, Scotland and Wales, but not Ireland.

[36] The 'Bantam' battalions were one result of the lowering of the height rule. As it would be unsafe to have very small men fighting alongside large men , they were formed into separate units.

[37] See *Winter* at pages 39–64.

[38] 1 October 1914–30 September 1915, the casualties among officers were 42.3 per cent. This figure omits the exceptionally heavy casualty figures during the Mons Retreat (See *Winter* at pages 87–88).

[39] The Edinburgh Academy is used as an example because it has good records in the form of its 'Register', as well as being a leading public school in Scotland, which R. B. Haldane had attended.

[40] See *Magnussson* at page 295.

[41] 97% of Oxford and Cambridge graduates and undergraduates who joined the Army served as officers (*Winter* at page 88).

[42] See *Magnusson* at page 295.

[43] See *Winter* at page 88.

[44] Ministers of Religion had absolute exemption from conscription under both Acts, provided they were in 'holy orders or were regular ministers of any religious denomination'.

[45] This transcript appeared in the *Kirkintilloch Herald* on 1 March 1916.

[46] This information is from accounts given by John to his family. There is no transcript of what was said at the second meeting of the Tribunal, and therefore it is not possible to know if *Cooneyism* was rejected as a denomination. John's bona fides as a conscientious objector seems to have been accepted; otherwise he would not have been put in a non-combatant unit. The pacifism of the Cooneyites or 'Testimony of Jesus', although well attested, was not accepted by similar Military Tribunals in Commonwealth countries because the sect was too informally constituted and a number went to jail (See *King and Country Call,* by Paul Baker,1988, Auckland University Press, N.Z., at page 171.).

47 See *Gilbert* at pages 224–225.

48 See *Keegan* at pages 310–321.

49 See *Ewing*, 102.

50 See *Ewing*, 138.

51 See *The Necessity of Poetry* by Robert Bridges, 1918, Oxford, Clarendon Press, at pages 41–47.

52 See *Selected Letters of Robert Bridges,* Donald E. Stanford editor, 1984, Newark, Delaware, page ii, 654.

53 Edward Bridges, future Cabinet Secretary Lord Bridges, won a Military Cross.

54 See *Alarms and Excursions,* by GTM Bridges, 1938, Longman Green and Co. at pages 75–77. The lieutenant, Charles Hornby, won the DSO for this act. According to General Bridges such acts by the *arme blanche* were not common later in the war.

55 Ordinary editions, February 1916, March 1916, August 1916, January 1917, March 1918, January 1919; India paper editions, January 1916, February 1916, January 1917, March 1918, January 1919. Also used for life of Bridges, *Robert Bridges 1844–1930,* by Edward Thompson, 1944, Oxford.

56 See *The Pageant of Greece,* by Sir Richard Livingstone, first published, Oxford, in 1923, at page 205. By 1963 it had been reprinted eight times, largely for use in the public schools.

57 Five poems were printed during Owen's lifetime mostly in *The Hydra, The Journal of the Craiglockhart War Hospital* (See *Wilfred Owen,* by Jon Stallworthy, OUP ,1974, at page xii.)

58 See *Ewing* at page 139.

59 See *Ewing* at page 143.

60 Diary entry of 21 August 1916.

61 See *Ewing* at page 148. This extraordinary truce was remarked upon by Hope Bagenal in an address to 27 Field Ambulance Veterans' Association as the most memorable incident for 27 FA at Vimy Ridge (St Clair Papers).

62 See *Ewing* at page 167.

63 There is at this place in the original of the letter a later hand-written note which states '*and theirs after that*' i.e. the trench or part of the line was recaptured later by the Germans presumably on the 'Somme retreat'.

64 The unit concerned was the London Division (See *Ewing* at page167).

65 'Bantam' battalions were made up of men of less than 5ft.3 inches in height. They were frequently coal miners, and, according to many accounts, some of the toughest soldiers in the British Army. (See *The Bantams, The Untold Story of World War I,* by Sidney Allinson, 1985,

London, and *Winter* at page 32.) The word 'Bantam' was taken from the type of fighting cock of that name, which came from Bantam in Java, and which, as well as being very small, was thought to be particularly 'conceited and pugnacious'.

[66] See *Ewing* at pages 176–177. John Ewing says that the trenches were deepened 'so that one could walk along the front line without being exposed from the waist upwards'.

[67] See *Ewing* at page 177.

[68] See *Ewing* at page 176.

[69] The actual figures for operations on 9 April, 12 April, 3 May and 5 June were 283 casualties among officers and 5,195 casualties among other ranks (see *Ewing* at page 408).

[70] See *Ewing* at page 218.

[71] Willie's family belonged to a very radical Protestant sect founded in 1897 among the small farmers near Enniskillen in Co. Fermanagh by William Irvine, a Kilsyth man, born in 1863, the same year as Willie's father. The sect rejected calling itself by any name, although it has been variously called by outsiders the 'Irvinites', or 'Cooneyites' or 'Testimony of Jesus'. It adopted the ways of the 1st century Christian Church, rejecting institutionalised structures and bodies of doctrine. In *The Impartial Reporter and Farmers' Journal* of 23.7.1908, Enniskillen, there is a long account of a sermon of William Irvine in which the rejection of doctrine and structures is given, including how the established clergy were going to Hell. Other issues of that newspaper in the preceding years give accounts of the growth of the sect. For further accounts of doctrine see *The Secret Sect*, by Doug and Helen Parker, 1982, N.S.W. Australia.

[72] See *Manchester* at page 622, and sources quoted.

[73] See *Gilbert* at page 365.

[74] See *Gilbert* at page 365.

[75] See *Gilbert* at page 363.

[76] See *Manchester* at page 624.

[77] Casualty figures were not made public at the time for obvious military reasons. More surprising is the fact that no proper figures were ever compiled of British war casualties, and therefore any figures must be treated with care (see *Winter* pages 65 – 99).

[78] See *Gilbert* at page 365.

[79] See *The Private Papers of Douglas Haig (1914–1919)* edited by Robert Blake, London, Eyre and Spottiswoode, 1952. Indeed Haig's son in the foreword to the diaries suggests that Haig even avoided visiting casualty clearing stations. He stated, 'The suffering of his men during the Great War caused him great anguish. I believe that he felt it was his

duty to refrain from visiting the casualty clearing stations because these visits made him physically ill.'(Private Papers at page 9).

80 See *Passchendaele*, by David Lloyd George, July 1934, Ivor Nicholson & Watson, London, at page 5. The account appeared later in 1934 as a chapter in Lloyd George's *War Memoirs*, Vol IV, October 1934, Ivor Nicholson & Watson, at page 2114.

81 See *Ewing* at page 226 for an account of the method of attacking the pillboxes.

82 See *Ewing* at page 409.

83 He was succeeded by William Croft, who, like Maxwell, very much led from the front, winning 4 DSOs before the end of the war.

84 High Explosive.

85 See *Ewing* at page 243. Originally pigeons were used for intelligence only. But they were later used as a back-up communication means. In 1918 there were 20,000 birds in the charge of 380 experts under Major A. Waley, who had been detailed by the General Staff in 1915 to organize the service, and 90,000 men were trained as fliers (see *OHW* at page 99).

86 See *Ewing* at page 243. The organization of a messenger dog service was not taken up officially until July 1917 (see *OHW* at page 99).

87 This account of the action on 12 October 1917 and the following days is taken from *Ewing* at pages 238–245, and the War Diary of 27 Field Ambulance (W.O 95/ 1758) and the War Diary of the 9th (Scottish) Division (W.O 95/ 1740).

88 The Official History of the War says that at this time (17 October 1917) at least a third of casualties at were caused by gas (see *History of the Great War based on Official Documents, Medical Services General History, Vol III,* by Major-General WG MacPherson, 1924, HMSO, at page 170). The gas hospital is referred to in a 27 Field Ambulance Veterans' Newsletter (St Clair Papers).

89 See *Croft* at page 161.

90 *WO 95/1758.*

91 See *Ewing* at page 409.

92 See *Croft* at page 162.

93 *WO 95/1758.*

94 See letter of 16 October 1917 and account of Richmond in the Introduction.

95 Major-General J.T. Hill.

96 From a tribute to Eustace Hill, by Colonel Eric Thompson, published in *The Johannian* – the School Magazine of St John's College (St Clair Papers).

[97] See picture of Padre Hill and Sister Flynn burying her dead brother Dudley Flynn at Delville Wood in 1919.

[98] *De Groot* at pages 218–219.

[99] The War Diary of 27 Field Ambulance (WO 95/1758) records in 1916, during the Somme Offensive, '18/19 October Bazentin-Rev Hill CFSAI wounded arm and thigh passed through ADS.'

[100] See *Gilbert* at pages 401–402.

[101] See *Manchester* at page 628.

[102] See *Churchill* at pages 410 –411.

[103] See *Strachan* at page 137.

[104] Brigadier-General Dawson was captured with Padre Hill in what was called the South Africans' Last Stand.

[105] See *Churchill* at page 410.

[106] See *Ewing* at page 318.

[107] The Germans' success of 21 March 1918 cost Germany 39,329 casualties (of whom all but 300 were killed or wounded), as against British losses of 38,512 (of whom17,512 were killed and wounded). See *Strachan* at page 146.

[108] See *Ewing* at page 409.

[109] This may be a reference to the flu epidemic, called 'The Spanish lady' of 1918/1919, which swept the world killing millions. See *The Plague of the Spanish Lady: The Influenza Pandemic of 1918 – 1919* by Richard Collier, 1974, Macmillan, London.

[110] See *Slings & Arrows – Sayings Chosen from the Speeches of D. Lloyd George*, edited by Philip Guedalla, 1929, Cassel, London, speech to House of Commons 24.10. 1917

[111] See *Morrow* at page 238.

[112] See *Morrow* at page 239.

[113] See *Morrow* at page 367.

[114] See *Morrow* at page 239.

[115] See *Keegan* at page 386.

[116] See *Morrow* at page 329.

[117] See *Keegan* at page 438.

[118] See *Ewing* at pages 336 and 337.

[119] *The German War Manual,* (*Kriegsbrauch im Landkriege*), translated by J.H.Morgan, under the title *The German War Book*, 1915, John Murray, London, at page 66.

[120] See *Albert Einstein,* by Albrecht Folsing, translated by Ewald Osers, 1998, Penguin Books, at page 345.

[121] See *Passchendaele,* by David Lloyd George, July 1934, Ivor Nicholson & Watson, London. The account appeared later in 1934 in Lloyd George's *War Memoirs* , October 1934, Ivor Nicholson & Watson.

[122] See *De Groot* at page 386.

[123] There were also 134,202 Irish volunteers, conscription never having applied in Ireland, despite a late attempt in 1918 to introduce it there (*Winter* at page 129).

[124] See as an example *Chambers's Patriotic Poems for the Young,* selected by S. Tait, 1915, W. & R. Chambers, London and Edinburgh. This anthology for use in the schools contains martial patriotic poetry of the British Isles, and the national anthems of the French, Russian, Japanese and Serbian allies. The purpose of this propaganda in the schools was to prepare the boys to volunteer to fight, or as stated in the Foreword 'to awaken and foster…such a love of their country and pride in their glorious heritage as will prepare them the better to fulfil in after years their duties as citizens of a great Empire'.

[125] See *Brave Deeds of War, told by Donald MacKenzie* (undated, probably late 1914), Blackie and Sons Limited, as an example of this genre. It is a beautifully illustrated book of imagined war, written for boys.

[126] Lt. Colonel Costello, the commanding officer of 27 Field Ambulance, wrote a small book about the march to the Rhine, which was published in Ohlrigs, Germany (St Clair Papers).

[127] See *The Modern Scottish Theatre,* by David Hutchison, 1977, Molendinar Press, Glasgow, one of the few books on the Scottish theatre at this period. There is no reference to or discussion of any influence of the Great War on the Scottish theatre.

[128] *No Leading Lady* by R.C. Sherriff, 1966, Victor Gollanz, at page 109.

[129] *The Great War and Modern Memory* by Paul Fussell, 1975, OUP, at pages 34 and 35.

Index

Aeroplanes 176-180
   German A.A. fire at British
      Aeroplanes, 21–2, 178
   German aircraft, 42, 43, 102,
      147, 154, 179, 185
   aerial dogfights, 127, 180
   British superior in 1918, 174
   forced landing of British aircraft,
      180
Air bombing, 164, 170, 174, 178,
      180, 192, 194
   unnerving effect of, 164, 174, 180
Albert I, King of the Belgians, 193,
      193 fn.
Aldershot, 10–11
All Quiet on the Western Front, 3
American Army, 18
American Civil War, 16
Amiens, 181
Ammunition accidents, 28, 126–7
   ammunition dump explodes in
      Arras, 142–3, 144
Ancre, River, 16
Annequin, 50, 57 fn., 59, 66
Antwerp, 149
Armenières, 94
Armistice, 194
Armoured cars, 112
Arnott, Private D., 10/ A. & S.H,
      killed in action, 29/04/1917
      (son of James Arnott of
      Kirkintilloch), 142, 145
Arras, 1, 132–144
   Cathedral, 139, 172
Arnim, General Sixt von, 150
Artois, 47, 109
Athens, 122
Atrocities, hints of, 140, 142

Bagenal, Philip 'Hope'
   background, 30–1, 32, 33, 106,
      119
   'Fields and Battlefields', 31, 220
   sonnet on Louis XVI coin, 33,
      220 fn.

awarded D.C.M., 119
   gives W.St.C. Robert Bridges' *The
      Spirit of Man*, 119–120
Bailleul, 94, 101, 105
Balkan Wars, 16
Baltic States, 166
Barlinnie Prison, 102
Bazentin-Le-Grand, 113
Bazentin-Le-Petit, 124, 124 fn., 172
Belarus, 166
Belgium, 4, 9, 16, 70, 109, 149–50
   Belgian civilians compared with
      French, 70
   Belgian refugees, 11
   alleged Belgian spy, 76
Begg, S., artist & illustrator, 172
Bell, Corporal P., M.M., 10 A. &
      S.H., killed in action
      30/12/1917, 163
Bemersyde, 183
Berlin, Kaiser Wilhelm Institute, 103
Bessarabia, 166
Béthune, 35–6, 45, 57, 58, 59–60,
      66, 68, 88
Blunden, Edmund, 172
Boer War, 158
Bordon, Hants, 14, 17, 33
Boulogne, 130
Bray, 113 fn.
Brest-Litovsk, Treaty of , 166–7
Bridges,
   Edward, 1st Lord Bridges, 120,
      224
   Robert, Poet Laureate, 119–122
   Thomas, Lieut.-Gen. Sir Tom,
      120, 224
Britain, 121–2, 176
   civilians, 20–1, 95–6, 152
   ignorance of conditions in France,
      16–7, 18, 97, 108, 164
British Army
   Bantam Battalions, see under 35th
      Division
   British Army of Occupation of the
      Rhineland, 195–6

231

Royal Artillery,
    W. St.C.'s high regards for, 42,
      54, 87, 126
Royal Army Medical Corps, 10,
    11, 12, 53, 82, 85, 123, 128
    reputation in B.E.F. 51–53
    laying barbed wire in front line,
    99
    41 Casualty Clearing Station
      R.A.M.C., 141.
    26 Field Ambulance, 69 fn.
    27 Field Ambulance, 10 fn., 13,
      18, 21, 24, 30, 64, 65, fn.,
      68–69, 80, 84, 116–117,
      135, 151, 157, 187–188,
      222 fn. 28, 224 fn. 61
    casualties and awards of, 84
      fn..
    28 Field Ambulance, 37, 50, 61,
      69 fn.
    46 Field Ambulance, 13
Royal Engineers, 19, 73, 88
Britton, Private Ernest, 27 Field
    Ambulance, date of
    death.19/07/1916 (Dive Copse
    Cemetery), 55–56, 113
Brooke, Major Alan (Field Marshal
    Viscount. Alanbrooke), 132
Brooke, Rupert, 8, 121
Brown, James, 188
Bruce, Brig.-Gen. C.D., 221
Busnes, 46

Cambridge University, 91
Cambrin, 50, 51, 53, 59–60, 61, 64,
    74
Canada, 122
Canadian Army, 77, 103, 133
Canadian Institute, 101
Caporetto, 166
Casualties,
    BEF, Autumn 1917, 149
    W.St.C. initial perception of
      casualties, 1–2 July 1916,
      112

9th Division at Loos, 49, 110
    Somme 1916, 117, 123–4
    Arras 1917, 133
    Sept. 1917, 150
    Oct 1917, 151
    Mar–April. 1918, 168, 171–2
    April–May, 117, 133–4
    20 Sep 1917, 150
    Mar/ April 1918, 168, 171–2
    27 Brigade, Jul 1916, 114
    27 Field Ambulance, Arras April
      1917, 135
    Sergeant-Major Richardson
      wounded, 136
    May 1917, 142
    Ypres, Oct 1917, 156
    April 1918 six members
      believed captured, 171
    27 FA. Captured POW
      reported, 175
    Sep 1918, 187–8
    South African Brigade, 168
    officers, 90

Caucasus, 166
Caurnie, see Kirkintilloch
Censorship, 2, 18, 38, 46
    diaries, 4, 4 fn.
    green envelopes, 6, 7, 38, 117,
      124, 126, 145
    corporal court-martialled for
      abuse of green envelope, 7,
      88
    censorship eased in
      communiques, April 1918,
      168–9
Champagne, 47, 109
Christ Church Oxford, 158
Churchill, Winston, 76
    colonel 6/Royal Scots Fusiliers 93,
      109–10, 122
    visiting 9th Division, Mar 1918,
      167–8, 196
Cigarettes, 18, 25–6, 55, 65,71
Clark, Alan, 121–2

233

238

239

Wulverghem, 103–4

Yeats, W.B., 120
YMCA, 101
Ypres, 6–7, 16, 46, 62, 70, 75,
    80–1, 87, 99, 150
  destruction in, 75–6, 78, 121, 191
  cathedral, 78

Cloth Hall, 78, 78 fn.
Ypres Comines Canal, 75

Zeebrugge, 149
Zillebeke, 75
Zululand, 158
Zulu Rebellion, 158